...otting and Beyond

ECKART VOIGTS-VIRCHOW
(ED.)

JANESPOTTING AND BEYOND

BRITISH HERITAGE RETROVISIONS SINCE THE MID-1990S

narr
VERLAG

Cover photograph:
Frances O'Connor (as Fanny Price) on the cover of the Miramax VHS package for *Mansfield Park* (USA/UK 1999).

Bibliographic information published by Die Deutsche Nationalbibliothek

Die Deutsche Nationalbibliothek lists this publication in the Deutsche Nationalbibliografie; detailed bibliographic data is available in the Internet at http://dnb.dnb.de.

Printed with contributions from *Zentrum für Medien und Interaktivität Gießen* and *Gießener Hochschulgesellschaft*.

© 2012 · Gunter Narr Verlag Tübingen
Dischingerweg 5 · D-72070 Tübingen

Internet: http://www.narr.de
E-Mail: info@narr.de

Printed in Germany

ISBN 978-3-8233-6096-4

Contents

Introduction

Eckart Voigts-Virchow
"Corset Wars": An Introduction to Syncretic Heritage Film Culture
since the Mid-1990s 9

The *Mise-en-scène* of Austen Powers

Andrew Higson
English Heritage, English Literature, English Cinema:
Selling Jane Austen to Movie Audiences in the 1990s 35

Pamela Church Gibson
Otherness, Transgression and the Postcolonial Perspective:
Patricia Rozema´s *Mansfield Park* 51

Raimund Borgmeier
Heritage Film and the Picturesque Garden 65

The Bardbiz: Heritage Shakespeare

Deborah Cartmell
Fin de Siècle Film Adaptations of Shakespeare 77

Roberta E. Pearson
Heritage, Humanism, Populism: The Representation of Shakespeare
in Contemporary British Television 87

From Auntie's Heritage to Anti-heritage

Sarah Street
"The Mirror Crack'd" :
Heritage, History and Self-reflexive Discourse 101

Carolin Held
From 'Heritage Space' to 'Narrative Space' – Anti-heritage Aesthetics
in the Classic TV Serials *Our Mutual Friend* and *Vanity Fair* 113

Barbara Schaff
Still Lifes – *Tableaux Vivants*: Art in British Heritage Films 125

Lucia Krämer
Subversion in Disguise: Oliver Parker's Adaptations of
Oscar Wilde's *An Ideal Husband* and *The Importance of Being Earnest* 135

Stefani Brusberg-Kiermeier
Stormy Novel, Thorny Adaptation:
Recent Appropriations of *Wuthering Heights* 149

Transnational Productions / Transnational Classrooms

Angela Krewani
Heritage as International Film Format 161

Carola Surkamp
A Plea for Varied Readings:
Teaching British Heritage Films to German Students 167

Monika Seidl
Kommissar Rex Meets Mr Darcy: Pedagogical Approaches
to Visualising the Past and Literary Classics 183

Index of Films 199

General Subject Index 203

List of Contributors 211

Introduction

Eckart Voigts-Virchow

"Corset Wars": An Introduction to Syncretic Heritage Film Culture since the Mid-1990s

1   Approaching Heritage Adaptations via *Dogville* and *The Lord of the Rings*

What is a heritage film? In view of the fact that for several years an entire journal has been devoted to investigating aspects of the heritage concept,[1] one might not expect an easy answer. Sarah Street (2001: 106) has opted for a loose definition, writing that it is a term "associated with costume/historical drama; identified with high production values and a quest for period authenticity". Andrew Higson's recent revisionist monograph provides a narrower version. He was interested in "English costume dramas" of the 1980s and 1990s that "articulate a nostalgic and conservative celebration of the values and lifestyles of the privileged classes" and in doing so, reinvent "an England that no longer existed [...] as something fondly remembered and desirable" (Higson 2003: 12). The OED definition of "heritage"[2] suggests that these films re-establish the past as a property or possession, which, by 'natural' right of birth, belongs to the present, or, to be more precise, to certain interests or concerns virulent in the present – to groups of people determined by nationality, ethnicity, gender, class or patterns of consumption.

A binary approach, dismissed by Claire Monk (2002: 178) as outdated, may define the genre *ex negativo*, as diametrically opposed to the aesthetics displayed, for instance, in Lars Von Trier's recent movie, *Dogville* (2003). Let us look at the business framework first. The core heritage film might be regarded as a particularly British phenomenon with a long-standing tradition of a predominantly English cinema on the British Isles,[3] but also (and increasingly so) tailored for American audiences. In this view, heritage films participate in a heritage culture that turns Britain into a hyperreal simulation. If one accepts this (arguably too narrow) definition, *Dogville*, which casts a critical,

---

1   The *International Journal of Heritage Studies*, now in its ninth year, is published by Routledge.
2   OED definitions include "any property, and esp. land, which devolves by right of inheritance" and "the condition or state transmitted from ancestors" For a critique of the passivity, materiality, and exclusiveness of the heritage concept, cf. Stedman (1997).
3   The term 'British cinema' refers to the category of state, 'English cinema' to a national metonymy (cf. Kumar 2001). There is also a European heritage film (cf. Monk 2002: 182), but it may have been invigorated by the British 1980s and 1990s success stories.

'European' view on the USA (using 'authentic' American actors) does not qualify. Although set in a Depression-era village in Colorado – and therefore strictly speaking a 'historical', 'period' film – *Dogville* provides the complete antithesis to a heritage space and clearly intends to disinherit the USA of an established cultural scenario in American 'heritage'.

True, the adult target group, the small to medium budget and the inevitable Hollywood star are comparable to core heritage films, but the money is spent on a very different audiovisual set-up. Neither Nicole Kidman, James Caan nor Lauren Bacall are employed to endear *Dogville* to a projected American audience – an almost necessary marketing ploy for any British-produced heritage film and even BBC-made heritage TV series (regularly co-produced by the Boston-based company WBGH). In fact, the work of Danish filmmaker Von Trier, who has never crossed the Atlantic in his life, is ideally suited to articulate an alien, 'non-heritage' perspective on the American past. Von Trier embodies a distinctly European tradition of artistic auteurism separate from the Anglo-American film world dominated by Hollywood (old and new) 'entertainment'.

Whereas core heritage films address a relatively mature, feminine middle-class audience and appeal to traditional quality beyond the experiments of modernism, the Bertolt Brecht-inspired *Dogville* by the legendary, obsessive movie monomaniac Von Trier exhibits precisely this experimentalism marked as modernist (and masculinist). Let us look, therefore, at the cinematic aesthetics of *Dogville*. Heritage adaptations align themselves to the implicit values of a literary canon, authorship, and (often theatrically trained) British quality actors. At least since *Sense and Sensibility* and *Middlemarch*, however, heritage films have not merely been 'subservient' adaptations of literary texts, but have sought to exploit the medium-specific potential of film in order to avoid the deadbeat accusations of 'staginess' or 'wordiness'.

In contrast, Lars Von Trier leaves the unmistakable imprint of a *film auteur* on his *Dogville*. Instead of providing a mere media change in literary adaptations, the conventional transfer from a 'classic' novel to the media film and TV, *Dogville* is an exercise in intermediality proper. Von Trier takes recourse both to the theatre and, more specifically, epic theatre and poor theatre. His Dogville is hardly more than Peter Brook's empty space: the Dogville "Elm Street"[4] is constituted merely by chalk lines in a more or less empty Swedish studio. The actors mime the opening and closing of doors, because props are minimal and the walls are missing in the transparent set. The photography is in typical 'visually challenged' *Dogme95* style marked by handheld cameras, violations of the 180° rule and wilful cuts. *Dogme95* could not be further from heritage photography, which is focused on the *mise-en-scène* of dialogue and setting, with formulaic stylistic means such as shot/reverse shot patterns, over-the-shoulder shots, long takes, and deep focus. Heritage films are rarely

---

4   This is an obvious reference to *Nightmare on Elm Street* (1984), Wes Craven's classic of the horror genre.

the site of formal experiments (even if there are exceptions such as the singular long take *Russian Ark* (2002) by Alexander Sokurov, shot in ninety minutes of real time in thirty-five rooms of the St. Petersburg Hermitage). Certainly, heritage films are not famous for rapid camera or object movements, even if Sarah Street and Stefani Brusberg-Kiermeier point out that there is a stylistic tinkering of heritage films with *Dogme95* aesthetics.

Dogville is unashamedly 'authorial' and literate in a way widely different from heritage adaptation literariness. There is voice-over narration (by John Hurt) – once thought to be uncinematic and shunned even by many adaptations of novels. There is writing all over the film – from the prop denotations to inserted chapter titles that emulate the explicitly appetizing and ironically distancing chapter headings in 18th-century novels. In spite of the period specificity of a 'classic' heritage comedy, *Dogville* has a classical, mythical, almost allegorical subtext in the names of character and place,[5] in the tragic patterns of rise and fall, hamartia and anagnorisis, and violent and sexual excess. All in all, the 'Brechtian' distancing devices point to the fact that *Dogville* addresses Thornton Wilder's *Our Town* on more levels than merely that of a cynicist send-up of American small-town values.

Heritage films are crucially determined by creating heritage space through location hunting, through 'authentifying' period settings and through lavish but 'correct' costumes. Viewers ascribe 'authenticity' to heritage films to some degree because of the presence of 'authority', i.e. canonical literary authors, such as Jane Austen, but to a considerably higher degree because of their 'heritage space'. Gerry Scott has commented on his production design for *Pride and Prejudice*: "Our aim was to film as much as possible on location because we wanted to use the English landscape as a player in the film." (Birtwistle & Conklin 1995: 37) According to Emma Thompson's shooting diary, Ang Lee felt similarly about Flete Estate (representing Barton Cottage in *Sense and Sensibility*): "For Ang, the house is as important a character as the women." (Thompson 1996: 237) Thompson's diary concentrates on the English weather, on Ang Lee wanting sheep in every exterior shot, on pulling "boobs up as far as they'd go" and on getting the season right by having onlookers picking daisies from the lawn (*ibid.*: 228, 259, 255).

Heritage films, then, are about both reading and showcasing landscapes and costume props. Heritage films construct landscapes and countryside as metonymies of 'Deep England' (Patrick Wright), and they have been criticised for their ruralist nostalgia, harking back the neo-Romantic 'picturesque' ideal developed in response to the threatening industrialism since the beginning of the 19th century.[6] The makers of *Middlemarch*, the quintessential and

---

5 The 'modern' malcontent-philosopher is called Tom Edison; the children in the family of apple growing rapist Chuck are named Athena, Pandora, Olympia, Dahlia, Diana and Jason.

6 Cf. for this the overview by Howkins (2001), and, of course, the classic account by Williams (1973). On the social and economic value of token-nature landscapes and the picturesque, cf. the pioneering work by Ann Bermingham (1987).

paradigmatic Andrew Davies heritage adaptation, spend much of the DVD special "The Making of *Middlemarch*" on their impressive feats in cinematic illusionism, turning Stamford 1993 into Middlemarch 1830. Whereas Von Trier merely wrote the name and outlines of the road in chalk, *Middlemarch*'s location manager, Sam Breckman, spent five months and £200,000 negotiating with residents, Stamford police and council, closing down two roads, removing cars, burglar alarms and power lines and laying a dirt road.

Whereas *Dogville*, therefore, is an antithesis of a heritage film in terms of its ideology, its marketing, and its aesthetics, one might hazard to argue a case for *The Lord of the Rings* trilogy as a ruralist heritage project. *The Lord of the Rings* is clearly a literary adaptation, and, what is more, it is an adaptation of the currently most popular British book, written by an Oxford don.[7] Without a doubt, *The Lord of the Rings* trilogy may also be described as costume films and as quasi-historical films. The trilogy is set in a mythical past, celebrating a lifestyle and character that can be traced to constructions of the rural British past. Whereas the Hobbits are supposed to speak variants of British regional vernaculars, the Cockney spoken by the Orcs is a marker of urban lower class. "Middle Earth", however, clearly transcends the specifically rural pastures of the green and merry Shire. On the one hand, the films are saturated in heritage actors (Ian McKellen, Ian Holm, Cate Blanchett, Sean Bean). On the other hand, the acting talent from Australia, the USA, Scotland and elsewhere reflects a globalised Hollywood. After all, this glorification of 'Britishness' was created for an American company, filmed by a New Zealand director (Peter Jackson) in New Zealand, using New Zealand special effects talent (Weta) and benefiting (in true heritage style) the New Zealand tourist industry. It is a blockbuster fantasy trilogy that clearly appeals to a global audience beyond the restricted, mature middle-class audience, driven by Empire or Shire nostalgia.

The medievalist fantasy characters, plots and locations are a far cry from the social observation within the country gentry[8] – the quintessential core heritage sujet. On the one hand, in proper heritage style, movie locations and costumes are almost as important as the actors are in Jackson's movies. Similar to the 'production values' ethos of heritage films, the bonus material published in the "Extended Version" DVDs takes pride in the exemplary care devoted to 'authentifying' "Middle Earth". On the other hand, the settings emulate European medievalism, and while there are occasional sheep, there is not a single country house in sight, even if the repressed sexuality associated with this setting hovers over the digitally animated mass slaughter.

---

[7]   Cf. the BBC's 2003 *The Big Read* poll (http://www.bbc.co.uk/arts/bigread/top100. shtml). The novel may owe its current popularity to the film trilogy. *The Big Read* demonstrates the degree to which successful adaptations determine the perception and marketing of literary works: *Pride and Prejudice* is second and the entire list is brimful of source texts of recent adaptations.

[8]   For the 19th-century dissemination of the gentlemanly ideal (birth, wealth, honour, integrity, etiquette, cultivation, politeness, and respectability), cf. Castronovo (1987).

The main difference between the core canon of heritage films and *The Lord of the Rings*, however, is that the Tolkien adaptation is action cinema and a big-budget special effects vehicle aimed at crossing the entire spectrum of nation, ethnicity, gender and age in the cinema-going public. The core heritage film audience does not flock to the cinema for digital effects, scary monsters or spectacular stunts. Similar to *Titanic* (1997),[9] the Tolkien adaptations, however, earned global revenue of more than 3 billion dollars (cf. Giles 2003) by transcending these boundaries; in the cinema as well as on DVD, VHS, and chocolate wrappings, in computer games and board games as well as in books and plastic figures. *The Lord of the Rings*, therefore, is a fine example of both convergent generic packaging of cinema products and successful crossover "regenrification" as explained below.

2   "Corset Wars" I: Meta-heritage, Anti-heritage, Alternative Heritage, Revisionist Heritage, Post-heritage, Not-heritage

In November 2002, with the world drifting painfully slowly towards the Iraq war, even the British quality press felt the need to resort to martial imagery in the entirely different field of TV programming. In *The Guardian*, Hadley Freeman picked up the term "corset wars" for the classic TV serials *Dr Zhivago* and *Daniel Deronda*, both adapted by Andrew Davies, which were scheduled against each other by ITV and the BBC, like "duelling juggernauts with rather fetching hood ornaments", as Gareth McLean put it, likewise in *The Guardian*, again resorting to bellicose imagery.[10] The metaphor of the "juggernauts with fetching hood ornaments" picks up the point that heritage films aestheticise the past and provide a cinema of attractions beyond or against narrative. Whereas the binary juxtaposition of 'heritage films' and 'not-heritage films' in the first chapter of this introduction seems to make clear what a heritage film is, the second chapter will render the category problematic indeed. In spite of the schematic opposition forwarded above, I am not arguing that heritage film is a 'monolithic' genre or that it is immune from generic proliferation. As has been demonstrated in more detail elsewhere (Griem & Voigts-Virchow 2003), the success of films marketed as English quality entertainment has created a site of "intense contestation" (Monk 2002: 193), triggering ideological debates concerned with major issues such as national and gender identities, taste cultures, and institutional communities. The cultural studies 'corset skirmishes' of the last decade, therefore, have been fought along different lines.

---

[9]   Monk (2002: 183) pins her attack on constructions of the heritage film in part on the fact that even "the record-breakingly expensive, big-spectacle Hollywood blockbuster *Titanic*" was named as a heritage film. For *Titanic* as heritage film cf. Terry-Chandler (2000); for *The Blair Witch Project* as a subversion of film heritage cf. Morgan (2001).

[10] Cf. for the 'corset wars' and the contributions by Davies and J. Winterson the documentation in the *Media Guardian*, http://www.media.guardian.co.uk (11 March 2003).

Charles Barr coined the term 'heritage film' in respect to "British under-statement and the rich British heritage" in wartime films such as Laurence Olivier's *Henry V* (cf. Barr 1986: 12). The term was rapidly applied to the 1980s-films by Ismail Merchant and James Ivory, dubbed the "Laura Ashley school of filmmaking" by director Alan Parker. These films were vicariously attacked as inherently conservative recreations of a fossilised past in the context of Thatcherite traditionalism and new liberalism. The political implications of the heritage film, therefore, dominated the first phase of the discussion. This line of criticism was directly inspired by the anti-Thatcherist refutation of a traditionalist English mentality evident in the writings of Patrick Wright, Robert Hewison or John Corner and Sylvia Harvey.[11] In this perspective, films such as *A Room with a View, A Passage to India* or *Howards End* seek the imaginary plenitude of the upper-class country house. They delight in an anti-narrative pictorialism and the bourgeois reinvention of a golden age (cf. Higson 1994, 1995). At best, therefore, the 'heritage' film was seen as catering for an individual, nostalgic desire to be part of a non-organic, indirect community.

Since the mid-1990s, however, a clear paradigm shift has become apparent. In view of the rearranged field of heritage film criticism, both film critics and the film industry decided that it was time to go beyond "Janespotting", to quote the memorable term coined by John M. Forde. Andrew Higson, for instance, has reformulated his critique of heritage films (1996, 2003), allowing for a wider spectrum of responses than his earlier political reading seemed to suggest (cf. Higson 2003: 261). Initiated above all by feminist and gay readings, the earlier critical obsession with issues of national identity gave way to a more pluralistic agenda focussing on questions of sexual politics and audience targeting and leaving room for functional differentiation. (cf. Hill 1999: 97). Gender is a decisive category, and it has been used to demolish the very term 'heritage film', which, according to Monk (2002: 195), only works within a framework of ideological criticism. On February 2, 2002, a BBC representative announced in *The Times*: "We will still do period drama, but right now we have a very strong slate of dramas with powerful central female performances. Women tend to be the largest consumers of drama [...]." The gender revision of heritage films comes in the context of renewed interest in the role of costumes, which for a long time had been marginalised as 'feminine and frivolous'. As the recent monograph by Sarah Street (2001) illustrates, critics such as Pamela Church Gibson, Pam Cook or Jane Gaines and Charlotte Herzog have rediscovered the category of costume in movies as a site of flexible identity performance (in the vein of Annette Kuhn or Judith Butler). Stella Bruzzi asked whether films look "at" or "through" the clothes, distinguishing between a pictorialist realism tacitly fetishising historical and literary authenticity and a foregrounding of the fetishistic function of clothes,

---

[11] Cf. also Paxman (1999) and Langford (2000) on mentalities; Lucas (1990) and Gervais (1993) for 'Englishness' in literature; Gikandi (1996) for the post-colonial perspective.

which can be mobilised to activate the pleasures of female spectators (cf. Bruzzi 1997: 35-36).

The increasing hybridisation of heritage film is also indicated by recent crossovers to the *Trainspotting* crowd, such as *Plunkett and Maclean*. One may also discuss the Film Council-sponsored *Revengers Tragedy* (2002) in this vein, which adapts a play by Shakespeare contemporary Thomas Middleton. The play is a violent, misogynistic and implausibly gory revenge tragedy. True, the Duke is played by veteran Shakespeare tragedian Derek Jacobi, but other lottery money is spent on maverick transvestite comedian Eddie Izzard, on crossover specialist Christopher Eccleston, and on the hybrid, dystopian near-future setting of 2012. Rather than showcasing rural countryside, veteran punk filmmaker Alex Cox and *24 Hour Party People* writer Frank Cottrell Boyce turn Liverpool into an urban wasteland corrupted by Murdoch-style media. *Revengers Tragedy* offers studies of problematic masculinities and a Liverpool football stadium setting – it clearly aims at a market identified as "masculine, populist and closely affiliated to youth-orientated style culture" by Monk (2002: 195). Cox's movie basks in sexual aberrance and even directly attacks the Royal family: During the final murders, the camera tilts upwards to expose a portrait of Elizabeth II. This revenge by the dispossessed security workers may be read as a grotesque comedy which mixes Chumbawamba (Liverpudlian 1980s and 90s disco music) and Fellini, and therefore it is a far cry indeed from the moral canon of the English gentry and more reminiscent of *Romeo + Juliet* or *28 Days Later* than of Kenneth Branagh's "Renaissance Films". One may argue that the commercial disaster results from the mutually exclusive audience ranges of "trashed" heritage (cf. Griem & Voigts-Virchow 2003: 325).[12]

Pamela Church Gibson (2000) argued that the visual style of 1990s heritage films departs from canonical movies. Let us return, therefore, to Claire Monk's point that, resulting from the climate of 'New Labour', 'Britpop'-marketing, and the projection of a renewed and progressive cultural industry in Britain, the character of heritage films has mutated. Against Cairns Craig and Higson, Monk argued that the category of heritage film is fraught with the general problems of genre, that it is constructed solely by criticism and valid neither for the industry nor for the consumers. According to Monk, recent heritage films attempt to go beyond the category in both content and marketing, while some 'contemporary' films (such as *The Full Monty, Notting Hill, Bridget Jones's Diary*) might be equally denounced as "cleansed of the urban poor, the homeless and ethnic minorities", conservative and nostalgic, with pro-enterprise messages and successful white professional scenarios, or even as "profoundly reactionary" (such as *Lock, Stock and Two Smoking Barrels*, cf. Monk 2002: 195). Regardless of whether one interprets this as an innovative or a true and tried formula, the presumed canon of generic formu-

---

12 The marketing of *Revengers Tragedy* was imperilled by a disastrous '18'-rating of the trailer by the British Board of Film Classification (BBFC).

lae has been splintered to include the terms 'alternative', 'revisionist' heritage or even heritage films projected as 'not-heritage' films, such as *Elizabeth* and *The Wings of the Dove*.[13]

Higson (2003: 44-45), however, remains unconvinced and continues to reject Monk's argument for a 'post-heritage' film: "[...] there is no clear break between these films and, say, Merchant Ivory's Forster adaptations." Following Monk, one might be tempted to abandon the term 'heritage film' entirely, but the terms 'period film', 'historical film' or 'costume film' merely open up different cans of worms and by no means lend themselves to clearer generic delineation. The very fact that the category has stimulated so much criticism illustrates how productive it continues to be.

While this controversy is palpably informed by the topical debates of cultural criticism, formalist approaches in film studies along the lines of David Bordwell *et al.* have more or less skirted the costume film, as too literary and therefore un-cinematic, in the words of Andy Medhurst (and Clarence in Quentin Tarantino's *True Romance*) as "film-for-people-who-hate-cinema".[14] At the same time, the literature on adaptation keeps burgeoning[15] in spite of the fact that the criterion of fidelity has long since been abandoned – or maybe for that very reason.

Even if the heritage market has reached the point of saturation (Higson 2003: 138-141) and the 'Austenmania' of the mid-1990s, therefore, has abated, heritage films continue to appear in various formats and particularly as TV miniseries. The 'heritage industry' did not simply vanish into thin air when the new Labour government renamed the Department of National Heritage the Department of Culture, Media, and Sport (cf. Worpole 2001: 235). In the cinema, *I Capture the Castle* and *Nicholas Nickleby* were released in 2003, and Roman Polanski has recently agreed to adapt *Oliver Twist*. On TV, Andrew Davies has moved on to a lesser-known Eliot novel, to lesser-known novelist Anthony Trollope (*The Way We Live Now* 2003, *He Knew He Was Right* 2004), to non-English novels (*Dr Zhivago* 2002, 6.5 to 6.2 million viewers), to 'sexier' contemporary recreations of Victorianism (*Tipping the Velvet*, 5 million viewers on BBC 2) and to 'sexier' ancient British history (the disastrous *Boudicca* for ITV in 2003). ITV 1 transmitted the Edwardian two-part miniseries *Plain Jane* to an audience of 5.5 million viewers and belatedly aired their 2001 *The Mayor of Casterbridge* in 2003. The classic TV serial tradition was also continued with the ITV remake of *The Forsyte Saga* (2002). This serial had 9 million viewers on the first night, but subsequently lost a quarter of its audience. The second series (2002) even sank below a 5 million rating. In general, the rat-

---

13 Cf. Powrie (2000: 325-326), Church Gibson (2000), and Monk (2002).
14 For Medhurst cf. Higson (2003: 71), who also quotes Bordwell himself; for *True Romance* cf. Lochhead (1995) in Vincendeau (2001: 14).
15 Cf. Cartmell (1999), Lothe (2000), Vincendeau (2001), Cardwell (2002). Recently, there have been publications on adaptations according to specific literary periods (Mayer 2002, on 18th-century fiction) and on adaptations of individual novelists (Troost & Greenfield 2001, MacDonald & MacDonald 2003, on Austen; Niemeyer 2003, on Hardy).

ings of these adaptations have dropped from the 10 to 12 million viewers who regularly watched *Pride and Prejudice* in 1995. The BAFTA-award winning, six-part *The Way We Live Now*, for instance, lost 1.3 million viewers in two weeks, dropping to a rating of 4.5 million.

The BBC contributed *Byron* (BBC 2) and *Charles II* in 2003. It is now seeking to expand the classic TV serial towards the 'soap opera' format, planning an Andrew Davies's adaptation of Dickens's *Bleak House* as a 20 episode half-hour series to be shown twice a week (cf. Cozens 2003). In general, expensive heritage television has suffered from sinking revenue in TV advertising and the crisis of drama on television. On the other hand, drama elements have infiltrated history programmes to create what has been dubbed "hybrid history" (Brown 2003). Probably as a consequence of generic diversification in a saturated market and of toying around with popular formats, heritage drama has also become part of the intense debate around 'dumbed down' television.

3   "Corset Wars" II: Heritage Films and Adaptation

Let us return to the case of the BBC's *Daniel Deronda*, which was moderately successful (5.5 to 5.8 million viewers). It is quite clear that Davies falls back on an adaptation such as *Daniel Deronda* because of the established reputation of his immensely successful earlier Eliot vehicle, *Middlemarch*. In the case of *Daniel Deronda*, George Eliot promises both an interest for female viewers and the cultural capital of an established Victorian novelist. It can be sure of an audience who "want to see what the book 'looks like'" (McFarlane 1996: 5), and it is clearly not at odds with the BBC ethos of public improvement and education, even if the director made his name in TV soap operas. Eliot's book is out of copyright so she won't claim royalties. The miniseries, however, spawned off an interesting debate between the British novelist Jeanette Winterson and Davies, the foremost heritage adaptor on TV. In fact, they re-iterated some of the attitudes that have become deeply entrenched in the public profile of the debate, however anachronistic they appear to anyone who is familiar with its recent developments. In a venomous letter to the *Guardian* editor, Winterson accused not just Davies but television itself of trivialising literary culture, arguing that the miniseries was incapable of conveying the subtleties of the book. Davies' riposte awarded bad marks for her reading of both, novels and TV serial, and pointed out how many new readers the miniseries would secure for *Daniel Deronda* and *Dr Zhivago*, the books.

This is general fare in the semiotic adaptation studies as summed up by Brian McFarlane (1996), Lothe (2000) and others: Film adaptations are most often adaptations of novels. Both novels and films, tell stories which unfold in space and time and components connected by causality. Films provide visualisations whereas novels provide printed text that must be mentally visualised by their readers. Both novels and films, however, require the meaning-making processes of comprehension. It is enormously difficult to adapt the discourse level of novels; the iconic and indexical process of mean-ing-making is necessarily specific and must represent objects. Outside of the symbolic order, this line of argument goes, adaptations have to show "how people live or lived", they have no grammar, they tend towards neutral nar-ration and they have difficulties in representing subjectivity and thought processes. Adaptation is but one instance of chronologically secondary in-termediality, and the novelisation of *The Piano* is but one example how this can be reversed from film to novel.

A look at some of the more influential adaptation typologies suggests that there are no hard and fast criteria on how to fit individual films into any of the categories established by critics. The criterion 'fidelity' is particularly problematic and has been unanimously criticised by 'adaptationists' such as McFarlane, Morris Beja, Helmut Kreuzer, and Irmela Schneider. Adaptation theory tends to view literary adaptations exclusively in these hierarchical terms, namely, as dependent upon the earlier *Ur*-text or source text, and therefore in terms of the media transfer. Other, no less relevant aspects, such as the remediation of literary heritage phenomena in tie-ins or merchandising and the appropriation of heritage cultures, had for some time been neglected. Shakespeare, for instance, caters to the Stratford-upon-Avon/London Globe tourist cluster and ranks as no. 17 in an ironic as well as idiosyncratic list of heritage clichés, the "Fifty Quintessences of Englishness" in Julian Barnes's *England, England* (1998).[16]

Table 1: Adaptation typologies

Geoffrey Wagner	Dudley Andrew	Helmut Kreuzer
Transposition: minimum interference	Fidelity of transformation	Appropriation of literary 'raw' material
Commentary: purposely or inadvertently altered	Intersection	Illustration: finding images for literary texts
Analogy: considerable departure, time shifts etc.	Borrowing	Interpretative transforma-tion: enunciation process (discourse) transformed
		Documentation: filming theatre

Erica Sheen (2000: 3) has argued against "a rhetoric of possession" and the concomitant restrictive ideas of meaning in adaptation theory. In view of a virtual literary culture recreated by classic films, she suggests a new New Criticism of "restoration" rather than "fidelity" (2000: 11). Sarah Cardwell similarly rejected the old medium-specific adaptationist approach, distin-guishing it from the more descriptive comparative approach culminating in McFarlane's *Novel into Film* (1996), and the pluralist approach of Erica Sheen,

---

[16] The BBC (no. 14), "TV classic serials" (no. 27), and "emotional frigidity" (no. 46) are also particularly relevant to our concerns.

Deborah Cartmell et al. Cardwell is also correct, however, to opt for a return to medium-specific issues (for example peculiarities of film vs. TV) and to a "renewed interest in close textual analysis" (Cardwell 2002: 73).

4   A Case Study: Syncretic Crossover Shakespeare

If there is a common critical consensus that fidelity and hierarchies of media change should not dominate research into adaptations, then one should discard typologies based explicitly or implicitly on these criteria. In the case of Shakespeare, for instance, one might ask the question as to whether similar typologies of Shakespeare films or even the very category of 'Shakespeare film' itself are still valid.

Not surprisingly, the existing typologies of Shakespeare films seem equally inadequate methodological tools for analysis. Neil Sinyard (2000: 69) has cordoned off three types of Shakespeare films. The *conservative* Shakespeare movie (such as Laurence Olivier's *Henry V*), he writes, is marked by a star cast, and aims for reverence, not relevance. The *updating* Shakespeare movie (such as Richard Loncraine's *Richard III*), opts for incongruous modernization. According to Sinyard, the *reconceptualising* Shakespeare movie (Baz Luhrmann's *Romeo + Juliet*) eventually arrives at a "cancelled out" Shakespeare by adapting him to the visual language and form of today. Sinyard seems to share Zeffirelli's prejudice against films in this category. He quotes the veteran Shakespearean director, who said of Baz Luhrmann that he "didn't update the play, [but] made a big joke out of it", pandering to the "pseudo-culture of young people of today".

Instead, Sinyard champions Al Pacino's *Looking for Richard* as an ideal *synthesis* of existing approaches to Shakespeare. According to Sinyard, Pacino offers a star cast, a congruous modernization, and reconciles its appeal to a young audience with a welcome preservation of the text's poetry.

Adaptationist critics have conventionally invoked a number of traditional problems in adapting Shakespeare: How does the director or the cinematic apparatus create an articulate visual language for Shakespeare? How does the film solve the particular question of manipulating a space that is virtually blank in the Shakespearean text (Davies 1988, Jackson 2000)? What is the particular predicament of films as (readable, repeatable) texts vs. the study of a Shakespeare performance, in other words, in what way is a Shakespeare film a Shakespeare "performance re-textualized" (Donaldson 1990)? The valid point has been made that the automatic need to "concretize" means more flexibility for a Shakespeare film than for filmic audiovisualizations of 19th-century novels (cf. Cartmell 2000). Finally, there remains the perennial problem of how to assess the rendering of Shakespearean language on film, with standard complaints about rhythmic problems with the blank verse or American accents fuelled by absurd notions of textual purity or authoritative Shakespearean acting.

What might a Shakespeare film studies look like which transcends questions such as these? First of all, it is important to go beyond the all-too-neat typologies. We need to develop a more flexible framework when dealing with the recent Shakespeare film, which is fragmented into a wild and syncretic variety of generic modes, reflecting the recent generic hybridity and splintered target groups of New Hollywood (cf. Schmidt 2002). Both in terms of film form and in terms of film audiences, therefore, we have seen art-house Shakespeare (*Prospero's Books*), horror Shakespeare (*Titus*), American war Shakespeare (*Henry V*), transatlantic "heritage" and "frock-flick" Shakespeare with crossovers into postmodern rom-com (*Much Ado About Nothing, Twelfth Night, Midsummer Night's Dream*), alternative heritage and action Shakespeare (*Richard III*), teen pop culture Shakespeare (*Romeo + Juliet, Almereyda's Hamlet, 10 Things I Hate About You*), and, finally, camp and subculture Shakespeare (Jarman's *The Tempest, Tromeo and Juliet*).

It is obvious that Shakespeare films are crossover products, which fill the bill for prestigious but comparably inexpensive art-house movies with a blockbuster potential. They are syncretic in the sense that they fuse supposedly incongruous genres into a new blend. The three most successful Shakespeare movies are teen films and a bio-pic which is only loosely connected with the plays, indicating that the category of 'fidelity' has been eroded (cf. table 2). After we have got rid of questionable typologies and the obsolete criterion of 'fidelity', it might be worth looking again at adaptation studies.

Table 2: Selected Shakespeare movies at the box office (LUMIERE database, figures: admissions in thousands)

Shakespeare in Love (John Madden 1998)	US: 19 423	EUR: 17 338
Romeo + Juliet (Baz Luhrmann 1996)	US: 10 466	EUR: 7 725
10 Things I Hate About You (Gil Junger 1999)	US: 7 515	EUR: 2 167
A Midsummer Night's Dream (M. Hoffman 1999)	US: 3 163	EUR: 1 850
Hamlet (Kenneth Branagh 1997)	US: 960	EUR: 1 033
Richard III (Richard Loncraine 1995)	US: 603	EUR: 666
Titus (Julie Taymor 1999)	US: 334	EUR: 140
Hamlet (Michael Almereyda 2000)	US: 286	EUR: 99

5   "Hybrid Heritage, Hybrid History": The *Mise-en-scène* of Historicity, Nationalism and Genre

The very title of Raphael Samuel's seminal work *Theatres of Memory* refers to the staging or *mise-en-scène* of history.[17] Terms such as re-enactment, dramati-

---

[17] The term appears in the 17th and 18th centuries in France, but in order to overcome an unnecessary distinction in Film Studies, one may also speak of a history *montage*, a

sation and re-creation refer to the indisputably constructed nature of our representations of the past. This constructedness has been highlighted in the constructivist paradigm of metahistorical thinking, the linguistic turn of historical research in the vein of Hayden White and his trenchant critique of the 'verbal fictions' of historical writings or of Robin G. Collingwood, whose *The Idea of History* from 1946 draws structural parallels between the narrative coherence of novels and history.

Since their beginnings, film and television have proved a useful and profitable medium for historical or heritage formats. Dominant concepts of the nation, for instance, are largely dependent on images in the media and in education. In her seminal book on *British National Cinema*, Sarah Street (1997: 1) points out that we "have inherited a dominant conception of what it is to be British, a collective consciousness about nationhood which has, in part, been constructed by cultural referents, including cinema". The rise of the multiplex cinema has both re-invigorated the cinema industry and increased the pressure on filmmakers to produce predictable rather than risky and daring movies. The proliferation of screens in the multiplex, therefore, has spawned the generic hybridisation of film beyond a monolithic mass audience, but has it also broadened the scope of the British collective consciousness?

Nationalism should be seen as the product of a hybrid amalgamation of national languages, histories, myths, traditions, and symbols. A nation is thus the effect rather than the cause of nationalism. Whereas the construction of a nation may be a conscious process, it must necessarily conform to a community sense of a shared heritage. Thus, a nation as a 'mental image' may appear, as Benedict Anderson's famous phrase goes, as 'imagined communities': Even if they don't know each other personally, members of the same nation develop a sense of togetherness from sharing a 'heritage', i.e. languages, novels, issues, and one might add, heritage films and history channels. This heritage function of possessing a cultural 'safe haven' is displayed affirmatively and unapologetically on the *Russian Ark* website:

> We have lost or forgotten some of our traditions; we have greatly altered our way of life, for better or for worse; and our social behaviour and attitudes towards each other have changed radically over the centuries. Only the creation of the finest art, architecture, music and literature can sustain the idea of a greater humanity, and give it a point of anchorage for the future, a safe haven from the storm.[18]

'We' presumably refers to the Russians. Or does it? And, if so, who are they really and are they such a homogeneous group? In his 1998 study, *Englishness and National Culture* Antony Easthope argued that Benedict Anderson's ubiquitously quoted notion of the 'imaginary community' still adheres to "a

---

'mounting' of history on a stage. History appears in some kind of virtual form or representation or imagination or re-enactment of the historical event that cannot be actual, present, or concrete.

18 http://www.russianark.spb.ru/eng/ (21 January 2004).

nostalgic and sentimental desire to believe that face-to-face contact is real, free from interference by signs, language, 'writing', while opposed to this the larger, more impersonal groupings constructed by modernity are imaginary, false, unreal" (Easthope 1998: 10). In contrast to Anderson, Easthope redefined national identity as an "effect of multiple identifications" which creates the impression of unity by overlooking the very conditions of its emergence: "Identity [...] arises as a necessary coherency which can never escape the operation of which its temporary fixity is an effect. In this sense all identity is plural and disjunct." (Easthope 1998: 22-23)

Among others, Pam Cook (1996: 2) has drawn on costume films to illustrate the doomed "quest for authentic identities", arguing that nationalisms

> which depend on a retreat to cultural purity, to unchanging ethnic identities and boundaries, appear to be a manifestation of cultural crisis, a last refuge from social change.

In the field of British cinema, Sarah Street (1997) pointed out both its diversity and the extent of the Hollywood influence. British film, therefore, is just as plural and disjunct as (national) identities, and its 'multiple identification' will, in part, include Hollywood film and (in some smaller part) even European film. Sargeant (2000) suggested a fine-tuning of heritage analysis considering the targeting of a 'glocalised' market, the democratisation and expansion of heritage culture and the increasingly complex tie-ins between tourism and the film industry. Analyses of Britishness and Englishness in film and TV, therefore, have become more complicated because of recent trends of a 'globalised' or 'glocalised' culture as described by Mike Featherstone or Robert Robertson. Robertson (1990: 20) analysed a relatively recent modern/postmodern "structuration of the world as a whole". Both Robertson and Featherstone (1990a: 1) insisted that this is a cultural rather than a political or institutional tendency. Robertson (1995: 28-29) has theorised 'glocalisation' in the business sense as "the tailoring and advertising of goods and services on a global or near-global basis to increasingly differentiated local and particular markets. [...] To put it very simply, diversity sells." This diversity has been fostered by the consumer society, and, more to the point, by global narrowcasting of multi-channel TV[19] and the rise of the fragmented audience multi-generic crossover film. Even if commentators such as Anthony D. Smith maintained at an early stage in the debate that strong anti-global forces remained, based on both an old and resilient "ethno-history"(1990: 182) and a new, pressing need for identity in the face of oblivion, these forces were somewhat mitigated through transnational "culture areas" (1990: 185) based on shared cultural assumptions.

---

[19] Cable and satellite channels catering to more specialised audience segments have appeared, such as The History Channel (since 1994) and the latest rival, UK History, which opened in 2002 on the cable network UKTV, co-owned by BBC Worldwide and Telewest.

The concept of 'culture areas' is useful for the discussion of the transnational appeal of heritage films that clearly transcend the boundaries of Britain. One may say that British heritage films speak to an international audience, for instance fulfilling heritage functions in Germany across a national divide (in the relative absence of a German 'heritage' film). In Germany, one certainly could not witness anything remotely equivalent to the wave of post 1980s or 1990s heritage films, to the Andrew Davies serials for the BBC and WBGH or the Merchant/Ivory industry or the transatlantic Edith Wharton and Henry James 'gang'. Even if there have been attempts at rejuvenating the Austro-German *Heimatfilm* one can hardly overestimate the influence of the British heritage formula on the German market.[20] In this sense, Germany and Britain seem to share a 'culture area', British traditions imaginatively replacing the lacunae of German heritage culture destroyed by militarism and fascism.

For Rick Altman, who argues about genres in a similar vein as Antony Easthope argues about nations, the formation of genres can also be explained as an attempt to cover up the instability of generic categories: "While at any given point a generic system may appear perfectly balanced and thus at rest, the look of stability is actually produced only by a momentary equilibrium of countervening concerns." (Altman 1999: 195) Echoing Easthope's critique of Anderson's 'imaginary community', Altman works within a functionalist and flexible framework of genre analysis, which might accommodate both generic approaches based on categories of both gender and ideology. Moreover, Altman's less deterministic approach implies that genres are often hybrid, that they look different to different audiences and that they have to be approached as "system and process", "constantly subject to reconfiguration, recombination and reformulation" (Altman 1999: 195). In this view, it makes little sense to argue that an audience is being 'positioned' by heritage films, entirely at the mercy of the hegemonic signification or at least preferred readings.

It makes equally little sense to argue that heritage films or costume films do or do not exist or to quibble over conflicting canons, when, according to

---

20 The Austro-German frock-flick or *Heimatfilm* (literally, 'hometown film') has a 1950s track record in the wake of *Schwarzwaldmädel* (1950) and the Karlheinz Böhm/Romy Schneider vehicle *Sissi* (1955). There have been alternative and post-heritage variants since the 1980s (for instance, *Heimat* by Edgar Reitz, the Eberhard Fechner/Walter Kempowski family saga of a Rostock family (*Tadellöser & Wolff* etc.), or the films of Joseph Vilsmaier and Jo Baier (thanks to Lucia Krämer for pointing this out in the discussion). One may also mention the drama-documentaries by Heinrich Breloer and Oliver Storz, German variants of the "history docusoap" modelled on Channel Four's *The 1900 House*, such as the SWR *Schwarzwaldhaus*, or the recent wave of post-1989 films aimed in various ways at defining a German post-unification identity: *Lola rennt (Run Lola Run)*, *Sonnenallee*, *Goodbye Lenin*, *Das Wunder von Bern*. The success of British heritage products in Germany as well as the the German 'trash heritage' TV productions of Mills and Boon novelist Rosamunde Pilcher speak for the scope of the heritage film formula, which reaches well into contemporary Germany.

Altman, "the diverse groups using the genre are considered together" and "genres appear as regulatory schemes facilitating the integration of diverse factions into a single social fabric" (Altman 1999: 208). *Bleak House*, the new BBC Dickens soap, is yet another attempt at finding an integrated audience (soap/period/costume/heritage) for a syncretic product. It remains to be seen whether Trollope and Dickens adaptations can really regenrify the heritage film in a manner similar to the remarkable syncretism of gender and heritage concerns in *Pride and Prejudice*.

The current heritage *mise-en-scène* is a nostalgic, historicist simulation. It is, however, also much more than that:[21] a lively exchange and interaction between communities who meet in this theatre of "resurrectionism", as Samuel famously called it (1994: 139). The 'resurrectionism' of the heritage community includes retrochic and conversationism, the revival of Georgian housing and high-waisted dressing in the mid-1990s, the rising memberships of the National Trust and JASNA (the Jane Austen Society of North America), the Janeite discussion groups and organisations – now a legitimate academic field of study (cf. Lynch 2000 and Wiltshire 2001), the popular commercial websites maintained by *ExxonMobil* [!] *Masterpiece Theatre*, or *Eras of Elegance*, the large community of 'living historians', the proliferation of history docusoaps, the resurrected Globe theatres around the globe, the immense success of Simon Schama's *A History of Britain* (on TV, DVD, VHS, WWW and in print), the history docu-soaps such as *The 1900 House* and, at the academic end, the *International Journal of Heritage Studies*. In order to discuss how strategies of what Altman calls "regenrification" (1999: 199) can be employed to offer various forms of national identity to highly differentiated target audiences, it may be useful to chart the criteria which have served to analyse and group together the so-called heritage films or costume dramas.

History or heritage programmes and films are necessarily spatial and concrete. In both historiographical and fictional re-imagining, identity is in part determined by décor, costume, and make-up, rather than by historical knowledge or literary fidelity. The generic indeterminacy as well as the key importance of exotic visuality of film and TV has probably contributed to coining another catchphrase, "retrovisions". The term was suggested by Cartmell and Hunter (2001: 2) for "countermyths" which "demythologise the past, gazing back sometimes with horror at its violence and oppression [...] and sometimes with nostalgia for lost innocence and style", for texts which "self-consciously reinterpret history through the meshes of genre and fictional precedent", and which are "both postmodern as academics understand the term – allusive, ironic, knowingly intertextual – and firmly in line with popular culture's playful and opportunistic treatment of history".

What has been lost in this trend towards retrovision, of course, is the clear distinction between 'historical film' and 'costume film', so that Andrew Hig-

---

[21] See the overview in Böker (2000), who takes cognitivist approaches to task, arguing that heritage culture is polyvalent rather than monolithically 'positioning' the audience.

son (2003: 12) rejects the category 'history'. He argues that traditional criteria – actual figures from history vs. fictional characters in historical settings, or public events vs. private matters – have been blurred in filmmaking as early as in the 1930s, and also in bio-pics such as *Elizabeth* (1998), *The Madness of King George* (1995) or *Mrs Brown* (1997).

This volume, therefore, reflects the multiplicity of retrovisual genres. It is opened by three papers that specifically address the *mise-en-scène* of 'Austen Powers' from widely different perspectives. Andrew Higson augments his recent *English Heritage, English Cinema* with his chapter on Jane Austen adaptations, arguing against an adaptationist or 'fidelity'- approach. 'Literariness' is but one of nine features that Higson isolates as typical of English costume films of this period. For him, these movies seek to extend the production trend in costume drama from the 1980s into the 1990s. Next, Pamela Church Gibson takes issue with Higson's focus on *Mansfield Park* as a marketing ploy. For her, the film indicates a pioneering political and feminist revision of the heritage genre. From still another point of view, Raimund Borgmeier attacks the harsh criticism of showcasing heritage landscapes in Austen movies, arguing that they debate "formal" and "landscape" garden concepts as essential components of their audiovisual signification.

The next section in this volume discusses the specific situation of filming *fin de siècle* Shakespeare. The notion of cultural capital figures prominently in Deborah Cartmell's reading, which assesses the contribution of Shakespeare movies to the breakdown of the clear audience segmentation between 'Trainspotters' vs. 'Janespotters', focusing on Michael Almereyda's 'teen-pic' *Hamlet*. Roberta E. Pearson takes issue with the 'capitalization' of heritage Shakespeare on television. She also offers a critique of rivalling concepts she names as 'humanist', universalist appropriations and as the prevalent facile Shakespeare populism, faulting all of these Shakespeare readings for their tendency to erase history.

The third section features various readings of 'post-heritage' products, and it also exhibits a timely emphasis on the somewhat neglected field of heritage television. Sarah Street reads classic TV serials in the climate of postmodernist historicity. Contextualising history documentaries (for instance, by Simon Schama) and TV programmes such as *The Lost Prince* and *The Other Boleyn Girl*, she argues that the current television syncretism allows for influences that go beyond a recycling of heritage aesthetics. Carolin Held locates a different kind of television hybridity that moves beyond heritage formulae. She reads recent literary adaptations on television for subversions of pictorialism and finds these both in an expressionist or grotesque *mise-en-scène* and, more generally, in a tendency to define space in narrational rather than pictorialist terms.

The following two papers focus on adaptations of Oscar Wilde. Barbara Schaff harks back to an issue raised in Sarah Street's paper, the problem of historicity vs. heritage. She accepts the idea (voiced, among others, by Baudrillard) that heritage films feature a 'display aesthetics', but then documents how *tableaux vivants* may contribute towards an intermedial camouflage of problematic notions of 'authenticity'. Next, Lucia Krämer's paper utilises a more adaptationist approach to make a similar point: For her, it is the Wildean intertextuality and theatricality that contributes towards the critical interrogation of authenticity in Oliver Parker's Wilde adaptations. Stefani Brusberg-Kiermeier brings this issue to bear on recent adaptations of *Wuthering Heights*. Revising adaptationist concerns, she concludes that only a departure from heritage conventions may, in the future, render productive audiovisual media transfers of Emily Brontë's difficult multi-perspective novel.

The final section of this volume provides papers that distinctly transgress the national boundaries of the heritage debate, rendering the category of 'target culture' or 'target audience' problematic both in terms of marketing and in terms of teaching these films. Picking up the cinema/television link mentioned by Andrew Higson, Angela Krewani is clearly indebted to his view of heritage film as an entertainment industry. She charts how a parochial British TV miniseries format has come to be part of international Hollywood entertainment, reflecting both the international component of the heritage concept and the diversification of Hollywood formulae. The contributions by Carola Surkamp and Monika Seidl provide glimpses into the foreign language classroom, arguing that heritage films play an increasing if problematic role in teaching key cultural manifestations of British mentalities and images to Austro-German students. For Surkamp, heritage films may disentangle the teaching of film from purely formalist concerns, while Seidl takes issue with adaptationist and fact-based transmission models in teaching cultural studies.

It follows from this diversity of approaches that Higson is right in warning against all too easy categorization, switching between the terms "heritage films, costume dramas, period films" (Higson 2003: 9). He argues that "genres and cycles are in fact best understood as loose, leaky, hybrid categories" (*ibid.*: 10). Following Samuel, Higson (2001: 258) has also taken to speaking of "heritages" in the plural. If we can still dissociate historical films, heritage films, costume films, or period films, then we do so only tentatively by the claims they make and by the degree to which their audience accepts these claims. Iser (1991: 35) calls this a contract between producer and recipient established through textual, paratextual and situational signals. The controversial generic markers of heritage itself, as well as historicity and literariness indicate, therefore, that all the other categories in the following matrix have to remain contested and fluid. Various concerns may position our papers at opposing corners in the grid below, but it is our shared notion that this collection of essays opens up new perspectives on the negotiation and commerce of values, histories and cultures in heritage retrovisions.[22]

---

[22] I would like to thank Julika Griem for developing some crucial ideas with me (cf. Griem & Voigts-Virchow 2003). Further thanks are due to Katherine Williams, Elaine Nowak,

Table 3: Criteria and conceptualizations of 'heritage/costume/period' films

Criterion	Conceptualization	
Mediality	Classic novel TV serial (CNTVS): residual ethos of education and betterment (Mackillop & Platt 2000: 71), traditionally national transmission, secondary markets, "soap classics"?	Classic novel film adaptation (CNFA): pure entertainment, crossover films and border genres: global niche audiences, "New Hollywood" and glocalisation (Robertson 1995)
Genre	Genre film, formula film, heritage film as part of heritage culture	Transgeneric, hybrid crossover film, revisionist heritage, alternative heritage, post-heritage und meta-heritage, heritage parody or pastiche, syncretic "regenrification" (Altman 1999)
Literariness	Literary adaptation (McFarlane 1996, Cardwell 2002): fidelity, adaptation studies, respect for books (Higson), hybridity of literary and film cultures: mutual tie-in vs. subservience, ex. *The Piano*	Original screenplays: 'sub-literary' or seeking to participate in literary culture
Historicity	Historical films (Mico *et al.* 1996, Rosenstone & Sobchack 1996, Rother 1998, Landy 1997, 2001, Monk & Sargeant 2002): set in public spheres, historical fictions, conservative retro-film: fossilization of past in nostalgia film (Jameson)	Costume films (Gaines & Herzog 1990, Harper 1994, Cook 1996, Bruzzi 1997 & 2000, Street 2001): set in private spheres, visual re-enactment of period supersedes questions of accuracy, period fictions (Monk 2002) vs. "progressive" or "contemporary" film
Classicality	Classic films: received notions of high culture, decorum, moderation, harmony, mimesis, tradition, stability (Giddings & Sheen 2000, Giddings & Selby 2000, Cartmell *et al.* 2000)	Contemporary films: excess, sensationalism, instability, intensity, taboo-breaking
Biographism	Bio-pic, tie-in specials: history or literature personified	Socio-historical or economic analysis, materialism
Iconography	Pictorialism, "Laura Ashley" cinema of attractions (Alan Parker): visual conservationism (Higson)	Stylistic excess or bricolage, mannerism, painterly tableaux, costumes vs. clothes
Englishness	Metonymic English south, rural-pastoral, pre-industrial, imperialist heritage film	Geo-social diversity, urban, industrial or post-industrial, postimperialist 'not-heritage' film
Formalism	Transparent, uncinematic, "film-for-people-who-hate-cinema" (Medhurst 1995)	'Modernist' or cinematic, "movie"
Politics	Right-wing, reactionary or conservative film	Left-wing, progressive film
Emotionality	Costume melodrama: idealised beauty, emotional, warm, feminine or gay (Dyer 1994), sexually repressed	Aesthetics of ugliness, harsh, cool, masculinist, brutal, sexually explicit
Mass appeal	Minority film, crossover film	Blockbuster
Class appeal	Middle-class film: occupational vacuum, recreation	Working-class film (Higson 1996: 232-233)
Age appeal	Mature film	Adolescent film, "teen-pic"
Gender appeal	Bourgeois feminist film, woman's film, gay film	Heterosexual masculinist film

Alexander van de Bergh, Sonja Peacock, Imke Neumann, Christian Kölzer and Meike Röhl. I also gratefully acknowledge financial support for this project by the Centre for Media and Interactivity, The British Council, and the Gießener Hochschulgesellschaft.

Bibliography

Altman, Rick (1999), *Film/Genre*, London: British Film Institute.

Anderson, Benedict (²1991), *Imagined Communities. Reflections on the Origin and Spread of Nationalism*, London – New York: Verso.

Andrew, Dudley (1984), "Adaptation", in Andrew, *Concepts in Film Theory*, Oxford: Oxford University Press, 96-106.

Ashby, Justine & Andrew Higson, eds. (2000), *British Cinema, Past and Present*, London: Routledge.

Barnes, Julian (1998), *England, England*, London: Jonathan Cape.

Barr, Charles (1986), "Introduction: Amnesia and Schizophrenia", in Barr, ed., *All Our Yesterdays. 90 Years of British Cinema*, London: British Film Institute, 1-29.

Beja, Morris (1979), *Film and Literature*, New York: Longman.

Bermingham, Ann (1987), *Landscape and Ideology: The English Rustic Tradition, 1740-1860*, London: Thames & Hudson.

Birtwistle, Sue & Susie Conklin (1995), *The Making of "Pride and Prejudice"*, London: Penguin Books/BBC Books.

Böker, Uwe (2000), "Der britische *heritage*-Film der achtziger und neunziger Jahre. Die vetrackte Entschlüsselung medialer Zeichenwelten", in Martin Huber & Gerhard Lauer, eds., *Nach der Sozialgeschichte. Konzepte für eine Literaturwissenschaft zwischen Historischer Anthropologie, Kulturgeschichte und Medientheorie*, Tübingen: Niemeyer, 593-608.

Brown, Maggie (2003), "Walking with Hybrids", *The Guardian*, 24 November.

Bruzzi, Stella (1997), *Undressing Cinema. Clothing and Identity in the Movies*, London: Routledge.

-----, ed. (2001), *Fashion Cultures: Theories, Explorations, and Analysis*, London: Routledge.

Burnett, Mark Thornton & Ramona Wray, eds. (2000), *Shakespeare, Film, Fin de Siècle*, Basingstoke – London: Macmillan.

Cardwell, Sarah (2002), *Adaptation Revisited. Television and the Classic Novel*, Manchester – New York: Manchester University Press.

Cartmell, Deborah & I.Q. Hunter (2001), "Introduction: Retrovisions: Historical Make-overs in Film and Literature", in Cartmell *et al.*, eds., 1-7.

Cartmell, Deborah & Imelda Whelehan, eds. (1999), *Adaptations. From Text to Screen, Screen to Text*, London, NY: Routledge.

Cartmell, Deborah (2000), *Interpreting Shakespeare on Screen*, Basingstoke, London: Macmillan.

Cartmell, Deborah, I.Q. Hunter & Imelda Whelehan, eds. (2001), *Retrovisions. Reinventing the Past in Film and Fiction*, London: Pluto Press.

Castronovo, David (1987), *The English Gentleman. Images and Ideals in Literature and Society*, New York: Ungar.

Church Gibson, Pamela (2000), "Fewer Weddings and More Funerals: Changes in the Heritage Film", in Robert Murphy, ed., *British Cinema of the 90s*, London: British Film Institute, 115-124.

Collingwood, Robin G. (1956), *The Idea of History* (¹1946), ed. T.M. Knox, London – Oxford – New York: Oxford University Press.

Cook, Pam (1996), *Fashioning the Nation. Costume and Identity in British Cinema*. London: British Film Institute.

Cozens, Claire (2003), "Great Expectations for Dickens 'Soap'", *The Guardian*, 19 December.

Craig, Cairns (1991), "Rooms without a View", *Sight and Sound* NS 1:2, 10-13.

Davies, Anthony (1988), *Filming Shakespeare's Plays*, Cambridge: Cambridge University Press.

Donaldson, Peter S. (1990), *Shakespearean Film – Shakespearean Directors*, London: Hyman.

Dyer, Richard (1994), "Feeling English", *Sight and Sound* NS 4:3, 17-19.

Easthope, Antony (1998), *Englishness and National Culture*, London – New York: Routledge.

Featherstone, Mike (1990a), "Global Culture: An Introduction", in Featherstone, ed. (1990b), 1-14.

-----, ed. (1990b), *Global Culture*, London: Sage.

Featherstone, Mike, Scott Lash & Robert Robertson, eds. (1995), *Global Modernities*, London: Sage.

Forde, John Maurice (1997), "Janespotting", *Topic* 48, 11-21.

Gaines, Jane & Charlotte Herzog, eds. (1990), *Fabrications. Costume and the Female Body*, London – New York: Routledge.

Gervais, David (1993), *Literary Englands: Versions of 'Englishness' in Modern Writing*, Cambridge: Cambridge University Press.

Giddings, Robert & Erica Sheen, eds. (2000), *The Classic Novel from Page to Screen*, Manchester: Manchester University Press.

Giddings, Robert & Keith Selby, eds. (2001), *The Classic Serial on Television and Radio*, Basingstoke: Palgrave.

Gikandi, Simon (1996), *Maps of Englishness: Writing Identity in the Culture of Colonialism*, New York: Columbia University Press.

Giles, Jeff (2003), "Secrets of 'The King'", *Newsweek*, 1 December.

Griem, Julika & Eckart Voigts-Virchow (2002), "Filmnarratologie: Grundlagen, Tendenzen und Beispielanalysen", in Vera & Ansgar Nünning, eds., *Erzähltheorie transgenerisch, intermedial, interdisziplinär*, Trier: Wissenschaftlicher Verlag Trier, 155-184.

----- (2003), "Trashing and Recycling: Regenrification in British Heritage Movies and Costume Films of the 1990s", in Ewald Mengel, Hans-Jörg Schmid, Michael Steppat, eds., *Proceedings Anglistentag 2002 Bayreuth*, Trier: Wissenschaftlicher Verlag Trier, 319-331.

Harper, Sue (1994), *Picturing the Past. The Rise and Fall of the British Costume Film*, London: British Film Institute.

Hewison, Robert (1987), *The Heritage Industry. Britain in a Climate of Decline*, London: Methuen.

Higson, Andrew (1995), *Waving the Flag: Constructing a National Cinema in Britain*, Oxford: Oxford University Press.

----- (1996), "The Heritage Film and British Cinema", in Higson, ed., *Dissolving Views. Key Writings on British Cinema*, London: Cassell, 232-248.

----- (2001), "Heritage Cinema and Television", in Morley & Robins, eds., 249-260.

----- (2003), *English Heritage, English Cinema. Costume Drama since 1980*, Oxford: Oxford University Press.

Hill, John (1999), *British Cinema in the 1980s. Issues and Themes*, Oxford: Clarendon Press.

Howkins, Alun (2001), "Rurality and English Identity", in Morley & Robins, eds., 145-156.

Iser, Wolfgang (1991), *Das Fiktive und das Imaginäre. Perspektiven literarischer Anthropologie*, Frankfurt/Main: Suhrkamp. [engl. transl. by Iser and David Henry Wilson:

The Fictive and the Imaginary: Charting Literary Anthropology, Baltimore: Johns Hopkins University Press, 1993.]

Jackson, Russell (2000), "From play-script to screenplay", in Jackson, ed., *The Cambridge Companion to Shakespeare on Film*, Cambridge: Cambridge University Press, 15-34.

Kreuzer, Helmut (1993), "Arten der Literaturadaption", in Wolfgang Gast, ed., *Literaturverfilmung*, Bamberg: C.C. Buchners, 27-31.

Kumar, Krishan (2001), "Englishness and English National Identity", in Morley & Robins, eds., 41-55.

Landy, Marcia (1997), *Cinematic Uses of the Past*, Minneapolis: University of Minnesota Press.

-----, ed. (2001), *The Historical Film. History and Memory in Media*, New Brunswick, NJ: Rutgers University Press.

Langford, Paul (2000), *Englishness Identified. Manners and Character 1650-1850*, Oxford: Oxford University Press.

Le Goff, Jacques (1977), *Geschichte und Gedächtnis*, Frankfurt – New York: Campus, 1992.

Lothe, Jakob (2000), *Narrative in Fiction and Film: An Introduction*, Oxford: Oxford University Press.

Lucas, John (1990), *England and Englishness. Ideas of Nationhood in English Poetry 1688-1900*, Iowa City: University of Iowa Press.

Lynch, Deidre, ed. (2000), *Janeites. Austen's Disciples and Devotees*, Princeton: Princeton University Press.

MacDonald, Gina & Andrew F. MacDonald, eds (2003), *Jane Austen on Screen*, Cambridge: Cambridge University Press.

Mackillop, Ian & Alison Platt (2000), "Beholding a Magic Panorama': Television and the Illustration of *Middlemarch*", in Giddings & Sheen, eds., 71-92.

Mayer, Robert, ed. (2002), *Eighteenth-Century Fiction on Screen*. Cambridge: Cambridge University Press.

McFarlane, Brian (1996), *Novel into Film. An Introduction to the Theory of Adaptation*, Oxford: Clarendon.

McKechnie, Kara (2002), "Taking Liberties with the Monarch: The Royal Bio-Pic in the 1990s", in Monk & Sargeant, eds., 217-236.

Medhurst, Andy (1995), "Inside the British Wardrobe", *Sight and Sound* NS 5:3, 16-17.

Mico, Ted, John Miller-Monzon & David Rubel, eds. (1996), *Past Imperfect. History According to the Movies*, New York: Henry Holt/Owl.

Monk, Claire & Amy Sargeant, eds. (2002), *British Historical Cinema. The History, Heritage and Costume Film*, London – New York: Routledge.

Monk, Claire (1995), "The British Heritage Film and Its Critics", *Critical Survey* 7:2, 116-124.

----- (2002), "The British Heritage-Film Debate Revisited", in Monk & Sargeant, eds. 176-198.

Morgan, Sally J. (2001), "Heritage *Noire*: Truth, History, and Colonial Anxiety in *The Blair Witch Project*", in *International Journal of Heritage Studies* 7:2, 137-148.

Morley, David & Kevin Robins, eds. (2001), *British Cultural Studies. Geography, Nationality, and Identity*, Oxford: Oxford University Press.

Niemeyer, Paul J. (2003), *Seeing Hardy: Film and Television Adaptations of the Fiction of Thomas Hardy*, Jefferson, NC: McFarland.

Paxman, Jeremy, (1999), *The English. A Portrait of a People*, London: Penguin.

Powrie, Phil (2000), "On the Threshold between Past and Present. 'Alternative Heritage'", in Ashby & Higson, eds., 316-326.

Robertson, Robert (1992), *Globalization. Social Theory and Global Culture*, London: Sage.

----- (1995), "Glocalization: Time-Space and Homogeneity-Heterogeneity", in Featherstone *et al.*, eds., 25-44.

Rosenstone, Robert A. (1996), "The Future of the Past: Film and the Beginnings of Postmodern History", in Sobchack, ed., 201-218.

Rother, Rainer, ed. (1998), *Mythen der Nationen: Völker im Film*, München – Berlin: Köhler & Amelang.

Samuel, Raphael (1994), *Theatres of Memory*, London – New York: Verso.

Sargeant, Amy (2000), "Making and Selling Heritage Culture. Style and Authenticity in Historical Fictions on Film and Television", in Ashby & Higson, eds., 301-315.

Schmidt, Johann N. (2000), "In Love with Shakespeare: Der Barde und das zeitgenössische Hollywood-Kino", *Shakespeare-Jahrbuch* 137, 86-99.

Schneider, Irmela (1981), *Der verwandelte Text. Wege zu einer Theorie der Literaturverfilmung*, Tübingen: Niemeyer.

Sheen, Erica (2000), "Introduction", in Giddings & Sheen, eds., 2-13.

Sinyard, Neil (2000), "Shakespeare Meets the Godfather: The Postmodern Populism of Al Pacino's *Looking for Richard*", in Burnett & Wray, eds., 58-72.

Smith, Anthony D. (1990), "Towards a Global Culture?", in Featherstone, ed. (1990b), 171-191.

Sobchack, Vivian, ed. (1996), *The Persistence of History: Cinema, Television and the Modern Event*, New York: Routledge.

Sonnet, Esther (1999), "From *Emma* to *Clueless*: Taste, Pleasure and the Scene of History", in Cartmell & Whelehan, eds., 51-62.

Stedman, Gesa (1997), "Austenizing Britain. Heritage Culture, Heritage Film and the Representation of 'Englishness'", *Hard Times* 61, 10-16.

Street, Sarah (1997), *British National Cinema*, London: Routledge.

Street, Sarah (2001), *Costume and Cinema. Dress Codes in Popular Film*, London: Wallflower.

Terry-Chandler, Fiona (2000), "Vanished Circumstance: *Titanic*, Heritage, and Film", *International Journal of Heritage Studies* 6:1, 67-76.

Thompson, Emma (1996), *The Sense and Sensibility Screenplay & Diaries*, New York: Newmarket.

Troost, Linda & Sayre Greenfield, eds. (²2001), *Jane Austen in Hollywood* Lexington: UP of Kentucky.

Vincendeau, Ginette, ed. (2001), *Film, Literature, Heritage: A Sight and Sound Reader*, London: British Film Institute.

Voigts-Virchow, Eckart (2003), "The Renaissance of British Cinema since the Mid-1990s (or just 'Brit-à-brac' and 'Tarantinospotting'?)", in Merle Tönnies, ed., *Britain under Blair. anglistik & englischunterricht* 65, 207-227.

White, Hayden (1973), *Metahistory. The Historical Imagination in Nineteenth-Century Europe*, Baltimore: Johns Hopkins University Press.

Williams, Raymond (1973), *The Country and the City*, New York: Oxford University Press.

Wiltshire, John (2001), *Recreating Jane Austen*, Cambridge: Cambridge University Press.

Worpole, Ken (2001), "Cartels and Lotteries: Heritage and Cultural Policy in Britain", in Morley & Robins, eds., 235-248.

Wright, Patrick (1985), *On Living in an Old Country: The National Past in Contemporary Britain*, London: Verso.

The *Mise-en-scène* of Austen Powers

Andrew Higson

English Heritage, English Literature, English Cinema: Selling Jane Austen to Movie Audiences in the 1990s

Janespotting in the mid-1990s was an easy game to play, as the Anglo-American film and television industries went out of their way to sell Jane Austen to audiences in cinemas and in the living-room. And there is no doubt they did a good job too, if we measure their success in terms of ticket sales and television ratings, critical adulation and audience interest. The release in cinemas of a further Austen adaptation at the end of the decade – *Mansfield Park* (1999), directed by feminist filmmaker Patricia Rozema, and supported by one of the most successful indie-major producers of the period, Miramax – should then have been a sure-fire hit, although, somewhat surprisingly, it wasn't.

In what follows, I examine the circumstances of the four Austen adaptations that found their way into cinemas and wore their Austen heritage on their sleeves. Three of the films will be very familiar. *Sense and Sensibility* (1995) and *Emma* (1996) were widely hyped at the time, had reasonably big stars, and did pretty well at the box-office, by any standards. *Mansfield Park* was much less successful at the box-office but is still quite well known, given its mild notoriety, its festival outings and the involvement of Miramax. The fourth title, *Persuasion* (1995), perhaps needs a little more explanation, since it was made and broadcast as a television programme in the UK. However, as it was given a theatrical release in art-houses in the USA, I'll treat it here as a film. I'll also refer to other Austen-related material in passing – much looser 'adaptations' of Austen's work, such as Amy Heckerling's High School romantic comedy *Clueless* (1995); films with strong Austen references for those who want to pick them up, such as *Bridget Jones's Diary* (2001); and the various TV adaptations of Austen's work that appeared in the 1990s.

There is now a surprising amount of published work about the four Austen films on which I am focusing, as well as all the other television adaptations of Austen's novels that appeared around the same time.[1] Much of this work deals with the films precisely as Austen adaptations, and is therefore interested in their relationships with the novels and with the historical period in which they were written. Much of it is written by literary historians and

---

[1] See, for example, Ballaster (1996), Pidduck (1998), Sidoti (1998), North (1999), Sonnet (1999), Sales (1996, 2000, 2001), Wiltshire (2001), Troost & Greenfield (2001b), MacDonald & MacDonald (2003).

critics who have an intimate knowledge of Austen's novels and their historical context. And of course much of this writing focuses on the way that the
novels have been adapted to the circumstances of the moving image business
and its audiences in the 1990s – that is, the changes that have been made in
order to sell Austen's work to late twentieth century consumers.

Much of this work on the Austen films is fascinating, but there is much
more to these films than the ways in which they compare to the Austen novels. Even if I don't ignore the literary connection and the question of adaptation in what follows, I want in due course to focus on some of the other circumstances of the films. Thus, I want to take account of the fact that the
Austen films are cultural products that were produced and then circulated in
a particular industrial context. From this point of view, it is important to
acknowledge the fact that the film business was more concerned to provide
experiences that might meet the expectations of 1990s movie audiences, than
it was to create texts that reproduced exactly what Austen intended, or which
represented the early nineteenth century world in precise historical detail. I
also want to consider some of the intertextual frames within which audiences
enjoyed and interpreted these films besides the adaptation frame or the Austen frame. To put it crudely, I want to examine how Jane Austen was sold to
non-Janeites, how period chick lit, albeit an upscale version of chick lit much
appreciated by male intellectuals, was transformed into the multiplex-
friendly frock flick.

For me, the problem with the adaptation debate is precisely that it situates
the films first and foremost as adaptations, affording far too much primacy to
the novels and to Austen's authorship. It assumes too often that film audiences only relate to the films through the novels – and that if they don't, they
should. It forgets that *Emma* could for some audiences be marketed as "based
on the story that inspired the hit movie *Clueless!*"[2] Adaptations are clearly
readings of the source text – and very public readings at that. But because the
adaptation debate generally starts from the point of view of the novels and
their canonical status, it too often sees the films as a form of cultural debase-
ment, what Austen scholars have referred to as "'E-Z' Austen" (Troost and
Greenfield 2001a: 9), or "the harlequinization of Austen" (Kaplan 2001: 178).
Too often, then, the adaptation debate will suggest that films offer inadequate, or inappropriate, or unfaithful readings. From this point of view, film
adaptations are seen as dreadful travesties of the source text, violations of its
cultural integrity, mass market commodities that fail to do justice to the cultural complexities of Austen's work.

As John Wiltshire (2001) points out, the debate very often seems to be
about trying to rescue Austen from the adaptations, and from popular culture in general, rather than about responding to the adaptations as films in
their own right. The adaptation debate will thus often focus on what seems to
have been lost in adapting a culturally prestigious source text as a film, or on

---

[2]   Video publicity in the USA – see Buena Vista's video.com website.

how the author of the source text has been misrepresented. Of course it would be silly to deny that the films give Austen's characters, plots and themes a late twentieth century slant, rendering them closer to Hollywood, recreating them for contemporary consumers. But then much of the literary-historical scholarship around Austen is about situating Austen in the culture, society and political economy of her period, explaining why her novels take the shape that they do, so it seems rash to admonish the film adaptations of the 1990s for being similarly steeped in the culture, society and political economy of the period in which they were produced.

In any case, it is important to recognise that if by some standards the films are closer to Hollywood, they try at the same time to keep their distance from Hollywood, by insisting on their literariness, by insisting on their fidelity to Austen, their historical authenticity, their English cultural refinement, their sense of good taste. It is also important to think about what has been *gained* in the process of adaptation, rather than lost from the 'original'. The most productive accounts of adaptation, then, are those which try to understand an adaptation in its own terms, as a product of the moment in which it was produced, and addressed to audiences with their own contemporary preoccupations and interests. Accounts of adaptations from this point of view will focus on the process of authorship involved in the production of the adaptation, rather than fetishising the author of the source text and focusing on the fidelity or otherwise of the adaptation. They will also take on board how the adaptation works for *all* of its audiences, and not just the dedicated readers of the source text. Literature is thus treated rather differently from this perspective, with the novel regarded as a cultural commodity that is bartered in the market-place, rather than as a text that needs to be examined subtly and in detail. What the film industry buys into, as much as anything else, is the cultural status of the novel and its author, from which point of view it is less a question of how faithful an adaptation is to its source text, and more about how the discourse of fidelity is mobilised in the promotion and reception of the film.

The ability to appeal to different audiences was important to the design of the Austen films of the 1990s. In effect, they were designed to work both for those who want to see a Hollywood love story or a romantic comedy and for those who want to see an 'authentic' Austen adaptation. The extensive debate about the films among reviewers, cultural commentators and academics is testament to their success in reaching different audiences. And the contrariness of that debate, the fact that there are so many divergent readings of the films, some seeing them as feminist, some as having edited out Austen's feminism, and so on, is, I would argue, testament to both the richness of the films and the fecundity of the reception process.

There have of course been numerous *television* adaptations of Austen's novels over the years – classic serials, one-off dramas, and mini-series. But until the mid-1990s, *film* adaptations intended for theatrical release were very rare indeed. There was of course the MGM production of *Pride and Prejudice* in 1940, starring Laurence Olivier and Greer Garson – and it is worth noting that this too was sold as both an Austen adaptation, and as a romantic comedy with no apparent literary reference points.[3] After that production, however, Janeites had to wait more than half a century for another immediately recognisable English-language Austen adaptation to appear in cinemas. And having waited all that time, what should happen but that several such adaptations should arrive all at once? Thus, both *Persuasion* and *Sense and Sensibility* were first shown in Britain in 1995, the same year as the BBC's hugely successful six hour television adaptation of *Pride and Prejudice*, and *Clueless*, the modern-day re-working of *Emma*. With both the film version of *Emma* and a television version for the ITV network seeing the light of day in 1996, Austenmania had really taken hold in the UK.

In the USA, too, Austen adaptations were experienced in a rush. Numerous heavyweight reviews in the press took advantage of the appearance between August 1995 and January 1996 of *Clueless*, *Persuasion* and *Sense and Sensibility* in the cinemas, and *Pride and Prejudice* on the Arts and Entertainment cable network. The press frequently referred to Austen as "the hottest writer in showbusiness" (Jacobs 1996: 74), or "the hottest script property in Hollywood these days" (Blake 1996: 20), while *Newsweek* ran a headline, "Jane Austen Does Lunch", and quoted Charles Denton, head of BBC drama, proposing that "Jane Austen is obviously the Quentin Tarantino of the middle classes" (Kroll 1995: 67-8). This rush of adaptations was clearly evidence that the cult of Jane Austen remained intensely fascinating. Did it also say something about the period through which we were living in the mid-1990s? Was there a good reason for so many Austen adaptations appearing at the same time? Several commentators argued that there was. It was a response to the loss of genuine social values, argued some, a response to the collapse of a caring, ordered society, a search for a more ethical stance in an increasingly unethical world. The films thus represented "nostalgia for a more decorous and polite age" (Thomas 1996: 61). Yet others argued that Austen's work had a timeless, universal quality which ensured that the films possessed a different sort of contemporary relevance – though this could hardly explain why so many Austen adaptations appeared in the mid-1990s, rather than in another period.

There is little evidence that film and television producers went out of their way to produce an Austen cycle, however – although apparently Orion Pictures did at one point at the height of Austenmania option Austen's unfinished novel *Sanditon* for production (Weiner 1997). And the marketing people of course had a field day, tying each new adaptation into the audience base and public awareness that had been established for the previous one. I have found little evidence, however, of producers carefully planning these films

---

[3] See e.g. advertisement in *Picturegoer*, 16 November 1940, 2; and posters and lobbycards on www.filmsite.org, www.movieposter.com, and at http://www.alyon.org/generale/theatre/cinema/affiches_cinema/p/p.../pride_et_prejudice.jp.

and television programmes as a coherent cycle at the production stage. In fact, like James Collins (1996: 70), I think the rush of Austen adaptations in the cinema is probably much more coincidental, especially given the length of time some of the films were in gestation, and the fact that there wasn't enough time between the success of one film and the appearance of another for the latter film to be conceived and produced.

We need then to situate the Austen films in a broader context, to look beyond the Austen connection – and I would argue that it is much easier to see the emergence of three Austen films in the mid-1990s as evidence of the intense exploitation of a broad industry production trend than it is to see them as evidence of a very specific cultural turn that required the rediscovery of Jane Austen. The audiences for Austen films were not simply, and in some cases not at all, looking back to Austen as a key woman writer of the early nineteenth century. Nor were they necessarily particularly interested in the historical details of the period. For many audiences, they were perhaps above all engaging with a particular type of film of the 1990s, namely the tasteful, middlebrow period drama with an English setting and characters, strong literary connections, and an intense appeal to female viewers. The Austen films are symptomatic of this production trend. That is, they are the products of a particular business strategy, a particular way of operating within the global film economy. *Emma, Sense and Sensibility* – and later *Mansfield Park* – were produced by a Hollywood fascinated by the potential of the co-production and the crossover film – that is, a relatively low budget 'indie-style' quality film that might work in both specialised, art-house cinemas, and in the multiplexes, a type of film that might cross over from the niche market to the mainstream. *Emma* and *Sense and Sensibility* simply ratcheted the strategy up a notch or two closer to the mainstream.

The Austen films were thus variants of the English heritage film, attempts by the industry to prolong the Anglo-Hollywood costume drama production trend (Higson 2003). Thus, while they share a great deal as Austen adaptations, they also share much with a great many other tasteful costume dramas, historical films and period literary adaptations of the last two decades, from *Chariots of Fire* (1981) via *A Room with a View* (1986) and the other Merchant-Ivory English films to more recent productions such as *Gosford Park* (2001), *I Capture the Castle* (2003), *Nicholas Nickleby* (2003), and *Bright Young Things* (2003). By situating the Austen adaptations of the 1990s in the context of this production trend, I want to divert attention away from the specifics of adaptation and the relationship with the source text. Clearly, the fact of adaptation is important to how these films are conceived, how they are developed by the filmmakers, how they are discussed by critics and how they are received by audiences. Adaptation is thus an important framing device, and an important promotional strategy. But fidelity to the source text is by no means the only interpretive frame through which audiences make sense of the films. Other frames of reference include the English costume film production trend; the television classic serial, and especially earlier television adaptations of Austen; the love story and the romantic comedy genres; and the heritage tourism industry. In this sense, each film is assessed in part by its audiences in relation to representational traditions with which they are already familiar – and that won't always be by reference to Austen. In order to unpick some of these other frames of reference, I want now to identify nine features of the Anglo-Hollywood costume drama production trend that I think are salient here.

First, we should simply note the number of frock flicks produced in the 1990s with British business connections, and/or which engage with the English past and the English cultural inheritance. While Austen's novels are historically specific, I think for many people the adaptations are simply period films, and so belong with other period films, almost regardless of the period in which they are set, so long as they are set sufficiently far back in the past. Even if we ignore films set in or after the Second World War, there were some eighty English period dramas produced between 1990 and 2000 that fall into this category – and the Austen adaptations clearly form only a very small proportion of those eighty films. This means that something like one in every ten British or Anglo-Hollywood films of the period was a frock flick set before the Second World War.[4]

The second feature of this production trend that I want to underline is the literary connection. Of the eighty pre-Second World War English frock flicks produced between 1990 and 2000, some fifty-five are literary or dramatic adaptations of one sort or another, while several others have strong literary connections, including the various bio-pics about writers, such as *Tom and Viv* (1994), *Carrington* (1995), *Wilde* (1997) and *Shakespeare in Love* (1998) – and more recently, *Iris* (2001), *The Hours* (2002) and *Sylvia* (2003). In other words, around seventy per cent of the English period films of the 1990s had strong literary connections. The Austen films are thus part of what might be called a literary cinema, or a literate cinema, a cinema addressed to audiences who have a strong attachment to literary culture. From the point of view of the film industry, as I suggested above, adaptation is very much a marketing strategy, a way of producing a film that is in some significant way 'pre-sold'. For the industry, the adaptation of canonical literature is thus both a way of engaging with particular niche tastes and niche audiences, and a way of ensuring that the film has an audience on its release. Hence my argument that what is important is less how faithful an adaptation is to its source text, and more how the discourse of fidelity and the cultural status of the source text and its author are mobilised in the production, promotion and reception of the film.

The links between literature and this type of cinema are also apparent in the publishing tie-ins that frequently occur. Thus, for instance, Bloomsbury brought out a British paperback edition of *Sense and Sensibility* to tie in with the film release, using the main publicity images, title design and stars'

---

4   These statistics are based on the Select Filmography in Higson (2003: 262-267), and on the table in Dyja (2002: 34).

names on the front cover. Meanwhile, in the USA, Signet Publishing printed 250,000 copies of the book rather than the usual 10,000 a year in their mass market tie-in, Everyman's Library/Knopf Publishing printed 50,000 hard cover copies, and Penguin Audiobooks brought out a version of the novel read by Julie Christie (Oder 1996).

The third feature to which I want to draw attention is the contribution female authorship made to the English frock flick of the 1990s. Thus, of those eighty pre-Second World War period films produced between 1990 and 2000, eleven were directed by women, including *Mansfield Park*; twelve were written by women, including *Sense and Sensibility* and *Mansfield Park*; twenty were adapted from novels by women, including all the Austen adaptations; twenty-one had female production designers, including *Sense and Sensibility*; twenty-five had female producers or executive producers, including *Persuasion, Emma* and *Mansfield Park*; and, perhaps least surprising of all, seventy had female costume designers, including all four Austen adaptations. All of these women – as well as the many female stars of these films – can lay some claim to having authored the films, shaping how they appear to audiences. Female authorship, in a broad sense, is thus a significant feature of the English heritage films of the 1990s, with the Austen films typical rather than distinctive in this respect.

Fourthly, the middlebrow costume drama production trend developed to cater for particular audiences – audiences, that is, that were more upscale than the mainstream, and more female-oriented (Higson 2003: 101-6). Choice of subject matter was thus to a great extent dictated by what it was felt this audience was interested in. In terms of the upscale female audience, Austen is obviously a real winner, especially when, as in *Sense and Sensibility* and *Mansfield Park*, the feminine tropes of romance, domesticity, strong female protagonists, and fine frocks could be given a modern feminist spin. Fifthly, and developing the previous point, the conventions of the romance are central to this production trend. While some of the films are played as straight romantic dramas, another variant is the romantic comedy – and *Emma* and *Sense and Sensibility* are clearly played in part as Hollywood romantic comedies, albeit in period garb. Two other films with Austen links make the romantic comedy connection even stronger: *Clueless* and *Bridget Jones's Diary*. In this vein, one might also situate the Austen adaptations alongside the broader cycle of Anglo-Hollywood romantic comedies with contemporary settings. Not just *Bridget Jones*, then, but also *Four Weddings and a Funeral* (1994) and *Notting Hill* (1999) – and of course each of these films in some way re-works or re-presents heritage England and heritage English culture. When placed in this context, it is hardly surprising that the Austen films play up desire and eroticise the characters, and especially the male characters, in a very 1990s fashion.

The sixth feature of the middlebrow costume drama production trend to which I want to draw attention is that these are films with strong connections to the heritage and tourism industries (Higson 2003). That is to say, these are

films in which a particular version of heritage England is presented as spectacle, a spectacle which tourists are encouraged to visit. For instance, the
upscale, Anglophile, American lifestyle magazine *Town and Country* ran a
lavishly illustrated six-page piece at the time of the release of *Sense and Sensibility*, under the title "Jane Austen's England" (Stanger 1996). The article
opens with a double page spread, a giant photograph of Elinor and Marianne
walking across a lush green hill, with heritage sheep in the background. The
text superimposed on this photograph informs us that "The film version of
Sense and Sensibility takes us to the England that was – and, in some places,
still is." (Stanger 1996: 78-9) In a trope typical of such journalism, it is suggested that "the English landscape itself plays a starring role", that England
"becomes a vivacious character in a roster already rich with personalities":
"With sweeping wide-angle shots of Devon and close-ups of the human
heart, it brings to life an era and a place, with present-day England doing a
thoroughly convincing imitation of the turn of the 18th century." (Stanger
1996: 78-9, 82, 81) The article then begins to sound like a tourist guide, listing
the various locations, noting that many of them are owned by the National
Trust and are therefore open to the public. This England, then, is a place that
can be visited, and every opportunity was taken to establish this fact. Thus
the press book (Columbia Pictures 1995) produced to promote *Sense and Sensibility* also listed all the locations used in the film, as did Emma Thompson's
Diaries (Thompson 1996), published as a tie-in with the film. And Austen film
and television adaptations do have a demonstrable effect on heritage tourism. Thus Lyme Park at Disley, Cheshire, saw a 178% increase in attendances
after featuring in the BBC's *Pride and Prejudice*, while Saltram House, in Devon, used in *Sense and Sensibility*, recorded a 57% rise (Meikle 1999). *Pride and
Prejudice* was even given an award by the British Tourist Authority, in honour of the series' "outstanding contribution to English tourism" (Culf 1996:
9).

     The seventh feature shared by so many of the Anglo-American period
films of the 1990s is their take on Englishness or Britishness (Higson 2003).
This is complex. One reading of the films, as in the article from *Town and
Country*, is that they are nostalgic, conservative visions of Olde England, a
green and pleasant land, pre-industrial, safe and welcoming ("impressions of
order are supplied by its deep, green, manicured farmlands..." Stanger 1996:
82). Reviewers who see the films in this way will frequently describe them as
"quintessentially British",[5] while the films themselves do seem to offer a very
class-bound vision of a national identity steeped in the past, but still heavily
traded in the global market-place today. It is also possible, however, to see
these same films as offering much more complicated and ambivalent versions of national identity. Thus, many of the films depend on the spectacle of
class privilege – grand houses, landscaped grounds, lavish interiors, extrava-
gant costumes, and so on – while at the same time weaving narratives in

---

[5]   In this case, a reference to *Sense and Sensibility* (Sloane 1996: 30).

which those privileges are critiqued or at least presented ironically, and class tensions are revealed. Arguably, too, some of the films, and especially the Austen films, offer a feminised vision of Englishness, telling stories of how women were disenfranchised, disinherited and disempowered in the past.

It is worth noting too the effect of the iconography of English heritage cinema on the Austen films. All four films – even those produced by American companies – were shot on location in England. In adopting this iconography, as Ros Ballaster (1996) and Julianne Pidduck (1998) have noted, the Austen films shift away from the domestic interiors of the novels to what Pidduck calls "the picturesque outdoors" (1998: 386). It is also worth noting that in the Austen films, as in so many other films of this production trend, we are invited to look at England from afar, and often from the perspective of another culture. This sense of cultural distance is built into many of the films from the moment of inception. So, for instance, all four of the Austen films were made for an international rather than solely English market, and all four enjoyed American financial involvement, some of it substantial. *Emma* was directed by an American, Douglas McGrath, *Sense and Sensibility* by Ang Lee, who hails from Taiwan, and *Mansfield Park* by a Canadian, Patricia Rozema. Even Roger Michell, director of *Persuasion*, was born in South Africa, while the lead characters in *Emma* and *Mansfield Park* were played by an American and an Australian, respectively. In this sense, then, it is a very familiar strategy to cast an un-English eye on Englishness in these films – although this doesn't stop reviewers from continuing to treat these Anglo-Hollywood productions as "quintessentially British". What this draws attention to is the paradoxical interplay in these films of the national and the international, the local and the global, something that is very much a feature of contemporary cultural activity. The concept of 'glocalisation' (Robertson 1995) describes what is at stake quite neatly – global, or at least transnational arrangements enable the development of very culturally specific, local representations (the leisured classes in southern England in the early nineteenth century), which are then circulated to audiences on a near-global scale.

This leads on to the eighth feature of the production trend: this un-Englishness will often allow a certain irreverence into the films. Or rather there is a constant tension between authenticity and irreverence, a tension that we can again see in the Austen films. On the one hand, they retain an affinity with traditional Austen, on the other hand, they sex up the novels, play on the relations between servant and master (Sales 2000), or pull at the threads of colonialism and slavery. Hence claims like that of Roger Michell, director of *Persuasion*, that "I'm trying to trash the hotel room of the BBC classic" (quoted in Davies 1995: 12). Hence too the radical revisionism of Patricia Rozema's *Mansfield Park*.

The ninth feature I want to discuss will be familiar from the above, and that is the fact that these films are the products of a particular business strategy, the carefully engineered Anglo-Hollywood crossover film. The Austen adaptations, but also the broader production trend, represent a particular way of operating within the global film economy, building on the successes of Merchant Ivory's E. M. Forster adaptations, for instance, but also on the success of self-consciously American heritage films such as *Little Women* (1994), produced by Columbia, the same company that produced *Sense and Sensibility*. Like so many of the other entries in this costume drama production trend, *Persuasion, Emma, Sense and Sensibility* and *Mansfield Park* are perhaps best classed as Anglo-Hollywood films. On the one hand, they all have English characters and settings; on the other hand, they all had American production involvement, although *Persuasion* and *Mansfield Park* were handled by British companies. And like most of the other films in the production trend, they were all low to mid-budget productions, with *Sense and Sensibility* commanding the biggest budget, thanks to the involvement of Columbia, one of the major American studios. All were carefully handled at the exhibition stage, *Persuasion* working as a traditional art-house film in the USA, but *Emma* and *Sense and Sensibility* leading double lives as both art-house releases and mainstream films. *Sense and Sensibility* went furthest into the mainstream and made the most impact at the box-office, but *Emma* too was a considerable success. *Mansfield Park* on the other hand was a major disappointment commercially.

The cinema/television link was an important element in the business strategy too, feeding Austenmania with its numerous adaptations, but also providing a more specific impetus to the film business. Thus *Persuasion*, as we know, was made as a one-off drama by the BBC, but released theatrically in the USA, while the BBC was also involved in the production of *Mansfield Park*. Channel 4 too played a vital role in supporting the development of the small-scale English costume drama on film and at the cinema, although it was not actually involved in any of the Austen films. Both the BBC and Channel 4 developed strategies of co-production and international sales to exploit to the maximum the potential of their television programmes and filmed dramas – and these strategies meshed well with those of the American film industry as it sought to engineer the crossover hit that might bring together a range of niche audiences. There is of course a long history of BBC television adaptations of Austen's novels, and that history, as Angela Krewani (2004) notes, as well as the history of the classic serial more generally, feeds in a number of ways into the 1990s Austen adaptations. Just as previous Anglo-Hollywood heritage films paved the way for later entries in the production trend, so television adaptations of Austen in a sense prepared audiences in both Britain and the USA for the film versions that were to follow. Thus they attuned audiences to what some saw as the commercialisation of Austen and her fellow literary gods, and what others saw as a tastefully refined version of screen entertainment. In this respect, previous television adaptations and period films are as important as the Austen source texts in terms of providing an intertextual frame through which audiences might make sense of the Austen film adaptations of the 1990s.

By the early 1990s, the English costume drama production trend was well-established. What the industry attempted to do over the next few years was to finesse the production trend, to refine its chances of succeeding in the market-place, to maximise its audience share, especially in the USA and the UK. For a start, there were almost twice as many period dramas made in the 1990s as in the 1980s (Higson 2003: 262-7). But it is not a question simply of quantity, it is also a question of the ways in which the production trend was exploited economically, and marketed to its potential consumers – and the four Austen film adaptations are each in their own way symptomatic of developments across the 1990s. Indeed, the critical but especially the box-office success of *Emma* and *Sense and Sensibility* might be seen in many ways as the highpoint of the strategy of deliberately engineering a crossover hit. As far as the middlebrow English period film was concerned, a number of specialised American companies began to take notice when earlier low-budget costume dramas like *A Room with a View* and *Enchanted April* (1991) reaped unexpectedly large profits at the box-office. Those companies became increasingly interested in buying into this end of the market at the point of production, and then carefully milking the box-office potential of the films as they moved through the cinema circuits (Higson 2003: 119-45).

Persuasion shares much with films like *A Room with a View* and *Enchanted April* in the sense that like them it was a small but tasteful English costume drama that was picked up by an American distributor to exploit on the specialised or art-house circuit in the USA. In fact, *Enchanted April* also initially only aired in the UK as a television drama, but like *Persuasion* it was given an art cinema release in the USA. One can see why *Persuasion* was picked up by its specialised American distributor too, given its Bergmanesque intensity and its self-consciously de-glamourised and austere *mise-en-scène*, but equally its constantly moving camera, its familiar heritage iconography and its slow-moving, character-based narrative. Plenty of upmarket critics were impressed with *Persuasion*, and what they saw as its restraint, subtlety and authenticity: as one critic put it, "Jane Austen would have approved" (Pearson 1995). But even this tasteful and restrained drama was promoted in part as a conventional romantic period piece. Thus the American poster for the film showed the central couple, Anne and Wentworth, kissing – a kiss which caused some consternation to Janeites, since it was added at the request of the American TV co-production company, in an attempt to give the film wider appeal (Davies 1995). That attempt to widen the appeal of the film was taken a step further when the film was released for video rental in the USA. Now the cover showed two entirely different actors involved in a much more passionate and revealing pose, suggesting a much racier drama.

This modification of the Austen story can be traced back to the involvement of an American company at the production stage. But while this was part of the emerging business strategy for the Anglo-Hollywood costume drama, what the American companies were increasingly interested in was those films that managed to cross over from the specialised market into the multiplexes. By the mid-1990s, the American majors had got interested in the sort of profit margins that could be achieved by such films. Such companies were prepared to invest more up front, but in return expected even more impressive returns at the box-office, a strategy that did seem to make sense, given the success of more mainstream productions such as Columbia's *Little Women*. *Sense and Sensibility*, *Emma* and *Mansfield Park* were all products of this strategy, with *Sense and Sensibility*'s Columbia connection enabling it to benefit from a relatively high budget for a middlebrow period piece. The other two films were handled by one of the key companies involved in the development of this strategy, Miramax. Initially a relatively small independent company, by the time *Emma* was made, Miramax had become part of the Disney family, which enabled it to establish a sizeable budget for such a film.

In order to make the most of their investments, Columbia and Miramax handled their films very carefully at the distribution stage. After all, the English costume drama was not everyone's cup of tea. Thus, they were released into cinemas relatively slowly by comparison with the mainstream film, where the opening weekend was everything. Their releases were also carefully tied into the Oscar season, to make the most of the publicity that Oscar nominations and awards generate. Both films were designed from the outset to win both the core English costume drama audience but also more general audiences. This was one of the reasons why Ang Lee was taken on as director of *Sense and Sensibility*. As the producer, Lindsey Doran, put it: "I didn't want this to be just some little English movie. I always felt it was more than that and could appeal to the whole world, not just audiences in Devon" (quoted in Moore 1995: 19). But the core audience, the Janeites and the fans of English period films, were not to be frightened away – and of course for these audiences, the film was a pre-sold property, given the prestige and familiarity of the title. The marketing people could also rely on quality, upmarket newspapers and magazines to take an Austen film seriously and to treat it to plenty of influential column inches.

In the case of *Emma*, the producers endeavoured to seduce multiplex audiences by casting an up and coming American star, Gwyneth Paltrow, as the eponymous heroine, while critics noted the way the director "keeps things moving at a delirious trot" (Eisner 1996), producing an "anachronistic snap bordering on irreverence", and "grasping the screwball possibilities" of the plot (Maslin 1996). Nor did the tagline used in publicity exactly stress that this was a Jane Austen film, although romance was very much to the fore: 'this season, cupid is armed and dangerous'. But if on the one hand this was a Hollywood romantic comedy, on the other hand, it was a film from what *Variety* referred to as Miramax's "traditional stronghold of upscale, specialised pics" (Roman 1997), and as another reviewer put it, the "speedy pacing" was achieved "without sacrificing period manners or the precision of the original language" (Eisner 1996), ensuring that "it has enough satirical edge to amuse audiences weary of big-screen explosions and computer wizardry" (Maslin 1996).

Films that could work both as mainstream romantic dramas and as tasteful and 'authentic' Austen adaptations; films that could be exhibited at both mainstream cinemas and specialised art-houses: this was what defined the crossover film. Of course, by attempting to address both the traditional audience for such films and the wider multiplex audience, the filmmakers were always running a risk. Thus for the *LA Times*, if *Persuasion* was "the most authentically British version" of the current crop of Austens, *Sense and Sensibility* was "the audience-friendly Hollywood version ... easygoing and aiming to please" (Turan 1995). But if that risk resulted in box-office takings on the scale of *Emma* and *Sense and Sensibility* then the strategy could be deemed a success. After all, these were exactly the sorts of profit margins that attracted American companies to invest in such English productions in the first place. For the companies interested in such productions, the question now became how to capitalise on the success of such films, how to exploit further the very specific cultural and economic possibilities that such films represented, how to develop the Anglo-Hollywood crossover strategy.

In the case of Jane Austen adaptations, a particular problem was the very limited number of commercially exploitable titles. After all, four of the six major novels had already been produced in one form or another, and sometimes in more than one form, in 1995 and 1996 – *Sense and Sensibility, Pride and Prejudice, Emma* and *Persuasion*. But it would be wrong, as I argued earlier, to see the Austen films in a vacuum. Rather they need to be seen in the context of the English costume drama production trend, and the genres of romantic comedy and romantic drama – and both of these could be exploited further without having to rely on Austen. Thus, for the film industry, films like *Sense and Sensibility* or *Emma* were not simply Austen adaptations. They were also part of the broader cycle of tasteful period adaptations of literary works with strong female central characters – in which context one might say that the successors to the rush of Austen adaptations in the mid-1990s were such productions as *Mrs Dalloway* (1997), as a small-scale art-house film, or *The Wings of the Dove* (1997), as a larger scale, Miramax production. One could play out this strategy in different ways. One could for instance make woman-centred period dramas that weren't actually literary adaptations, but bio-pics of key historical figures, such as *Elizabeth* (1998), or key literary figures, such as Virginia Woolf in *The Hours* (although that of course was a literary adaptation!). *Shakespeare in Love* works in a similar way, playing up the romantic comedy while retaining both the fascination with heritage England and the fascination with literary culture.

Another way of building on the success of films like *Sense and Sensibility* and *Emma* was to produce further female-oriented English romantic comedies, but without the period setting. From this point of view, as I suggested earlier, one might cite Anglo-Hollywood films such as *Bridget Jones's Diary*, which of course directly referenced the Austenmania – and especially the

Darcy-mania – of the mid-1990s, and *Notting Hill*, one of whose central characters is a Hollywood actress who plays in an English costume drama adapted from a Henry James story. (And of course both films could boast Hollywood stars.)

Of course, there was one further Austen adaptation, *Mansfield Park*, and in many ways this production is symptomatic of how the production trend was developed in the late 1990s. Like other costume dramas of the late 1990s, such as *Elizabeth*, *Plunkett and Macleane* (1999), *Shakespeare in Love* and *The Wings of the Dove*, *Mansfield Park* was an attempt to update and open up the period film, to make it more relevant to contemporary multiplex audiences, while not ignoring the niche art-house audience. Thus while retaining the veneer of the authentic period adaptation, it attempts to incorporate more recent readings of Austen's work, and more modern representations of desire.

Like *Elizabeth*, a major success in 1998, *Mansfield Park* incorporates touches of the grotesque, the gothic and the expressionist, blatantly eroticises its themes and characters, and in various ways tarnishes the charms of the English national past. Advance publicity made much of the fact that the actor who played Austen's hero had previously played Sick Boy in *Trainspotting* (1996), while more upmarket commentators noted the extent to which the adaptation drew on feminist and post-colonial readings of Austen's novel (Johnson 1999, Bradshaw 1999, Sales 2001). The film was promoted in terms of its difference, its cutting edge qualities. The tagline, "Jane Austen's wicked comedy", certainly sounded most un-Austenish, as did the sex scenes in the film itself. But the promotional strategy failed to secure a box-office hit, and by the time the film appeared on video it was being promoted primarily to the core Janeite audience – "will delight Austen fans everywhere".[6] Thus the very same film had become another 'faithful' adaptation, rather than the radical, audience-grabbing film Miramax had evidently been hoping for, or the "bodice-ripping shagfest" (CW 2000) some of the initial publicity seemed to suggest.

The film seemed to have all the right business ingredients: the backing of Miramax; a UK production company, HAL, that was run by people that had been key figures at Channel 4's FilmFour; funding from the BBC and the Arts Council's lottery scheme; and a budget the same size as *Emma*. Despite such strong credentials, the film failed at the box-office in both the UK and the USA. Why did it fail? I would suggest that it fell between audiences. Thus, it was not Austenish enough, too radical, and too overtly eroticised for the Janeites. But it was also too knowing, too revisionist in its approach to the past, too austere, without all the traditional period clutter, for the costume drama aficionados. And it lacked the big stars, the fast-paced narrative, the accomplished story-telling and the lavish spectacle necessary for multiplex success. More generally, so many companies had tried so hard to get on to

---

6   Back cover blurb on the British retail video sleeve (Miramax Home Entertainment/ Buena Vista Home Entertainment).

the crossover band wagon that by 1999 the market was saturated, with even the majors producing films like *American Beauty* (1999). Thus, too many indie films had been produced, too much had been spent on them, and they were all competing for the same screen time. This was then partly a problem with the Austen adaptation, partly a problem with the market for costume dramas more generally, and partly a problem with the even broader category of the specialised indie film that had been designed to have crossover potential...

The bubble had burst; the strategy had been over-played. Even so, this was not the end of the frock flick, the costume drama, the heritage film, as a number of more recent productions demonstrate. It is worth noting, however, that most of the recent Anglo-Hollywood costume dramas have been set in the first half of the twentieth century, with several set in 1920s and 1930s – including *Gosford Park*, *I Capture the Castle*, *The Heart of Me* (2002) and *Bright Young Things*. It would be easy to say that such films have little to do with Jane Austen, but what I hope I have demonstrated above is that it is not enough to treat the Austen films of the 1990s simply as adaptations of the work of a woman writer of the long eighteenth century. Adaptation and literary culture are certainly important intertextual frames through which to view these films, as we have seen, but they are by no means the only ones. To look at the details of the particular production trend to which the films belong is to suggest an additional set of circumstances that might explain why the films take the shape that they do, reach particular audiences, and generate certain sorts of debate. The films clearly do have a strong relationship to their source texts, but they also have a strong relationship to the other non-Austen films around them, and for the film industry, they are cultural commodities designed to exploit a fairly clearly delineated market, and are promoted accordingly.

Bibliography

Ballaster, Ros (1996), *The English Review*, September, 10-13.

Blake, Richard A. (1996), "Plain Jane", *America*, 9 March, 21.

Bradshaw, Peter (1999), "Licence pays off in modern look at Austen", *The Guardian*, 16 November, 5.

Cartmell, Deborah & Imelda Whelehan, eds (1999), *Adaptations: From Text to Screen, Screen to Text*, London: Routledge.

Collins, James (1996), "Jane reaction", *Vogue*, January.

Culf, Andrew (1996), "Pride wins over tourist prejudice", *The Guardian*, 13 March, 9.

CW (2000), "Mansfield Park", *Empire*, October, 126.

Davies, Tristan (1995), "To kiss or not to kiss", *Daily Telegraph*, 7 January, 12.

Dyja, Eddie (2002), *BFI Film and Television Handbook*, London: British Film Institute.

Eisner, Ken (1996), "Emma", *Variety*, 17 June.

Featherstone, Mike, Scott Lash & Robert Robertson, eds. (1995), *Global Modernities*, London: Sage.

Higson, Andrew (2003), *English Heritage, English Cinema: Costume Drama since 1980*, Oxford: Oxford University Press.

Jacobs, Laura (1996), "Playing Jane", *Vanity Fair*, January, 74.

Johnson, Claudia L. (1999), "The authentic audacity of Patricia Rozema's *Mansfield Park*. Run mad, but do not faint", *Times Literary Supplement*, 31 December, 16-17.

Kaplan, Deborah (2001), "Mass Marketing Jane Austen: Men, Women, and Courtship in two Film Adaptations", in Troost & Greenfield, eds., 177-187.

Krewani, Angela (2004), "Heritage as International Film Format", in this volume.

Kroll, Jack (1995), "Jane Austen does lunch", *Newsweek*, 18 December, 66-68.

Lynch, Deidre, ed. (2000), *Janeites. Austen's Disciples and Devotees*, Princeton: Princeton University Press.

MacDonald, Gina & Andrew F. MacDonald, eds. (2003), *Jane Austen on Screen*, Cambridge: Cambridge University Press.

Maslin, Janet (1996), "*Emma*", *New York Times*, 2 August, C1.

Meikle, James (1999), "Movies redraw the tourist map: Visits to locations featured in popular films provide profitable new dimension in the travel business", *The Guardian*, 16 June.

Moore, Oscar (1995), "Sense and Sensibility", *Screen International*, 7 July, 18.

North, Julian (1999), "Conservative Austen, Radical Austen. *Sense and Sensibility* from Text to Screen", in Cartmell & Whelehan, eds., 28-50.

Oder, Norman (1996), "Sensible tie-ins", *Publisher's Weekly*, 1 January.

Pearson, Allison (1995), "Television: the fine art of *Persuasion*", *Independent on Sunday*, 23 April.

Pidduck, Julianne (1998), "Of windows and country walks: frames of space and movement in 1990s Austen adaptations", *Screen*, 39:4, 381-400

Robertson, Robert (1995), "Glocalization: Time-Space and Homogeneity-Heterogeneity", in Featherstone *et al.*, eds, 25-44.

Roman, Monica (1997), "Arthouse, haunted house buoy Miramax", *Variety.com*, 9 January.

Sales, Roger (1996), *Jane Austen and Representations of Regency England*, London: Routledge, revised edition.

----- (2000), "In Face of All the Servants: Spectators and Spies in Austen", in Lynch, ed., 188-205.

----- (2001), "Jane Austen at the Movies: A 1990s Kind of Gal?", *Jane Austen Society (Midlands) Transactions*, 12, 22-45.

Sidoti, Concetta (1998), "An evening with Jane Austen. National pride and audience prejudice: re-writing the heritage text", *Cultural Studies from Birmingham*, 2:1, at http://artsweb.bham.ac.uk/bccsr/issue1/sidoti.htm.

Sloane, Judy (1996), "Emma makes sense", *Film Review*, March, 30.

Sonnet, Esther (1999), "From Emma to Clueless: Taste, Pleasure and the Scene of History", in Cartmell & Whelehan, eds., 51-62.

Stanger, Ila (1996), "Jane Austen's England", *Town and Country*, January 1996.

Thomas, Evan (1996), "Hooray for Hypocrisy", *Newsweek*, 29 January.

Thompson, Emma (1995), *Sense and Sensibility: The Diaries*, London: Bloomsbury.

Troost, Linda & Sayre Greenfield (2001a), "Watching Ourselves Watching", in Troost & Greenfield, eds., 1-12.

-----, eds. (^{2}2001b), *Jane Austen in Hollywood*, Lexington: University Press of Kentucky.

Turan, Kenneth (1995), "An Austen-tatious year", *Los Angeles Times*, 13 December, F1.

Weiner, Rex (1997), "More Jane Mania: Orion Buys Austen's Sanditon", *Variety.com*, 17 January.

Wiltshire, John (2001), *Recreating Jane Austen*, Cambridge: Cambridge University Press.

Pamela Church Gibson

Otherness, Transgression and the Postcolonial Perspective: Patricia Rozema´s *Mansfield Park*

Even the term costume drama is hilarious to me – what's dramatic about a piece of fabric? (Patricia Rozema)

Finally a director has taken real risks and reaped real rewards...treating Jane Austen's novel not as a museum piece or sacred text but as a living presence whose power inspires. (Claudia Johnson)

Mansfield Park (1999) was largely misunderstood when first released; subsequently it has been unjustly overlooked and strangely neglected by the academy. For it is an extraordinary reworking of Jane Austen's most overtly political novel, itself highly 'political' but in various different and contemporary modes.

And how wonderful it is to find a truly progressive heritage text, rather than searching hopefully for 'progressive' readings within less critical – and formally sterile – celebrations of the past. Perhaps – as this essay will suggest – it is the plethora of progressive qualities within this film which have rendered it so unpalatable, not simply to those who desire the reverential treatment of any high-canonical literary source', but also to those scholars who were, perhaps, unprepared for and unwilling to accept such a deeply transgressive text. For Rozema's adaptation of the novel and her cinematic treatment are unparalleled even within the many changes taking place in and around the 'heritage' film. It is not merely radical in its politics and anti-realist in its formal innovations: it goes beyond its foregrounding of the novel's thematic subtext, its complete reinvention of the central protagonist and its deployment of innovative cinematic techniques, ranging from Brechtian address and alienation to self-conscious use of slow-motion and expressionistic lighting – it is, arguably, both the first truly 'queer' heritage text and the first to be an overtly postcolonial polemic.

The novel itself poses problems for many modern readers – not only does it concern itself with the theme of ordination and the duties of a clergyman, but it has as its emotional epicentre a curiously meek and timid heroine. Fanny Price is a strange contrast to Elizabeth Bennett and Emma Woodhouse – even Marianne Dashwood, who conceals her true feelings and submits obediently to social constraints, is positively rebellious by comparison. Fanny is, however, the heroine who seems to embody certain of Jane Austen's own documented thoughts and ideals, about Christianity itself, and the kind of behaviour demanded of a clergyman. Fanny's object of desire is her cousin Edmund, intended for holy orders and – unlike so many of the other parsons within her fictional world – one who takes his duties, both spiritual and pastoral, very seriously.

Although this might seem unappealing to modern sensibilities, there is one particular thematic concern to tempt readers and to have provoked the scrutiny of postcolonial literary theorists – which also explains the interest of Rozema, not only as art-house director, but also as a native of Canada, formerly colonised. For interestingly, it is the only one of Austen's novels to specify and discuss the source of the wealth and privilege enjoyed by the central protagonists – and here, that wealth does not come from the rents of tenant farmers or the other benefits provided by large estates. Here, it is directly and unequivocally dependent on the income from Sir Thomas Bertram's sugar plantations in Antigua, part of the rapidly expanding British Empire. It is slave labour, with all its implications, which permits the lavish lifestyle of the Bertram family. Austen was aware of both the abolitionist movement and of the sufferings of the slaves themselves – her brother, Francis, had written an impassioned letter home on a visit to Antigua, so her choice of location is quite deliberate – but Rozema takes the topic into terrain where Jane Austen could not or would not go.

Her adaptation is a radical one – herself the author of the screenplay, she takes the plot and social context of the novel and develops, even inverts, a number of the narrative and thematic strands. Slavery, in the novel, is mentioned half-a-dozen times, while the visit to the West Indies is merely a narrative device whereby Sir Thomas is conveniently absent for a long period and his restraining paternal voice silenced. Here, however, it is the very fulcrum of much of the action. It is seen to be the cause of Tom Bertram's near-fatal illness, which in the novel is caused by injudicious behaviour; here, Rozema makes it much closer to a breakdown, caused through his witnessing of the brutalising of the Antiguan workforce by those 'masters' who include his own father. The second major change is the transformation of Fanny from the submissive heroine of the novel into a spirited girl who has always been, herself, a writer of stories – and who possesses not only a desire for knowledge but a talent for argument. A child who needs to be told by Mrs Norris on her arrival at Mansfield that "You speak only when you're spoken to", she grows up into a lively adult who, in the opening five minutes of the film, is reproved by Sir Thomas –"Fanny Price", he shouts, "can you please try to behave yourself with more decorum?" It is, for Austen devotees, as much of a shock as if Hamlet were to be told, "Do try to be more philosophical". But Rozema's Fanny is a self-proclaimed 'wild beast' – and has, as her adoring sister Susie tells her, a "tongue sharper than a guillotine." Interestingly most of the sentiments Fanny voices were taken by Rozema from Austen's own letters, diaries and juvenilia – the rest are Rozema's invention.

Rozema set herself certain important tasks, discussed in interviews but overlooked by critics involved in the heritage debate, who have either misunderstood or ignored this seminal text. Her comments on the foregrounding of the slavery issue are a straightforward declaration of intent:

> When I was first approached to do an adaptation, I reread the novel and was struck by the fact that the source of income for all this leisure was finally acknowledged. I was often disturbed, when reading novels from this time or watching adaptations of them, that nobody seemed to lift a finger – I wanted to know who was paying for the party. (Allen 2000: 24)

This last phrase she incorporates into her screenplay and gives this line to Tom Bertram on his return from the West Indies, so traumatised by his experiences that, we find later, he cannot, now, bear to be in the same house as his father. She continues: "Jane Austen can choose not to describe – but in a contemporary movie I can't choose not to show that – unless I just film the words on the page." (Allen 2000: 25)

Instead, she shows us Tom's own graphic drawings, which include one based directly on Blake's *Man on a Meat Hook*, well-known in Austen's lifetime, brings in a reference to Clarkson's abolitionist polemic, and alters the plot. As we will see, she is following suggestions implicit in the analyses and post-colonial critiques of *Mansfield Park* by Edward Said (1993) and Maaja Stewart (1993).

She hopes that she has "taken what was implicit in the novel and made it explicit for a new set of readers" (Allen 2000: 25). It was necessary to make drastic changes in order to achieve this – for the "connections between domestic realities and imperial fictions remained necessarily weak, unfocused, and fragmentary in the culture in which Jane Austen wrote" (Stewart 1993: 122).

She also gives the novel a feminist perspective it lacks through – ironically – the use of Jane Austen's private voice for that of Fanny Price in much of the voice-over commentary and addresses to camera which run throughout the film. She explains that what was needed was a central force of 'energy'– Fanny is so "incredibly retiring [...] that without the authorial voice [...] there would have been a gap in the middle of the narrative"(Allen 2000: 25), so she "decided to go directly to Jane Austen herself, to use those early novels to add layers to the character, to make her a writer like Austen herself and so give the audience a privileged view. She's just given a little more edge" (*ibid.*).

Already, it is clear, the concerns of postcolonialism and a feminist presence are now integral to the film. What is totally new within a film of this sort – apart from the avant-garde style which prevails throughout – is a sustained 'otherness' of sexuality. Yes, Claire Monk and others have found – correctly – 'queer' moments in the main body of heritage texts; however, this is the first to be infused throughout by a queer sensibility and by the deliberate introduction of different modes of transgressive sexuality. Interestingly, within literary criticism there was a brief furore around the sensibilities – or sexuality – of Jane Austen herself, set in motion by the deliberately provocative article "Was Jane Austen Gay?" which caused such a commotion when it appeared in the *London Review of Books* (Castle 1993). Jane Austen certainly did, as Castle explains, share virtually everything – including a room and a bed – with her sister, Cassandra, writing to her several times a day when circumstances kept them apart. The level of intensity within this relationship is undeniable. Furthermore, Jane Austen did develop attachments to younger women – including her own niece, Fanny Knight – but Castle later explained that she had not necessarily accused Austen of acting upon any of the "unconscious narcissistic or homoerotic impulses" she originally delineated when writing in response to the "spluttering tabloid mini-frenzy, fanned by the depraved rank and file of various local Jane Austen societies, that the piece elicited on both sides of the Atlantic" (Castle 1995: xxi). She insisted however that she was right, in her original article, to emphasise not only the "particularly intense nature of their sisterly bond" but to stress, too, Austen's "homophilic fascination with female bodies" (*ibid.*: 131).

A homophilic fascination with female bodies is certainly to be found in Rozema's film – and both lesbian and incestuous thoughts and even behaviour are clearly on display. Mary Crawford, still the embodiment of metropolitan sophistication, is now seemingly bisexual – while it is clear to us, as it is not in the novel, that Sir Thomas' approval of his niece's looks and manner when he returns from Antigua gives rise to more than avuncular interest. Fanny is certainly aware of his overly physical interest: she saddles up a horse and gallops off into the stormy night to escape his unwanted attentions – and to vent her anger at being the object of male discussion and interest. And when she returns to Portsmouth as an adult woman, her father moves towards her – "Come here, and give your coarse old father a squeeze." Behind him in the frame, Fanny's mother turns significantly away, with an ambiguous expression – it is suggested that this is not the first time he has displayed a more than paternal interest in his children. Finally, in the closing moments when the characters' final destinies are displayed, we are told in voice-over that the *roué*, Henry Crawford, and his sister Mary "soon found other partners who shared their more (pause) modern tastes". This is spoken over one of the *tableaux vivants* which make up the last sequence – as we see the four posed around a tea-table, the new partners surreptitiously clasp hands beneath the white cloth. It is clear that we are being shown a possible *ménage à quatre*.

It is, however, not merely the impulses of the characters that make for the transgression that infuses the film. Everywhere there are the 'unruly bodies' of Foucauldian analyis, here on display and in action as as never before in the heritage genre, giving in to impulse, refusing to be restrained by convention – or even clothing. Not only are the breeches as tight and revealing as ever – there are tracking shots up the men's' bodies, and mid-shots aplenty. And all the women – even the young Susan – display a great deal of décolleté at most inopportune moments – Fanny wears a very low-cut red dress for breakfast in Portsmouth, for instance. This is, after all, the first Jane Austen adaptation in which we see two characters caught *in flagrante*, both totally naked. And Henry's adultery with the newly-married Maria Bertram now takes place under the parental roof; Fanny herself walks in upon the scene. Most disturbing, perhaps, is the revelation of Sir Thomas' firm belief that his female slaves are there to provide him with sexual pleasure. It is as if the English characters here, usually forced into sexual conformity and repression, have refused to become 'docile bodies'; the black and 'mulatto' women, of course, whose 'well-shaped bodies' Sir Thomas so lasciviously describes to his family, are synonymous with unfettered desire – but, like their male counterparts, they are chastised and subjugated to become the ultimate 'disciplined bodies' of which Foucault writes. Lady Bertram, incidentally, is here depicted as having created her own 'subjugation' and docility through an addiction to opiates.

It is not just the profusion of physicality – nor the polymorphously perverse desires exhibited – that make this a truly 'queer' text. It is also the lack of any one continuous or fixed point of view within the text – and the multiplicity of 'gazes' shown. Although Fanny is the central figure and controls the verbal commentary, she does not have the same power over the 'look' of the camera or the object of whatever scopophiliac gaze may be currently conveyed on screen. Fanny is herself observed – by the heterosexual looks of Edmund and Henry, by the enigma that is Rozema's Mary Crawford, and – furtively – by her older male relatives, while the clearly-outlined bodies of Edmund, Henry and Mary are also offered up for our delectation. We as audience are never quite sure who is looking at who – there are so many glances, glimpses, changes of perspective that this is a text of multiple, fleeting and finally perplexing cathexes and decathexes.

Although she freely discusses her own lesbianism and moments of bisexuality, Rozema rejects all attempts to label her as 'lesbian *auteur*' – and, indeed, even rejects the notion that she is primarily a feminist *auteur*, angering Teresa de Lauretis among others (de Lauretis 1990). But it is this very rejection of any sexual identity or label – the only group with which she will agree to be identified is the Ontario New Wave – that makes her a truly 'queer' director. For she wants to evade any fixed gender position, to seek true fluidity of positioning.

> I don't want to be a professional homo. It's not enough [...] to be in the position of being called a lesbian filmmaker frightens me, because I see it as one category among many. (Bailey 1995: 7)

It was a critic discussing the London Film Festival who was the first to misinterpret this film, calling it merely "a raunchy bodice-ripper",[1] as if the sole desire of the director were to titillate. But Rozema makes the reason for the focus on sexuality quite clear:

> There is an atmosphere in the book of sexuality, sometimes unwholesome sexuality that I think I'm completely justified in bringing to the fore. I think there's a very

---

1   Cf. *London Evening Standard*, 19 October 1999, 11.

good chance that a wealthy group of attractive young people with time on their hands and no work to do would have been very physically aware of one another. (Allen 2000: 25)

Perhaps most important for this particular anthology, however, is her clear, cheery disrespect for heritage conventions, deliberately flouted at every turn. In cinematic – and generic – terms, the most striking thing about this adaptation is the avant-garde visual style that is so deliberately anti-heritage. All our visual expectations are crushed, all heritage pleasures denied us, from the very first shots of the gaunt buildings of Mansfield Park (filmed at Kirby Hall, Northamptonshire), where peacocks prowl and shriek, to the bleak, whitewashed interiors that we see next, curiously reminiscent of Dutch seventeenth-century paintings of the Delft School – all this is a world away from the fatly-upholstered, over-decorated rooms of the conventional heritage film. There are none of the usual tracking shots designed to showcase elaborate carved or gilded furniture, sumptuous sofas and lavish draperies – the interiors here are almost minimalist. The garret to which the young Fanny is banished – here a sheeted lumber room – is quite in keeping with this strangely bare stately home. Lady Bertram cannot loll on a daybed as in the novel – she's consigned to a rather uncomfortable-looking chair. The house actually shown here, with its bleak, baroque façade, is, in fact, a partial ruin – ironically enough, one under the protection of the English Heritage body itself. It is not surrounded by lush lawns or elegant formal gardens – but dominated by a hard, severe courtyard, paved and gravelled. Throughout the film, there is a complete absence of that pictorialism – in landscape and interior shots – usually found within this genre and the traditional sensuous pleasures provided by décor, dress and setting are either confounded or thwarted in some way.

Costume, too here denies us the usual heritage pleasures; it is often deliberately anachronistic – though it refers to a 'period', the question 'Which one?' may spring to mind at times. Mary Crawford, for example, looks at moments like a member of the Bloomsbury group – while in her very first appearance she sports a toque which could be worn as fashion statement in 1912. Later, after playing billiards in a black dress with lace sleeves, she leans against the table, smoking a small cheroot. The adult Fanny is first seen wearing the garb of the quasi-emancipated Edwardian 'New Woman' – a long black A-line skirt and waistcoat with a white blouse. The men, it is true, wear breeches and soft, high leather boots – but the fidelity to period dress which forms so central a feature in the pleasures usually afforded to the discerning audience, where they may congratulate themselves on their taste and discrimination in identifying it correctly and appreciating it to the full, is missing.

It is necessary to think of the intended audience now, before moving on, later and for the remainder of the essay, for a swift, sequential canter – with asides – through the text itself. This journey will be rather like the ride taken by Fanny and Edmund at the start of the film, where our view of the landscape is continually curtailed as the camera stays in mid-shot to show us these two protagonists discussing Sir Thomas' worries about his Antiguan affairs. This 'canter' will move through the director's thematic preoccupations to focus on the visual style in which they are configured.

The question of audience is an important one – for in one of the few mentions of the text within film scholarship, Andrew Higson makes this assertion about the positioning of this film by its producers and distributors: "[...] the films of the late 90s [...] were specifically designed to widen the appeal of the costume drama, and thereby to address more diverse audiences" (Higson 2003: 3). A still from the film is captioned "Addressing the Multiplex audience" (*ibid.*: 144).

Surely both Rozema herself and Harvey Weinstein, of Miramax, who asked her to adapt the book have other constituents in mind: the extraordinary and knowing liberty taken with the way in which the novel has been adapted, together with the anti-realist formal strategies and the wit, even playfulness, that characterise this anomalous film suggest an appeal to arthouse sensibilities rather than to mainstream audiences. In Higson's other reference to the film, it is described as "a self-conscious attempt to modernise the heritage film" by packaging costume drama and literary culture for a "more youthful and less reverential audience" which was "a comparative box-office failure" (*ibid.*: 145) But Rozema's work – here and previously – mitigates against any appeal to such an audience. Yes, it is an "attempt to modernise", but for a political purpose connected to Rozema's ideological stance and to the kind of thematic and technical explorations to be found in her previous films.

Harvey Weinstein recruited her immediately after the success – critical not commercial – of her first feature *I've Heard the Mermaids Singing* (1987). This film – a mixture of whimsical comedy and lesbian love story – mixed reality with fantasy and was notable for its self-reflexive formal strategies. It was hardly a multiplex film, but it was her adaptation that Weinstein wanted. And the traditional heritage audience – middle-aged and middle-brow - were also likely to be alienated, for one of the pleasures seemingly found in the conventional heritage film is that of recognition, of a novel half-remembered, a favourite character faithfully realised, a stately home once visited. If one is to use Bourdieu's notion of cultural capital as a useful analytical tool – and so far none of the writers on heritage have done this – then, perhaps, it is those in pursuit of this particular type of middle-class cultural capital who so far have formed the main audiences for these films. Until the middle of the 1990s, most heritage films gratified them by sticking – relatively closely – to the literary texts selected for cinematic adaptation.

This is precisely the kind of audience that Rozema does not, it seems to me, want to reach. Indeed she wishes to confound them. In the film *Sense and Sensibility* (1995), as I have mentioned elsewhere (Church Gibson 2000: 118) there is the cinematic invention of the young Margaret, a silent presence in the novel, as a tomboy heroine who wants to become a pirate. When Edward

Ferrars jokingly says to Marianne, discussing solutions to their financial difficulties, "Perhaps Margaret is right – piracy is our only option", he has in fact
hit upon an underlying truth. Rozema shows us how this jokey aside in
Emma Thompson's script is in fact an underpinning rule of their society.
Financial piracy forms its part of its foundation, for piracy and plunder are
the true basis of colonialism.

Rozema wishes not only to upset the cinema-goers who expect conventional middle-of-the-road heritage. She wants to go much further, even perhaps to engage the academy with the nature of the changes she implements –
the literature faculty, maybe, through her radical alterations – and maybe to
please its more progressive members, through the foregrounding of imperialist concerns and the feminist slant. There is now no need for the famous
Sotherton sequence of the novel, where Fanny is forced to watch the others
escape across the ha-ha and past the confines of the gate to freedom, while
she herself remains on the other side, confined, proper, concerned and aware
– as with the doomed production of the play *Lover's Vows* – that she is doing
the right, the moral thing. Fanny herself can here make good imaginative
escapes through her writing and her radical ideas. And her adored brother
William, so central to the novel, is now superfluous – this Fanny, like Jane
Austen, has a sister, who waits daily for the next instalment, the next letter.

We have seen feminist heroines in revisionist heritage film before – *Washington Square* (1997) ends with Catherine running a crèche in her family
drawing room, rather than hovering bitterly on the stairs like Olivia de
Havilland in *The Heiress* (1949). But this film is pushing the boundaries far
beyond that modest enterprise. It is also the first adaptation of Jane Austen
where the addresses to camera throughout and the mannered ending draw
attention to the fact that we are watching a film, a construct. Again, the audiences of conventional heritage – or within the multiplexes – are not perhaps
at the forefront of the director's mind. It is unsurprising that the multiplex
audience of which Higson writes should eschew it. It is equally unsurprising
that the traditional heritage audience – identifiable since the early eighties –
should be so outraged. Even the review in *Empire*, a magazine for the young,
complained that "flouting the spirit of a classic original is not imaginative"
(Errigo 2000: 37).

It is important to note that despite these radical upheavals, the ordination
of Edmund is still central to the dialogue, and both he and Fanny are advo-
cates of what he here describes to the mocking Mary as "a life of compassion
and contemplation". Nevertheless, it is the darker side that dominates – and
there is an interesting comment on the economic subservience of women.
Here, Fanny, while in Portsmouth, briefly accepts the rake Henry's proposal
of marriage – and it is made clear that her economic situation is as much a
factor as her belief that Edmund will definitely marry Mary. Her defeated,
exhausted mother warns her, "Remember, Fanny, I married for love." And
Fanny herself tells Henry, "Poverty frightens me – and a woman's poverty is
slavery worse than a man's."

Here it seems relevant to return to the work of Edward Said. He examines the novel at some length and notes that while "Jane Austen subjugates the agonies of Caribbean existence to half-a-dozen passing references" (Said 1993: 69), she tells us that on the one occasion where Fanny directly questions her uncle about "the slave trade", there follows "such a dead silence" – this he sees as a figurative display of the way in which the novel is circumscribed, no "common language" possible (*ibid.*: 115). It is "precisely because Jane Austen is so summary in one context, so provocatively rich in another, precisely because of that inbalance we are able to reveal that interdependence" (*ibid.*: 116) scarcely mentioned – between the domestic and the imperial. Maaja Stewart, writing from both a subaltern but a feminist perspective, examines the imperialist underside of the novels – in particular the "dark shadow behind the country house" of Mansfield Park (Stewart 1993: 105-37). She suggests that Fanny's name itself is telling – 'Fanny' was slang for 'whore' – while the surname 'Price' suggests that she is indeed a chattel to be bought and sold by men. Even the name of the house itself she sees as reinforcing the patriarchal structure of the novel (*ibid.*: 17).

Furthermore, she disentangles the relationship between white planter and female slave – the woman onto whom he can project his own transgressive sexuality and who can be controlled as is the "sexuality of the women in his own English domestic space" – what Stewart calls the "idealisation of domesticity" (*ibid.*: 128). In the film Sir Thomas plans – yet more worryingly – to mix the two, to bring back a "mulatto woman" to Mansfield Park itself. It is strange that the question of slavery – and the imperialist context – were ignored for so long, even by such authorities as Marilyn Butler and Tony Tanner.

The West Indies is "a space of the other, a counter image to the respectable domesticity in England" (*ibid.*: 106). This way of thinking, and Sir Thomas' own sexual behaviour, is in the film forcibly conveyed to Fanny – after he has sung the praises of "the well-formed mulatto women" he then offers her a ball at which to show off her own new beauty. It is at this point that she escapes into the night – as Edmund tears after her, she gallops off though the wind and rain, crying out: "I won't be sold off like one of your father's slaves … find yourself another adornment".

As a child in the opening moments, being herself transported, unwillingly, by coach to Mansfield, she sees and asks about a moored three-masted schooner, hearing from below its decks a kind of singing and chanting unfamiliar to her. And that same 'other' music is heard at the very end; when all has been resolved and Sir Thomas has finally abandoned his "interests in Antigua", which he does not do in the novel, it is the voice of the African singer, Salif Keita, that we hear as the closing credits roll up the screen. The song he is singing –"Djongna" – translates as 'slavery'.

It is through repetition of images as well as her dialogue that Rozema keeps these concerns at the forefront of our minds. The ship reappears, while Tom – whose first words in the film are "Even I have principles, Sir" – records the sights he has seen in Antigua in his sketchbook, ironically entitled *Our Neighbours*. Fanny finds this book when tending Tom in his illness – and we see the drawings from her own horrified perspective. The images fill the screen – the gang rape of a young black girl by white boys, Sir Thomas himself flogging a slave, a close-up of wrists chafed to the bone through bondage, and finally Sir Thomas once more, this time forcing a woman to fellate him. At this point Sir Thomas enters and rips the book from her hands, shouting at her "My son is mad": later he burns it.

However, he finally admits – if indirectly – his responsibility for Tom's condition. As they wait by his bedside, he tells Fanny that, as a child, Tom had frequently played at being a knight – and demanded "Give me a noble mission, father". He continues sadly "That's all he ever wanted – forgive me, Tom, I'm so very sorry" – and grasps his unconscious son's hand. Tom recovers – father and son are reconciled – and the patriarch rearranges his sources of income, abandoning Antiguan sugar for shares in tobacco.

The transgressive sexuality which pervades the film is shot rather differently, using tracking shots around the bodies in question, and moving swiftly into close-up at times – when Mary has persuaded Fanny to read the play with her, she winds her arms slowly around Fanny's waist. There is a cut, first to her hands roving over Fanny's back and then another, to the watching Edmund. But the second Sapphic interlude is more protracted. Caught in heavy rain very near the parsonage, the drenched Fanny is coaxed inside by Mary. She is taken upstairs and Mary helps her out of her clothes, slowly removing her dress and chemise to reveal her bosom – as she comments on her "fine form", the camera moves in again to corroborate this sentiment. Then she inveigles Fanny downstairs to play the harp to her. Once again, we cut to the figure of Edmund, who has just arrived and has been hovering outside, looking and listening to the women together.

Are these lesbian moments merely sensationalist? Or are they part of what Castle would call the "grooming behaviour" of young females of the time, the rituals in which they participated in the long hours spent in each other's company in a homo-social society (Castle 1995: 132)?

Castle talks here of the part clothes play in "the subliminal fetish life of women" (*ibid.*: 132) and in their physical intimacy at that time. Certainly there is something caressing in Mary's undoing of hooks and buttons, and Fanny seems to accept that not to submit would be strange, impolite. It is the knowing way in which the camera constantly moves in and away that gives this to this scene – as to so many – a sharp, sexual edge, and a self-conscious voyeurism – underlined by the lurking presence of Edmund.

Rozema has talked explicitly about her cinematic style in the film – and made it clear that she wants to subvert expectations: "I tried to stay with the people and their humanity and to acknowledge that I've done a contemporary interpretation [...] I stayed in close for a lot of the time."(Allen 2000: 25) So the traditional languorous pans are replaced at times by jerky movements, mid-shots, and the overhead tracking shots of the carriage in landscape in fact serve to locate it in relation to the sea and the slave ships.

She is openly critical of the heritage tradition in the same interview: "Even the term costume drama is hilarious to me – what's dramatic about a piece of fabric? What that term does reveal is that the focus of a lot of these things is an almost materialistic thrill in the clothing and furniture which I had to minimise." (*Ibid.*)

The lush orchestration so often found within the genre has been replaced by music composed with a different aim. The composer, Lesley Barber, explained in interview: "One of the things we wanted to do was have music that reflected the era but also gave it a contemporary feel – an accessibility." (*Ibid.*) And what the music also provides at moments is an element of pastiche, which coincides perfectly with the post-modern, self-reflexive visual strategies at work – the music at times has a tongue-in-cheek quality, seeming to echo, if not parody well-known movements and moments in eighteenth-century music.

The opening credits are a portent of what is to follow – dark semi-abstract shapes are seen, which are difficult to decipher. We glimpse what seems to be a dark pool of water – and what look like fallen leaves – moving on to what may be, perhaps, swatches of fabric. These puzzling shapes are explained when the camera pulls further back; we have been looking at close-ups of a pen dipping into ink, and moving swiftly across manuscript – we glimpse several pages of what seems to be a story and then there is a jump-cut, to an overhead shot of the bedroom in Portsmouth, where the child Fanny is telling one such story to her sister.

An element that is missing from traditional heritage – or the despised 'costume drama' – is humour, but it is deployed here in visual terms. Two examples may serve as illustration – the humour in both, furthermore, is at the expense of traditional narrative technique. In the first, Fanny's voice-over narration tells us that "Mr. Norris died" – and we see him, seated at the dining-table, pitch abruptly forward so that his face lands in his plate of soup, while the unseen Fanny continues mercilessly, "which did not seem to inconvenience Mrs Norris at all". She is seen busily engaged in ringing the handbell to summon the servant, presumably so that he can clear away both the spilled soup and the untidily sprawled-out body of her deceased husband at the same time.

The second instance parodies the love-at-first-sight moment of conventional cinema – replacing it with an extraordinary group performance of lust-at-first-glance. When Henry and Mary Crawford come to live across the park at the parsonage, they straightway call on their neighbours the Bertrams. Before they arrive, Maria, her dull fiancé Mr. Rushworth and her sister Julia are preparing without enthusiasm for a game of cards. Suddenly the Crawfords are announced – and as they enter the room we see firstly the effect that they have on the assembled gathering. All the faces reflect a transfixed admiration and sexual appreciation – even Lady Bertram is jolted out of her laudanum-induced stupor and a *louche* smile crosses her normally blank face. We then cut to the subject of the group gaze – through a tracking shot up the bodies of both elegantly-dressed Crawfords, starting with their boots and moving upwards, the camera seemingly approving what it sees since the music starts up and its pace and tempo echoes that of the camera. It cuts back to Maria, who allows the entire pack of cards to slip through her nerveless fingers – and as they fan out around her, the film goes into slow-motion. There are other postmodern touches: Fanny's midnight ride is filmed close-in, lit in a way that suggests expressionist painting – the film is temporarily tinted blue, and small circles of lighter blue move across the screen. And the penultimate shot of Fanny is her knowing smile to camera, her acknowledgement of its presence and recording gaze, as Edmund finally declares his love for her.

Rozema's use of images, here, reinforces those very subtleties of the novel which she wishes to retain and re-present for a modern sensibility. Although the Sotherton sequence of escape and intrigue may be missing, Rozema takes the image of an imprisoning cage and uses it as a kind of trope. The image of a caged bird, wanting to be set free, occurs throughout; when Henry Crawford displays his sensibility by reading aloud, he reads to Fanny from Sterne rather than, as in the original, from Shakespeare. He chooses the passage from *A Sentimental Journey* about the caged starling which the narrator is unable to liberate. "I fear, poor creature I cannot set thee at liberty", laments Sterne, and the bird itself reiterates pitifully "I can't get out.... I cannot get out". So when wooing Fanny, he sends a basket of white doves to her in her Portsmouth exile – but these birds are set free, to the sound and sight of a firework display which, as his messenger explains to her, was supposed to be accompanied by some words he has unfortunately forgotten and so cannot recite as instructed, "about starlings flying or summat". Later, when Fanny rejects him and he seduces Maria out of pique, she echoes the very words of the reading from Sterne to Edmund when he walks in to find her in adulterous dalliance with Henry. "Don't look at me like that, Edmund", says the cinematic Maria. "You know that my husband is a fool, and that I cannot get out." And like the starling, she repeats forcefully, "I can't get out – I can't get out." At the very end of the film, when Tom is declared to be out of danger, we see a flock of migrating birds – and we see them through what have been until that moment the confining window-panes of his sickroom.

Images like this stress the respect that Rozema has for the novel itself, which, she claims, "remains unsullied" and has now been reinterpreted "for a contemporary audience" (Allen 2000: 25). Since Miramax have asked her to do two more films, it will be interesting to see if she chooses again to make a literary adaptation – or whether she will return to contemporary Canada.

So - is she the first truly postcolonial heritage filmmaker? Shekar Kapur's *Elizabeth*, as I have argued elsewhere (Church Gibson 2002: 135), fights shy of examining the basis of the political power he portrays so forcefully. Although his rewriting of the biography of Elizabeth I is a true sea-change within heritage, he does not – oddly, given his upbringing in postcolonial India – make much of the imperialism of her reign. The closing credits proclaim that "Elizabeth ruled for another forty years...and at the time of her death, England was the richest and most powerful country in Europe". Yet for some reason, he omits to tell us exactly how those riches and power were obtained – through the ruthless colonial expansion of the latter half of Elizabeth's reign.

So perhaps the redoubtable Rozema is truly a pioneer. Certainly, this film is a remarkable achievement – and it is sad that the world of cinema scholarship has been so negligent in its response. It is unsurprising that Middle England Jane Austen devotees were so hostile, and the multiplex audiences were perplexed – but the seemingly misguided reaction of film scholars is both puzzling and disappointing.

Bibliography

Allen, Carol (2000), "Empowering Austen", *The Times*, 30 March, 24-5.

Bourdieu, Pierre (1984), *Distinction*, London: Routledge.

Butler, Marilyn (1976), *Jane Austen and the War of Ideas*, Oxford: Clarendon Press

Castle, Terry (1993), *The Apparitional Lesbian: Female Homosexuality and Modern Culture*, New York: Columbia University Press.

----- (2002), *Boss Ladies Watch Out: Essays on Women, Sex and Writing*, New York – London: Routledge.

Church Gibson, Pamela (2000), "Fewer Weddings and More Funerals: Changes in the Heritage Film", in Robert Murphy, ed., *British Cinema of the 90s*, London: British Film Institute, 115-124.

----- (2002), "From Dancing Queen to Plaster Virgin : *Elizabeth* and the End of English Heritage?", *The Journal of Popular British Cinema*, 5, 133-141.

De Lauretis, Teresa (1990), "Guerrillas in the Midst: Women's Cinema in the 1980s", *Screen*, 31:1, 6-25.

Foucault, Michel (1977), *Discipline and Punish: The Birth of the Prison*, transl. Alan Sheridan, London: Penguin.

Higson Andrew (2003), *English Heritage, English Cinema*, Oxford: Oxford University Press.

Johnson Claudia (2000), *Introduction to Screenplay of "Mansfield Park"*, New York: Talk Miramax Books.

Said, Edward (1993), *Culture and Imperialism*, London: Chatto & Windus.

Stewart, Maaja A. (1993), *Domestic Realities and Imperial Fictions: Jane Austen's Novels in Eighteenth-Century Contexts*, Athens, GA: University of Georgia Press.

Tanner, Tony (1986), *Jane Austen*, London: Macmillan.

Raimund Borgmeier

Heritage Film and the Picturesque Garden

This essay addresses picturesque and beautiful gardens in so-called heritage films, and, encouraged by the title of the volume – *"Janespotting" and Beyond: British Heritage Retrovisions since the Mid-1990s* – and by the name of this particular section – "The *Mise-en-scène* of Austen Powers" – I shall take the liberty of concentrating exclusively on the four Jane Austen films that came out in 1995 and 1996, namely *Sense and Sensibility, Pride and Prejudice, Emma,* and *Persuasion.*

Viewers generally liked these films.[1] Quite a few of my students have told me that their fondness for Jane Austen's novels started when they saw one of these adaptations. Many critics of both film and literature, however, view these films often in a much less benevolent light. According to them, such films "feed the still insatiable appetite for spectacle, period costume and picturesque setting" (Church Gibson 2000: 115). Andrew Higson criticizes: "The self-conscious visual perfectionism of these films and their fetishization of period details create a fascinating but self-enclosed world." (Higson 1993: 113) He notes with particular displeasure: "Almost all of these films contain a recurrent image of an imposing country house seen in extreme long shot and set in a picturesque, verdant landscape." (*Ibid.*: 115)

Landscape and gardens come in for especially harsh criticism in this debate. H. Elisabeth Ellington, for example, in her article with the significant title "'A Correct Taste in Landscape'. Pemberley as Fetish and Commodity" maintains that in the BBC version of *Pride and Prejudice*, the protagonist "is superseded by the real star of the show, Old England, bucolic and gorgeous." (Ellington 2001: 92) In comparing the original with the screenplay, she finds:

> In the novel, the viewer's scopophilic pleasure and desire are constantly undercut and thwarted, while the film exploits the scopophilic potential of Austen's text by eroticizing and commodifying a fine view. (*Ibid.*: 97)

This line of criticism is (at least in the case of Ellington) directly inspired by the 1970's distrust of cinema as a source of mere pleasure. According to, among others, Laura Mulvey, mainstream cinema created an "illusion of voyeuristic separation" (Mulvey 1975: 9). Mulvey, therefore, championed

---

1 The paradigmatic BBC miniseries *Pride and Prejudice* had a rating of about 12 million viewers when it was first aired on British TV in 1995, the BBC video is a best-seller, and the series has currently a 9.2 (out of ten) rating on the Internet Movie Database. *Sense and Sensibility* had an attendance of more than 8 million viewers in the US and more than 10 million in Europe (cf. the Lumiere database at: http://lumiere. obs.coe.int/web/EN/ search.php).

"the destruction of pleasure as a radical weapon" (8) a 'counter cinema' which undercuts the inherent 'scopophilia' of narrative film. From this perspective, the bucolic and gorgeous English garden of heritage cinema is the commodified object of the (predominantly female?) gaze.[2] In her discussion of landscape and gardens, Ellington comes to the negative conclusion that:

> [...] visions of "OLD ENGLAND" [as presented in the Austen films] are conservative and attempt to sell a lifestyle – and a landscape – that no longer exist (if they ever did). Adaptations of *Pride and Prejudice* draw our attention to landscape instead of to people or social problems and thus strip Austen of her social awareness [...]. (Ellington 2001: 108)

Of course, it is true that the different media of fiction and film work under different conditions. While a novelist can use gaps (which Iser in his influential theory has called *Leerstellen*, lacunae or indeterminacy gaps), filmmakers inevitably have to provide specific pictures. This necessity and priority of pictorial presentation seems to be the decisive difference between the two media. Where Austen can leave out detailed descriptions of the gardens and parks that surround the mansions and houses of her characters and tell us only in general terms, or not at all, through what kind of landscape her heroines take their favourite walks, the filmmakers have to show us concrete pictures of specific gardens and landscapes. The question is then whether these presentations indeed "supersede" the characters, and "by eroticizing and commodifying a fine view" make the setting, which was subservient and peripheral before, take on a false importance.

I would hold that this is not the case. On the contrary, together with most viewers, I am convinced that the filmmakers in general have done a good job with their adaptations of Jane Austen's novels.[3] The picturesque gardens are not only used to provide "scopophilic pleasure" for the audience but, above all, they invariably carry certain meanings, and clearly have a symbolic function. Especially, I think, the concept of the English Garden – for some historians England's greatest contribution to the history of European art – is employed to bring out important aspects and features of particular characters. I would like to show this with some examples. First of all, however, as a

---

2   Women, costumes and gardens cannot be construed as mere objects of the scopophilic 'gaze'. Mulvey theorized how mainstream film constituted viewers as masculine, catering to the 'male' gaze and turning women into objects. She had notorious problems in accounting for a 'female' gaze and was criticised for failing to account for the breadth of viewer responses. This causes severe problems for a group of films that particularly address women, both as characters and audience and, interestingly, Ellington must reverse Mulvey's subject-object positions. But is it really an indicator of "repressed exhibitionism" when female spectators look at the Pemberley of the BBC *Pride and Prejudice*?

3   Brownstein (2001: 17) argues convincingly that the visual and narrative style of *Sense and Sensibility* has veered away from exhaustive, slow, and dull drawing room 'classics'. The impressive location photography in these movies clearly reflects technological advances in the heritage *mise-en-scène*.

preparation for the discussion of the main subject, let me briefly look at Jane Austen's attitude to gardens and the way she uses them in her novels.

The chapter "Gardens" in *The Jane Austen Handbook* is a very short one, shorter than the one on "Dress and Fashion" and only half as long as the one on "Food and Drink", yet Marion Morrison, the contributor, rightly points out the importance of gardens in Jane Austen's life:

> She [Austen] certainly enjoyed her own gardens and those of her well-connected friends. She was a country girl, her life not all tea and backgammon in the drawing room or flirtation at the local balls. "Matters concerning the garden" were important (*Letters*, April 21, 1805) [...] (Morrison 1986: 184).

Thus, it is only natural that Austen uses horticultural technical terms connected with contemporary garden practice again and again, and when, for example, she writes to her sister Cassandra, "I have lop't and crop't" (January 13, 1813), she is not "referring to seasonal pruning, but to her meticulous revision of the early script of *Pride and Prejudice*" (*ibid.*: 186).

At the same time, Morrison understandably acknowledges the secondary position of gardens in Austen's novels when she states:

> One does not, of course, think immediately of Jane Austen as writing about gardens at all. People were her main concern. But on closer inspection one observes that the people she created have fine houses and the houses have fine gardens, superb back cloths for the stage on which she brings her group together. [...] In her novels, the elegant gardens [...] bring her characters to life, and although they are only lightly sketched, the reader immediately fills in the picture. (*Ibid.*: 184)

(These are the gaps I mentioned before, which the reader may fill in, which the filmmaker, however, cannot avoid replacing with complete pictures and sequences.) It is correct that the gardens in the novels serve both as backgrounds, but in many cases, also as symbols which convey a certain meaning. Even the garden at Hunsford, for example, belonging to "the insufferable Mr. Collins", who is "the only gentleman in her novels who digs his garden himself" (*ibid.*: 184), is not only the practical means for Charlotte to keep her moderately beloved husband out of the house, but may also be intended to represent a redeeming feature which prevents this simple-minded clergyman from becoming a mere caricature.

The best-known landscape garden in Jane Austen's novels is, of course, Pemberley in *Pride and Prejudice*. (That is why Ellington chooses it as a subtitle and talks of "Pemberley as Fetish and Commodity".) Elizabeth's visit to Pemberley constitutes a turning-point in the plot of the novel since it makes her begin to think differently about Darcy as a person. The strong impression she receives starts to make her aware of the heritage, the tremendous cultural and aesthetic (as well as social and economic) values he represents. Significantly, it is not the stately house that causes these feelings but the gardens. A long time before Elizabeth has entered and seen the "lofty and handsome" rooms the narrator tells us about her epiphany: "[...] at that moment she felt that to be mistress of Pemberley might be something!" (Austen 376, ch. 43)

The description Jane Austen gives of this wonderful estate seems, in some way, rather vague, yet two points stand out clearly. The first one is its enormous extent, which is emphasized before everything else:

> The park was very large, and contained great variety of ground. They entered it in one of its lowest points, and drove for some time through a beautiful wood stretching over a wide extent. (*Ibid.*)

Darcy is an aristocratic landowner, and the sheer size of his possessions denotes his importance. At the same time there is a connection with the second point, the garden.

Landscape gardens had a tendency to become much more extensive than the formal gardens they supersede in the history of garden design, and Jane Austen makes it perfectly clear that Pemberley is an English or landscape garden. Because this is so central, I have to quote the passage in full which describes the experience Elizabeth and her relatives have when they drive through the park:

> They gradually ascended for half-a-mile, and then found themselves at the top of a considerable eminence, where the wood ceased, and the eye was instantly caught by Pemberley House, situated on the opposite side of a valley, into which the road with abruptness wound. It was a large, handsome stone building, standing well on rising ground, and backed by a ridge of high woody hills; and in front, a stream of some natural importance was swelled into greater, but without any artificial appearance. Elizabeth [...] had never seen a place for which nature had done more, or where natural beauty had been so little counteracted by an awkward taste. (*Ibid.*)

Pemberley presents itself like a painted landscape, like a picture, it is picturesque in every sense of the word. There are particular views and prospects to be enjoyed by the spectator as he or she moves through the park. The phrase "the eye was [...] caught" reminds one perhaps that "eye-catcher" is a technical term in contemporary garden theory. Characteristically, the grounds are not flat and two-dimensional like a French or formal garden but three-dimensional and hilly. Most important of all, all traces of wilful human interference with the country have been removed, the whole scenery looks natural, nothing seems artificial (though Elizabeth and every informed person of her time must be fully aware that great pains had been taken and enormous costs incurred to achieve this effect).

Elizabeth immediately associates Pemberley with its owner. For her it is, to some extent, a reflection of Darcy's personality. In this respect it seems important that the park of Pemberley is an English garden, as was fashionable in the 18th and early 19th centuries. This not only demonstrates that the owner is a man of superb taste who endeavours to improve his estate as he should do. What is more relevant is that the particular kind of garden can be seen, above all, as an objective correlative of the owner's character. While the outmoded French garden, with its straight and symmetrical gravel walks, its regularly clipped hedges and geometrically shaped bushes and trees stands for coercion and inhuman clichés and stereotypes, the English garden is associated with positive ideas and ideals. Instead of constraint, it rather expresses liberty, liberality, and a mature respect for the interests of others. It reveals an attitude of naturalness and a movement towards a closer relationship with nature in the Romantic sense. In this way, Pemberley and, to a lesser degree, other gardens in Austen's novels, play a significant role.

The makers of the films seem to have understood this significance of the picturesque garden, or at least, they used the various gardens in an analogous way. First, there is, as I pointed out, the prestige value of a garden. Apart from in London and Bath, all the houses are, of course, country houses, and they need a suitable park or garden to set them off properly. Since Austen's main characters belong to the landed gentry or the land-owning aristocracy, sometimes one has the impression that the priority is even reversed, and that the grounds are the most important thing and the house or mansion comes second. So it is quite appropriate when in the filmed version of *Emma* the new Mrs Elton, who vicariously likes to boast about the country estate of her rich relatives, Maple Grove, talks about "people who have extensive grounds" (instead of 'large houses') and then revels in fantasies about Surrey as "the garden of England".

The prestige value of the country estates becomes most manifest probably in the screen adaptation of *Pride and Prejudice* directed by Simon Langton (1995). In their interesting report on *The Making of Pride and Prejudice* (1995), Sue Birtwistle and Susie Conklin relate in a special chapter on "Location Hunting" how they tried to set up a regular hierarchy of the houses and gardens they chose as locations. They write:

> We were all keen to establish a relationship between the sites and grandeur of the houses [and the gardens – one might add]. Pemberley, which is Darcy's house, has to be the grandest. Then, in descending order of importance, we placed Lady Catherine de Bourgh's house, Rosings Park, followed by Netherfield, which Bingley rents, Longbourn and finally Hunsford Parsonage, where Mr Collins lives. Having found Longbourn, we decided to look for Pemberley next and then fit the other houses in between. (Birtwistle & Conklin 1995: 24)

Sam Breckman, the location manager, is quoted on the difficulty of finding a suitable property:

> Houses on the scale of Pemberley are few and far between. It is supposed to be in Derbyshire, which would give it a distinctive northern look, and it has to be very big and set in stunning scenery. It has to say, "I am powerful, I am wealthy, but I have taste". (*Ibid.*)

With Lyme Park, situated on the Cheshire/Derbyshire border, an appropriate estate was found, and it was decided on in spite of the fact that the interiors could not be used for filming (which, obviously, shows the prior importance of the garden). For Lady Catherine de Bourgh's house, Rosings, Belton House near Grantham in Lincolnshire was chosen. Netherfield was found near Banbury in the north of Oxfordshire. The most important location of all, the place for Longbourn, Luckington Court, was discovered early on in the location hunting near Great Sherston in the vicinity of Malmesbury. The Old Rectory at Teigh near Oakham in Leicestershire had to serve as Hunsford Parsonage.

Likewise, the filmmakers apparently appreciate the opposition 'French vs. English garden' and put it constructively into practice. When, for example, we first see Rosings, it is unmistakably shown as a formal garden, stiffly regular with symmetrically arranged, carefully clipped evergreen shrubs and trees. Elizabeth and her companions slowly walk down the gravel drive towards the stately house and Mr Collins is talking about costs. This, of course, is a proleptic symbolic expression of Lady Catherine de Bourgh's autocratic character and the ruthless way she deals with other people.

Conversely, Pemberley is, first and foremost, presented as an English or landscape garden. Only at the very end of the visit after Elizabeth and the Gardiners have unexpectedly met Mr Darcy, when Darcy, the proud owner, says farewell to his visitors, only then do we see that there is also a formal part of the garden. Before this we can admire the wonderful English garden with its beautiful lake. To prepare us, a remark was made at the inn, "The grounds are delightful". After we have accompanied the visitors to the house and get glimpses of the landscape through the windows, we see Darcy riding through the splendid park. He comes to the lake and decides to dive in. According to the stage directors of the script, this new scene, which does not occur in the novel, is meant to give Darcy "a brief respite from duty, and from the tumult of his tormented and unhappy feelings" (quoted Birtwistle & Conklin, 1995: 5): But I think it is no over-interpretation if one understands this scene also as a communion with nature: Darcy comes into bodily contact with the picturesque garden, which, in turn, to some extent also represents himself. Afterwards, he takes his visitors on a walk and shows them (and us) the beauties of the grounds. Again, the next morning when he sets off for a ride, we are provided with another opportunity to enjoy the marvellous estate, and perhaps we remember that in the very first scene of the film, two riders, Bingley and Darcy, approached an impressive country seat: Netherfield – admired it, but remarked that Pemberley, of course, surpasses it in beauty.

Nature and garden scenery also play a heightened role in the love scenes of the film. When Darcy first, unwillingly and in an awkward, ungentlemanlike manner, declares his love to Elizabeth, the scene is indoors, but we look out of the window and see leaves moving in the wind. There is some slight occasion for hope. When Elizabeth goes for a walk in the park the next morning she is met by Darcy who hands her the letter which explains his actions in the past and thus improves his chances as a lover. As the two finally declare their mutual love, the bucolic scene is set under trees, and in clear symbolism, there is a cornfield ripe for harvest in the background.

The garden of Longbourn, which is naturally more modest than that of Pemberley and consists of a mixture of formal and English elements, similarly has symbolic connotations. When Elizabeth and her new brother-in-law

Wickham take a turn in the garden, she gives him to understand that she knows about his questionable past behaviour, but she also declares that as brother and sister they must not quarrel in future. Nature with its manifold kinds of growth reflects the great variety of human nature. Also the decisive final altercation between Lady Catherine and Elizabeth significantly takes place in the garden. The proud lady, whose bombastic formal garden we have seen before, pretends to admire a "prettyish wilderness" in the slightly neglected garden of the Bennets. Again, the contrast between two garden styles, French vs. English, mirrors the conflict between two ways of life, constraint vs. relative freedom: the lady wants Elizabeth to conform and obey, whereas the young woman claims the right to make her own decision.

In the other Austen films, picturesque gardens play a comparable part, least of all perhaps in *Persuasion*, which does not project landscape as a mere space of recreation and pleasure. Here the picturesque beauty of the sea, connected with the location of Lyme and the naval profession of some of the leading characters, comes into prominence. Yet in the very second sequence of the film, which alternates with a rowing boat trip in the initial sequence, we accompany a coach and slowly approach a stately English manor house, Kellynch Hall, surrounded by a beautiful park, which sets the keynote for the film. As Dole (2001: 61-62) has noted, however, the presence of filed workers and fishcutters renders the heritage space less picturesque – paying for this lack of prettification with only modest success, primarily on the art-house circuit.

In *Emma*, directed by Douglas McGrath (1996) with Gwyneth Paltrow in the title role, there are many scenes set in picturesque gardens, starting with the opening scene, a picnic arranged in a garden with blossoming flowers. Knightley is presented as a landed squire when he engages in a playful archery competition with Emma in his impressive park at Donwell Abbey. That the many flowers we see in the gardens are not merely beautiful background decoration, but may, to some extent, symbolize the metaphorical flowers of love, becomes particularly evident in one scene in the final part of the film. There, Emma is sitting in her garden and pulling the petals off a daisy. She has just discovered that she loves Knightley, but does not like the insecurity and painful feelings of love. So she calls daisies "drab little flowers" and voices the opinion that they have no right to be in the garden at all.

How the expressive potential of the picturesque garden can be employed to good advantage is to be observed particularly well in the award-winning *Sense and Sensibility*, directed by Ang Lee (1995), for which Emma Thompson wrote the script and in which she played the leading role. The dualism of the title, the contrast between rational and emotional attitudes, is mirrored in the antithesis of art vs. nature, the formal garden vs. the English garden concept. We find a whole range of outdoor scenery, from wild nature to the highly artificial design of a French garden.

Wild nature is the setting in the crucial scene when Marianne first meets Willoughby, and gives expression to the romantic quality of her personality and this incident. Marianne, the extravagantly emotional and romantic young woman, is dragging her unwilling little sister Margaret up a hillside, with forest trees in the background. The weather is bad and there is a thunderstorm in the air. But this scenery is just to Marianne's liking, and she exclaims: "Is there any felicity in the world superior to this?" Then she has a bad fall, and as she lies helplessly on the ground, suddenly, like a knight in shining armour, the rescuer, Willoughby, on a huge white horse comes out of the fog and rain.

Barton Cottage, where Mrs Dashwood and her daughters find refuge after they have been expelled from their family home, Norland Park, is almost in a state of nature. The neglected and overgrown condition of the small garden is distinctly shown when the family arrives. Most of all, it probably denotes the Dashwoods' seclusion and isolation from civilized society.

The English garden concept, as a middle position between the extremes of wild nature and the artificial manipulation of natural objects, is used for the Dashwood family's original home, Norland Park. Saltram House near Plymouth in south Devon, the film location for this place, is a stately country mansion surrounded by an impressive landscape park. Through this park, Edward and Elinor take a walk (and subsequently a ride) and talk about their prospects in life. Though Elinor, in the attitudinal configuration of Jane Austen's novel, represents sense or common sense, a preponderantly rational attitude to life, she also holds a middle position since her love for Edward and her final union with him are basically irrational. So it is quite appropriate that this important scene takes place in a landscape garden.

Here Edward, talking about his chances in different professions, expresses his love for the country and his aversion to life in the big city: "I hate London. No peace. A country living is my idea." (Thompson 1996: 49) 'Fidelity criticism' may note that at this point, Emma Thomson's script takes the liberty to deviate slightly from the original. In the novel, Edward is much more clearly a practical and rational man, who unhesitatingly voices his dislike of the ideal of the picturesque when he says in a conversation with Marianne:

> I like a fine prospect, but not on picturesque principles. I do not like crooked, twisted, blasted trees. I admire them much more of they are tall, straight, and flourishing. I do not like ruined, tattered cottages. I am not fond of nettles, or thistles, or heath blossoms. (Austen 58, ch. 18)

In the film, such an open approval of the credo of the practical and functional would probably be misleading.

The formal garden concept appears in Sir John Middleton's home, Barton Park, represented by Trafalgar House near Salisbury. The festive grounds provide the location for a game of lawn bowling played by the Dashwood sisters and for the generous and splendid hospitality Sir John and Mrs Jennings show to their guests. The regularly round trees in the background make us aware that all this is planned and organized, and that this is contemporary civilization at its best.

Even more formal is the garden of Montacute House near Yeovil in Somerset, which doubles for the Palmer's estate at Cleveland, where Marianne undergoes her decisive crisis. Although Marianne has promised her sister, "I will keep to the garden, near the house", she breaks her promise, and two scenes later, a stage direction reads: "*Marianne* walks purposefully towards the garden wall, beyond which lies a hill." (Thompson 1996: 174-175) The fact that the romantic young woman leaves the formal garden with its straight walks and its regularly clipped evergreen trees has an unmistakably symbolic meaning. But Marianne's breakout from the constraints of society is doomed to fail. Soaked with rain and senseless, she has to be carried back to the safety of the civilized house by Colonel Brandon, the representative of orthodox society. When she finally recovers from her severe illness, we are given glimpses through the window of the formal garden with its magnificent fountain installation and its impressive intersection of gravel avenues: Marianne will have to learn to accommodate to and accept the constraints of civilization.

I will refrain from giving further examples. Before I close, however, let me just mention one 'garden' device in the screen version of *Sense and Sensibility*, namely the tree-house which little Margaret has both in Norland Park and later on in Barton Cottage. At first, it seems a nice, but gratuitous element invented by the filmmakers. But towards the end of the film when Margaret's superior view from the tree-house is used by the adults to 'reconnoitre', in a humorous way, the advances Edward has made towards Elinor in the cottage, then we begin to understand that the tree-house may also be understood as a charming little symbol about the special world of children and the both innocent and precocious character of Margaret in particular.

My essay has sufficiently demonstrated that picturesque gardens in the Jane Austen films are not just unnecessary additions, which are merely intended to delight the spectators with fine pictures and thereby increase the commodity value of each film. I would rather suggest that gardens and landscape are important means of expression and can be interpreted by a specific expressive grammar, which is based on the significance of gardens in contemporary culture.

Bibliography

Austen, Jane (n.d.), *The Complete Novels* (The Modern Library), New York: Random House.

Birtwistle, Sue & Susie Conklin (1995), *The Making of "Pride and Prejudice"*, London: Penguin Books/BBC Books.

Brownstein, Rachel M. (2001), "Out of the Drawing Room, onto the Lawn", in Troost & Greenfield, eds., 13-21.

Dole, Carol M. (2001), "Austen, Class, and the American Market", in Troost & Greenfield, eds., 58-78.

Ellington, H. Elisabeth (2001), "'A Correct Taste in Landscape'. Pemberley as Fetish and Commodity", in Troost & Greenfield, eds., 90-110.

Church Gibson, Pamela (2000), "Fewer Weddings and More Funerals: Changes in the Heritage Film", in Robert Murphy, ed., *British Cinema of the 90s*, London: British Film Institute, 115-124.

Higson, Andrew (1993), "Re-presenting the National Past: Nostalgia and Pastiche in the Heritage Film", in Lester Friedman, ed. *British Cinema and Thatcherism. Fires Were Started*, London: UCL Press, 109-129.

Morrison, Marion (1986), "Gardens", in David Grey, ed., *The Jane Austen Handbook*. London: Athlone Press, 184-186.

Mulvey, Laura (1975), "Visual Pleasure and Narrative Cinema", in *Screen* 16.3, 6-18.

Thompson, Emma (1996), *The Sense and Sensibility Screenplay & Diaries. Bringing Jane Austen's Novel to Film*, New York: Newmarket Press.

Troost, Linda & Sayre Greenfield, eds. (²2001), *Jane Austen in Hollywood* Lexington: UP of Kentucky.

The Bardbiz:
Heritage Shakespeare

Deborah Cartmell

Fin de Siècle Film Adaptations of Shakespeare

If, as Michael Bristol has asserted, Shakespeare, the name, in popular usage, often symbolises "privilege, exclusion, and cultural pretension" (Bristol 1996: ix), then, according to James Quinn and Jane Kingsley-Smith, Shakespeare on film must be aligned "with the notion of 'heritage cinema'" (2002: 167). In other words, the critical constructs of literary adaptation and heritage film intersect in the Shakespeare film; but while heritage films (in the narrowest sense of the term) imply a closeness to and reverence for their literary and/or historical sources (adhering to what Andrew Higson has called "the discourse of authenticity" (2003: 42)), recent adaptations of Shakespeare increasingly and emphatically do not. A survey of major Shakespeare films from 1990 to 2000 reveals a trend of both invoking and censoring associations of "privilege, exclusion and cultural pretension" or, in other words, notions of 'heritage'. Indeed, Shakespeare on screen, at the *fin de siècle*, stands in direct opposition to Fredric Jameson's assertion that "all that is left is to imitate dead styles" (2000: 18).[1] Undoubtedly, successful Shakespeare adaptations at the end of the 20th and the beginning of the 21st century increasingly turn away from so-called heritage production approaches (arguably Jameson's 'dead styles'), especially in their apparent abhorrence of British period set and costumes.

1   Shakespeare and Heritage

In 1996, Martin Wroe, in a tongue-in-cheek article, claimed that film audiences can be polarised into two types – the Janespotters and the Trainspotters – those who seek solace in nostalgic re-enactments of the past and those who are firmly devoted to the popular culture of the present. Wroe was commenting on *Sense and Sensibility* and *Trainspotting* (both films released in 1996) as "two films that define the sensibilities of the nation" (as discussed in Paget 1999: 128). Wroe's argument is that the former is aimed at well-to-do ageing baby-boomers and beyond who are nostalgically revisiting a much-loved classic, while the latter appeals to a youthful audience whose interests are more likely to be drugs, football and popular music. Shakespeare films, however, especially at the close of the century, call attention to just how indistinguishable these categories have become. If anything, films of Shakespeare's

---

[1] Some of the material in this chapter on *Hamlet* (2000) appears in A. Stock, ed. *Plotting Early Modern London*, Ashgate (forthcoming).

plays at the *fin de siècle* tend to be targeted at an audience more likely to watch *Trainspotting* than *Sense and Sensibility*, more interested in drugs, popular music and America, than in what has become known as 'British heritage' cinema.[2]

As has been well documented, Shakespeare was one of the first authors to be adapted for cinema, with the first Shakespeare film, Herbert Beerbohm's *King John*, appearing in 1899. The reasons for the popularity of Shakespeare as a source for early filmmakers are various. Clearly, Shakespeare was seen as providing cultural capital for the audience as well as for the industry. The stories, being so well-known, are easily communicated; and the plays are exceptionally visual, inspiring Laurence Olivier to claim that Shakespeare virtually "wrote for the films", his writing is seen as a gift for filmmakers (1984: Preface n.p.). In many respects Olivier was responsible for the 'look' of Shakespeare in the mid 20th Century – his Henry V, Hamlet and Richard III visually anchored the protagonists in the minds of the public; and these Shakespearean representations became themselves, a part of the British heritage and/or 'authentic'/'traditional' Shakespeare. While it would be absurd to uphold Olivier's claim that Shakespeare was a would-be screenwriter, the playwright's appeal to filmmakers has remained undiminished. Indeed, by the 1990s, Shakespeare on screen has become part of the English syllabus. Its inclusion in edited volumes is virtually obligatory, there has been a huge growth in books devoted to the subject and it is now taught as a subject in its own right. This would have been unthinkable twenty years earlier. As I have argued, where Shakespeare goes, others – Austen, Dickens, Eliot, for starters – are likely to follow (1999: 29-37). And there is, undoubtedly, at the end of the 20th century and the beginning of the 21st century, an increasingly anti-reverential, meta- and/or anti-British heritage approach to Shakespeare's plays on screen. This is a far cry from Olivier's *Henry V* (1944), when British audiences left the cinema, full of national pride, epitomised by James Agee's reaction shortly after the release of the film:

> I was persuaded, and in part still am, that every time and place has since been in decline save one, in which one Englishman used language better than anyone has before or since ... and that some of us are still capable of paying homage to the fact. (1946; rpt. in Mast & Cohen 1974: 336)

---

[2]   I do not wish to enter into the debate as to what does and does not qualify as 'British heritage'; as Claire Monk has indicated, it is a critical construct rather than descriptive of any single film genre. In terms of its constructions, Monk points out that a film does not even need to be British or set in the past in order to be included under the umbrella of 'British heritage' (Monk 2002). For a lucid account of the bewildering directions of the debate, cf. Eckart Voigts-Virchow's introduction to this volume. For the purposes of this chapter, the British heritage aesthetic is interpreted in the narrower, often derogatory sense, as defined by Paget (1999) and Church Gibson (2000) below.

According to Agee, one great Englishman (Shakespeare) passes the baton to another (Olivier) who pays homage to his inheritance on screen – and this, it seems, is Shakespeare heritage cinema *par excellence*.

2 Representing 'Heritage' in Shakespeare on Screen: 1990 to 2000

A survey of (albeit, what I consider to be) the mainstream Shakespeare films from 1996 onwards reveals a definite trend, in what would be almost unthinkable in the mid 20th Century, of "reconceptualising Shakespeare" (Voigts-Virchow 2004), significantly, taking the plays out of their historical context:[3]

> *Looking for Richard*, 1996 (Pacino)
> *Richard III*, 1996 (Loncraine)
> *Hamlet*, 1996 (Branagh)
> *William Shakespeare's Romeo + Juliet*, 1996 (Luhrmann)
> *Shakespeare in Love*, 1998 (Madden)
> *Titus*, 1999 (Taymor)
> *Ten Things I Hate About You*, 1999 (Junger)
> *William Shakespeare's A Midsummer Night's Dream*, 1999 (Hoffman)
> *Love's Labour's Lost*, 2000 (Branagh)
> *Hamlet*, 2000 (Almereyda)
> *O*, 2000 (Blake Nelson)

While all these films employ, as Roberta Pearson observes, "dense, multiple and diverse intertextual and generic references" (2002: 155), their popularity is also attributable to their various takes on 'heritage' or the notion of 'authentic Shakespeare'. From the above list, Pacino in *Looking for Richard* dresses the cast in period costumes, while thematising the relation of the past to the present with the actors shown in and out of their parts. Similarly, Madden's *Shakespeare in Love*, the most lucrative of the Shakespeare films at the end of the century (Voigts-Virchow 2004), is a meta-heritage film; while seemingly painstakingly reconstructing the theatre and its inhabitants, it is playfully anachronistic and historically inaccurate, on one hand endorsing the Shakespeare heritage industry, while, on the other, sending it up. The souvenir Stratford-upon-Avon mug on the desk of sexy Will Shakespeare, in the opening of the film, is a reminder of the impossibility of historical re-enactment as the film parodies the heritage approach to Shakespeare which, it seems, is doomed.[4] The mug is a visual acknowledgement of the impossi-

---

3   Of course, there are exceptions to this case, but consider the consternation caused by Derek Jarman's *Tempest* (1978) – although, the country house setting can be seen to pay homage to heritage productions.

4   Richard Burt quotes Sandy Powell, the costume designer for the film: "On *Shakespeare in Love*, the studio was worried about the pants. It's a difficult period for men not to look

bility of historical reconstruction, what Stephen Greenblatt has referred to as the new historicists' desire to "speak with the dead" (1992: 1) while at the same time knowing that all they can hear is their own voices. In *Shakespeare in Love*, the souvenir mug is thrown in on purpose (not by accident, such as in the trumpeter wearing a watch in *Ben-Hur*, 1959) to call attention to the film as adaptation rather than historical re-enactment. Appropriately, the film ends with Viola in America, signalling the fate of Shakespeare and Shakespeare on film at the turn of the century – Shakespeare is no longer British heritage, but contemporary American. Significantly, none of the other films on the above list set Shakespeare in the Elizabethan/Jacobean period; rather they wilfully turn their backs on any futile attempt to recreate the past on screen. Whilst Taymor's *Titus* alludes to the period in which the play was set, the costumes and set disturbingly represent a variety of periods, from the Romans to our own time.

A list of mainstream film adaptations in the first half of the 1990s reveals a different story to that of the latter half:

> *Hamlet*, 1990 (Zeffirelli)
> *Prospero's Books*, 1990 (Greenaway)
> *Much Ado About Nothing*, 1993 (Branagh)
> *Othello*, 1995 (Parker)

With the exception of Branagh's film, all these films are set at the time of the original production or at the time in which the plays were set. Although Branagh's film is set in rural Tuscany sometime in the 19th Century, the villa and painterly attention paid to the idyllic Tuscan landscape recall heritage films such *A Room with a View* (1985). Uniquely, *Prospero's Books* can be seen as meta-heritage (like Madden's *Shakespeare in Love*) in that Greenaway's costumes are exaggerated versions of Jacobean garments and, as such, mock at the same time as endorse the heritage treatment of Shakespeare.[5]

---

stupid, so the exec types kept asking, 'Will there be tights?' So we made the jackets a little longer, the pants a little longer. You want to have believable clothes for the period, but you don't want your actors to look silly" (203-231).

5 Film should be distinguished from theatre, which has been much freer and much earlier, in adopting other periods and in taking greater risks. The first black actor to play Othello on stage was Ira Aldridge in 1833 while it wasn't until 1995 that a black actor played the part in mainstream cinema (Parker). With regard to period detail, in Shakespeare's own day, the plays were, of course, not given the 'heritage treatment' but set in the contemporary period. Perhaps the most noteworthy staging of the play after Shakespeare's own is John Philip Kemble's acclaimed production of *Henry V*. The play ran between 1789 and 1806 with a set that included 'modern furniture, anachronistic costuming, and inaccurate weaponry' (Loechlin 1997: 18). This anachronistic, seemingly 'anti-heritage' costuming is also present in a number of 20th century stagings, including Terry Hands' RSC production of 1975 and Michael Bogdanov's English Shakespeare Company production of 1986.

Clearly, at the turn of the century, Shakespeare films steer clear of heritage associations, defined by Derek Paget as a "nostalgic harkening back to the imagined elegance of a former period" (1999: 129), as depicted in the majority of Jane Austen adaptations. Indeed, these adaptations tend to be defiantly 'anti-heritage' and/or 'meta-heritage'– note the hybrid casting, intertextual references to other films, anti-picturesque settings, absence of dainty, period costumes, or costumes that try to be historically accurate (Church Gibson 2000). In addition to these, the films call attention to themselves as adaptations, not to be mistaken for 'the real thing'. For instance, the desecration of the statue of Hamlet Senior at the end of Branagh's 1996 film implicitly presents the film as an adaptation that simultaneously preserves and destroys the 'original'. The presence of new technologies in Shakespeare films at the turn to the century serves to remind the audience of the productions as adaptations in an age of mechanical reproduction. This is evident in films such as Michael Hoffman's *Midsummer Night's Dream* (1999). Although, to a certain extent adhering to the heritage genre in its lush Italian setting and beautiful nineteenth century costumes, the 'new' inventions of the gramaphone and the bicycle are constantly foregrounded, calling attention to the technical reproduction that is the film. In Baz Luhrmann's *William Shakespeare's Romeo + Juliet* (1996), we are made aware of the intrusion of technology through the television screen which introduces and concludes the film and in Michael Almereyda's *Hamlet*, we are overwhelmed with media images. Hamlet, in Almereyda's film, is trapped by consumerism; he is virtually lost in his hotel room amid the obscene heaps of expensive electronic equipment that he has accumulated.

3   Shakespeare Films and the Youth Market: The Case of Michael Almereyda's *Hamlet*

A striking development of turn of the century film adaptations of Shakespeare is the teenpic, in particular, Luhrmann's *William Shakespeare's Romeo + Juliet*, *10 Things I Hate About You*, and *O*. These films re-package Shakespeare for teen audiences. Like *Bill and Ted's Excellent Adventure* (1988), the grand narratives of the past (that is, Shakespeare's plays) are juxtaposed with the ill-read American teenager of the present, surprisingly, in a merging rather than a clash of cultures. Given the number of recent teen adaptations of Shakespeare, Hollywood backers obviously believe that there is cash in infantilising Shakespeare's plays, reconfiguring them for a teen or twenty-something audience. Both *Ten Things I Hate About You* and *O* not only change the context but also translate the once sacred words of Shakespeare's plays. *Ten Things I Hate About You* (directed by Gil Junger) modernises the language (retaining only the words 'I burn, I pine, I perish', I.i.149) and restructures the play according to the conventions of the teenpic. Accordingly, the film features a high school setting, distinct social cliques, a comic/ineffectual father, a drunken house party and a preoccupation with dating. The film's heritage (i.e. Shakespeare) makes only cameo appearances, in an English teacher's lesson and in a minor character's obsession with all things Shakespearean (thus he appears on a poster inside her locker door).

Perhaps the most surprising of the turn of the century films of Shakespeare is Almereyda's *Hamlet* which positions Shakespeare's most wordy play between the 'two cultures' outlined at the beginning of this chapter. Firstly, it reminds us that Shakespeare is no longer the exclusive property of the British – this is a quintessentially American adaptation of Britain's 'finest writer'. The film calls attention to its teenpic or Generation-X credentials right from the start in the casting of actors from well-known and successful teenpic adaptations of Shakespeare: Diane Venora (from Baz Luhrmann's *Romeo and Juliet* and Julia Stiles (who is also in *O*) from *10 Things I Hate About You*). In keeping with the *fin de siècle* trend of targeting Shakespeare to a young audience, Almereyda seems to be at pains to emphasise the youthful credentials of Laertes, Ophelia and Hamlet, thus accounting for their bad or impetuous behaviour. Bill Murray's Polonius regards Ophelia and Laertes as children; unbeknown to Laertes, he stashes money in his son's jacket while helping him pack. At one point, he even ties Ophelia's shoelace and rather than discourage, he encourages her to "think herself a baby" (I.iii.105), stressing that Hamlet "is young" (I.iv.124) and therefore not to be taken seriously.

As one reviewer notes, Ethan Hawke transforms Hamlet into a spoilt rich kid, 'or wet whining wanabe' whose 'intelligence and imagination are disturbingly dulled – presumably the effect of watching far too much TV' (Errigo: 2001). Although Hawke sees Hamlet more as Holden Caulfield (Almereyda 2000: xiv), he appears more like Bill or Ted, a 'Last Man', a victim of sloth and consumerism (cf. Hunter 1996: 113), and you cannot help wondering throughout why this humourless, seemingly unemployed youth (significantly, the first spoken words are about Hamlet having "lost all his mirth") is not in therapy like all normal Manhattan rich kids. There is no attempt in this film to explain the question of the succession: it is instantly apparent that Hamlet could not possibly cut it in the corporate world alongside his father and uncle. Beside Kyle MacLachlan's debonair, well-groomed Claudius, Hamlet is sulky and childish, wearing an absurd woolly hat, completely unnecessary in New York at the end of October (Halloween) when the film is set. It is likely that the final stages of filming, Almereyda decided to drop the line about Claudius popping "in between th'election and my hopes" (V.ii.65) due to the absurdity of Hamlet succeeding his father.[6]

Features of the teen-pic genre, the dysfunctional family, complete with amusing father, conspicuous consumption, the brat pack (as represented by Rosencrantz and Guildenstern), and the loner are imposed onto the play.[7]

---

[6] This line remains in the screenplay (116).
[7] For conventions of the teen-pic, cf. Bernstein (1997), Burt (1998), Doherty (2002), and Lewis (1992). Teen adaptation is an area with surprisingly little literature. These films

However, this is not to imply that the film simply 'dumbs down' Shakespeare in order to appeal to a youthful audience incapable of understanding *Hamlet* in its entirety. Almereyda parodies the process of adaptation, like Luhrmann, by inserting laughs within the narrative, such as old words in new contexts, visual jokes, such as the drinking of Danish beer, and quotations to 'heritage Shakespeare', such as the appearance of John Gielgud playing Hamlet on a video in Blockbuster's.

The ending of this version of *Hamlet*, unashamedly, relies on Baz Luhrmann's *Romeo and Juliet* with the news anchorman taking over the final lines of the play. Fortinbras's, the 1st Ambassador's and the Player King's words are together, joined ending with "Our thoughts are ours, their ends none of our own" (III.ii.209). We see the words repeated on the teleprompter and the final shot of the film is of words – according to Almereyda, "Shakespeare's words, ascending a glowing screen" (2000: 143). The Player King's words offer an excuse for the adaptation – "Our thoughts are ours, their ends none of our own". These lines call attention to the adaptation as a good-intentioned but ultimately doomed attempt to do justice to its source. These words which announce the difference between intention and result, provide a motto for recent film adaptations of Shakespeare, which self-consciously highlight (rather than attempt to conceal) the gap between then and now, Shakespeare and ourselves.

Recent film versions of Shakespeare call into question their heritage credentials through invoking a multiplicity of source texts rather than revering and seeking to preserve an 'original'. Shakespeare remains the common denominator of these films, but he is not the Shakespeare he once was. These recent films insistently combine the past with the present and are a far cry from the adaptations of Laurence Olivier or the BBC/Timelife series of the late seventies, early eighties, epitomised by Jonathan Miller's attempts at 'faithful' reconstructions of the Elizabethan and Jacobean periods. In fact, none of these films make any attempt at faithful historical re-enactment. It is without doubt that, at the turn of the century, Shakespeare is no longer given the kid glove 'heritage treatment' that he once was and that Shakespeare adaptations, in the mainstream, are constructed to appeal to an audience somewhere between the Trainspotters and Janespotters, referred to at the

---

tend to be noticeably formulaic or alike in their construction and usually include a majority or all of the following features:

- School or college setting
- Ineffectual parents – often single parents
- Distinctive groups within the school – such as jocks, skateboarders, etc
- Drunken parties and school proms
- Makeovers – including the central pair
- Large and luxurious houses
- Time spent in the central girl's bedroom – the bedroom is presented as an area of refuge

Thanks to Lucy Browster for helping me compile this list.

beginning of this chapter. In fact, Shakespeare on screen has come full circle; at the beginning of the 20th century, Shakespeare was used to uplift the status of film while at the end of the century, film is used to bring Shakespeare down to a more popular level. Adaptations of Shakespeare at the *fin de siècle* call attention to themselves as adaptations by both invoking and repudiating their 'heritage' associations; and as Shakespeare is the acknowledged leader of a pack of authors and a trend setter in film and literature studies, this may be a sign. Where Shakespeare goes, others are likely to follow.[8]

Bibliography

Almereyda, Michael (2000), *William Shakespeare's "Hamlet": A Screenplay by Michael Almereyda*, London: Faber & Faber.

Bernstein, Jonathan (1997), *Pretty in Pink: The Golden Age of Teenage Movies*, New York: St.Martin's Griffin.

Bristol, Michael D. (1996), *big-time shakespeare*. London – New York: Routledge.

Burt, Richard (1998), *Unspeakable ShXXXpeares: Queer Theory and American Kiddie Culture*, New York: St Martin's Press.

Burt, Richard (2000), "*Shakespeare in Love* and the End of Shakespeare", in Mark Thornton Burnett & Ramona Wray, eds. *Shakespeare, Film, Fin de Siècle*, London – New York: Macmillan, 203-231.

Cartmell, Deborah & Imelda Whelehan, eds. (1999), *Adaptations. From Text to Screen, Screen to Text*, London – New York: Routledge.

Cartmell, Deborah (1999), "The Shakespeare on Screen Industry", in Cartmell & Whelehan, eds., 29-37.

Church Gibson, Pamela (2000), "Fewer Weddings and More Funerals: Changes in the Heritage Film", in Robert Murphy, ed. *British Cinema of the 90s*, London: British Film Institute, 115-124.

Doherty, Thomas (2002), *Teenagers and Teenpics: the Juvenilization of American Movies in the 1950s*, Philadelphia: Temple University Press.

Errigo, Angie (2001), Review of *Hamlet* (Almereyda), *Empire*, January, 62.

Greenblatt, Stephen (1992), *Shakespearean Negotiations: The Circulation of Social Energy in Renaissance England* ([1]1988), Oxford: Oxford University Press.

Greenblatt, Stephen, Walter Cohen, Jean E. Howard, Katherine Eisaman Maus, eds. (1997), *The Norton Shakespeare: Comedies*. New York – London: Norton.

Higson, Andrew (2003), *English Heritage, English Cinema: Costume Drama Since 1980*, Oxford: Oxford University Press.

Hunter, I.Q. (1996), "Capitalism Most Triumphant: Bill and Ted's Excellent History esson", in Deborah Cartmell *et al.*, eds. *Pulping Fictions: Consuming Culture Across the Literature/Media Divide*, London: Pluto, 111-124.

Jameson, Fredric (1988), "Postmodernism and Consumer Society", in E. Ann Kaplan, ed., *Postmodernism and its Discontents*, London: Verso, 13-29.

---

[8] This is not to ignore the fact that there have been a number of meta-heritage and teen adaptations of other authors, *Clueless* (1995) as adaptation of Jane Austen's *Emma*, being the most notable example. Nonetheless, unlike Shakespeare adaptations, this still remains the exception rather than the rule.

Lewis, Jon (1992), *The Road to Romance and Ruin: Teen Films and Youth* Culture, London
– New York: Routledge.

Loehlin, James N. (1996), *"Henry V": Shakespeare in Performance*. Manchester: Manchester University Press.

Mast, Gerald & Marshall Cohen, eds. (1974), *Film Theory and Criticism*, Oxford: Oxford University Press.

Monk, Claire (2002), "The British Heritage-film Debate Revisited", in Monk & Sargeant, eds. 176-198.

Monk, Claire & Amy Sargeant, eds. (2002a), *British Historical Cinema. The History, Heritage and Costume Film*, London – New York: Routledge.

----- (2002b), "Introduction: the Past in British Cinema", in Monk & Sargeant, eds., 1-14.

Olivier, Laurence (1984), "The Making of *Henry V*", in Olivier, *Henry V.* London: Lorrimer, 1984.

Paget, Derek (1999), "Speaking Out: the Transformations of Trainspotting", in Cartmell & Whelehan, eds., 128-140.

Quinn, James and Jane Kingsley-Smith (2002), "Kenneth Branagh's *Henry V* (1989): Genre and Interpretation", in Monk & Sargeant, eds., 163-175.

Shakespeare, William (1982), *Hamlet*, ed. Harold Jenkins, London: Methuen, 1982.

Voigts-Virchow, Eckart (2004), "'Corset Wars': An Introduction to Syncretic Heritage Film Culture since the Mid-1990s", in this volume.

Roberta E. Pearson

Heritage, Humanism, Populism: The Representation of Shakespeare in Contemporary British Television

1   Introduction: Heritage, Humanism, Populism

In the first four years of the twenty-first century, British television continued the celebration of the life and works of William Shakespeare that had begun with the Bard's establishment as the national poet in the eighteenth century. Between them, the BBC and ITV broadcast the following programmes that focused in whole or in part on the poet whom his countrymen had voted the man of millennium: *South Bank Show: Shakespeare, Man of the Millennium* (ITV, 2000); *The Genius of Shakespeare* (BBC 2, 2000); *Changing Stages* (BBC 2, 2000); *Happy Birthday Shakespeare* (BBC 1, 2000), based on a novel by Mark Wallington; *Great Britons* (BBC 2, 2002); *The Adventure of English* (ITV, 2002) as well as Michael Wood's four part biography *In Search of Shakespeare* (BBC 2, 2003). These programmes are but the latest additions to a group of British film and television screen texts so large that it constitutes its own genre. Rooted in the newsreels, travelogues and feature films of the British silent cinema and representing the man rather than the plays, this Shakespeare genre, like any other, must constantly renew itself. The several texts discussed in this article accomplish this generic reconfiguration by attacking what they position as old-fashioned heritage appropriations of Shakespeare. Having rejected heritage and yet still themselves part of the 'bardbiz', the Shakespeare industry composed of educational, media, and tourism institutions, the programmes then make their own arguments for the national poet's continued relevance by invoking his humanism or populism.[1]

2   Heritage Shakespeare

Using heritage as an adjectival qualifier of Shakespeare requires narrowing its polysemy, for in Britain the term labels everything from gardens to paint

---

[1] On the bardbiz and Shakespearean reconfiguration generally, cf. Taylor (1990) and Hodgdon (1998).

to living history museums to cinema.[2] The vastness of a Shakespeare industry that encompasses everything from souvenirs to guidebooks to particular ways of mounting the plays compounds the potential polysemy. In this article the phrase 'heritage Shakespeare' indicates a static and narrow conception of British history, national identity and the national poet that has in the past lent unity to the diverse components of the bardbiz. In an earlier article (Pearson 2002), I examined the representation of Shakespeare in British silent newsreels and travelogues, beginning with the example of a 1926 travelogue titled *Shakespeare's Country*, an episode in the series *Wonderful Britain* (A Harry B. Parkinson Production for British Screen Classics). The film starts with an intertitle: "Shakespeare found success in London – but his heart, from his earliest days, was in his native Warwickshire. In the little village of Wilmcote, lived Mary Arden his mother." We see an exterior of a stone house, followed by a dissolve to a gate in a stone wall, then another intertitle: "And in the country around Stratford on Avon there breathes the very spirit of the Bard." A shot of a bridge over the river Avon is followed by a shot from one of the riverbanks. The rest of the film consists of similarly pretty 'chocolate box' shots of an old-fashioned, cosy England composed of thatched houses, cottage gardens and half-timbered buildings. This film, like other cinematic texts, travel books, biographies, and the like, constructed a Shakespeare who was strongly allied with a rural and idyllic Stratford. This Stratford stood synecdochically for the rural South in which English national identity was heavily invested during the 1920s. Functioning as a marker of the stability of English national identity, this timeless and eternal heritage Shakespeare was enshrined in the tourist industry, embodied in the national curriculum and performed by the Royal Shakespeare Company while buttressing conservative politicians and defending the British Empire.

Several of the programmes under discussion in this article contain sequences that ritually reject this heritage Shakespeare, with Stratford now serving as a bad rather than good object, emblematising an embarrassingly outdated image of the national poet. *Changing Stages* intercuts 1950s black and white travelogue footage of a boat floating down the Avon near the Shakespeare Memorial Theatre with presenter Richard Eyre on a boat in the exact same location. Says Eyre, "Visiting Stratford's like entering a time warp. It's an island of heritage Britain." The *South Bank Show's* anti-heritage sequence also uses Stratford travelogue footage, this time from the 1930s. Over the travelogue's shot of an Elizabethan-clad arm and hand holding a quill pen, presumably intended to represent Shakespeare, presenter Melvyn Bragg says, "In the 20th century Shakespeare's status as national poet has often obscured the true nature of his genius by turning him into a national treasure." The programme cuts to a talking head, Shakespeare scholar Jonathan Bate. "Part of the Shakespeare story is to do with heritage. You only

---

[2]   On the multiple meanings of the term heritage, cf. Samuel (1994). For a discussion of
      British heritage cinema, cf. Higson (1995).

have to look at the Stratford tourist industry." Bate continues to speak over shots of contemporary Stratford – the tour bus, the sign at the Shakespeare birthplace:

> The danger of that is that it makes Shakespeare into this old fashioned, cosy establishment figure, but that's not what Shakespeare's about. Shakespeare uses heritage in his plays, but he does so in order to say vital things to the present. His plays have got to be adapted in order to evolve. That's how he stays alive. Antiquarians, doublet and hose will be the death of Shakespeare. The best Shakespeare is always Shakespeare made contemporary.

In *Great Britons*, actress Fiona Shaw attempts to persuade the audience to elect Shakespeare as the greatest Briton of them all by wresting the poet from Stratford and the past and, as Bate advises, making him contemporary. Shaw tells us that Shakespeare is "possibly the most famous person in the English speaking world. He symbolises things, he's famous for being famous." The image track shows close-ups of Shakespeare items: a sign for the Bard's Walk; Shakespeare's blend English Breakfast tea; a Stratford souvenir plate with the famous First Folio portrait; the Hathaway Tea Rooms. Shaw continues, "He is also the most loathed writer seen by many as irrelevant and old fashioned, an embarrassing symbol of 'ye olde England' [...]." Shaw then visits Shakespeare's birthplace, the holiest of holy of Shakespeare shrines. As she walks from the bedroom to the kitchen, she says, "This unfortunate reputation is in part due to the Shakespeare industry. Shakespeare's imagination has little to do with this sanitised museum world." By contrast to the sanitised museum world, *Great Britons* offers a series of close-ups of the operations of a modern-day tannery, while Shaw tells us that Shakespeare's father was a butcher, a tanner and a glover. The earthy reality of the past is set against the sterility of the present, a common tactic in these programmes.

What do these texts gain from their anti-heritage stance? The rejection of heritage stems partially from the need to reconfigure the Shakespeare genre. In an age of devolution, multiculturalism and the split, fragmented national identity concomitant with these social trends, heritage's associations with a fixed and stable 'ye olde England' render its Shakespeare as antiquated as the quill pen. The rejection will presumably appeal to many in the audience who may have been force-fed a version of heritage Shakespeare as part of a national curriculum intent upon perpetuating the bardbiz. As artistic director of the Globe, Mark Rylance, says in *The Genius of Shakespeare*:

> The text has such big sticks attached to it because of how you meet it as a young person at school. There's usually an exam and some kind of gateway and if you say the wrong answer [...] the gates' gonna close and your options as a person will be limited.

The reconfiguration of the Shakespeare genre has the same ideological overtones as do the reworkings of other popular heroes, but a more specifically televisual requirement also accounts for the anti-heritage sequence.³ Like many documentaries, the programmes under consideration are primarily a compilation of talking heads, anathema to producers mandated to grab and keep viewers' attention. The talking heads may occasionally address the camera, but must deliver the bulk of their comments as voice-over accompaniment to compelling visuals. The many forms of heritage Shakespeare embodied in the built environment and the tourism industry provide obvious points of visual reference: Stratford buildings; Shakespeare tea-rooms; souvenir plates and the like. The old footage used to emblematise heritage Shakespeare in both *The South Bank Show* and *The Genius of Shakespeare* not only provides visuals to accompany the talking heads' voice-overs but also helps to decrease production costs.

Happy Birthday Shakespeare enacts the rejection of heritage Shakespeare in fictional form. The hero, aptly named Will, met his wife on Shakespeare's birthday, an event they celebrate annually and which gives the programme its title. Will is discontented both with his job (a driver of tourist coaches) and his personal life (stuck with his wife and two young sons in a small crowded London flat over a laundrette and overlooking the motorway). He dreams of buying a Stratford cottage, turning it into a tourist-haven tea-room and moving several rungs up the heritage-industry ladder. After a series of disasters, including a brief affair with a tour guide, the deus ex machina of his father's death gives him £250,000. Will uses the inheritance to buy a semi-detached house and, rather improbably given the London housing market, has enough left over to set himself up in a vacuum cleaner business completely removed from the heritage industry.

Despite the romantic significance of the title, Shakespeare functions in the text primarily as an illusion that causes Will to misinterpret the real conditions of his existence. The programme begins with Will dreaming of a rural idyll. He lies in his wife's lap reading Sonnet 116 while his young sons romp nearby in flower strewn woods. The excerpt from the sonnet is one of only two sustained passages of Shakespeare in the programme. The other occurs when Will and his new love interest, on an overnight tour to Bath, participate in Karaoke Shakespeare, reciting a passage about elopement from *A Midsummer Night's Dream*. This sequence is, in its own way, as unrealistically romantic as the opening dream images, for both participants are married and have no intention of abandoning their partners. Will's first encounter with the Stratford cottage he so desires cruelly mocks his doomed hopes for an idyllic heritage existence in a time-warp insulated from the realities of contemporary Briton. The romantic music from the opening dream idyll returns, accompanying slow travelling shots of the cottage and surrounding garden. Will enters the cottage to discover a downstairs tea-room stocked with plastic chairs, plastic tables and plastic ketchup bottles and an upstairs in which a fat

---

³   For discussions of other popular heroes cf. Bennett & Woollacott (1987), Brooker (2000) and Pearson & Uricchio (1991).

woman snores on a sofa amidst blaring television, empty wine bottles and dirty clothes. But Will's commitment to a heritage idyll is not easily discouraged, for, as the romantic music returns, he looks out the window to see a totally transformed garden, with happy tourists scoffing down cream teas, his sons playing on a swing set and his wife and himself acting as genial hosts.

The programme contrasts the heritage Shakespeare of Will's imagination with the heritage Shakespeare of the tourist industry as manifested in Stratford. Having negotiated a horrendous traffic jam, Will deposits his Japanese and American charges in the town to watch the Shakespeare birthday festivities. Jugglers, Morris dancers, men on stilts and faux Elizabethans all parade in the town centre. Some of the Japanese tourists show him a T-shirt they have just purchased. He reads it aloud: "To be or not to be." The tourists ask for more Shakespeare. "Friends, Romans, countrymen – that's from Caesar, I think." A juggler stops in front of them, catches a cabbage on a fork and declaims, "Alas, poor Yorick." A later scene reinforces the connections amongst Stratford, tourism and a meaningless heritage Shakespeare. At a faux Elizabethan banquet in an English country house an American tourist says, "We went to Stratford. Turns out Shakespeare wrote everything. If music be the food of love, play on; frailty thy name is woman; the world's your oyster; beware the Ides of March; all the world's a stage, all Shakespeare." At this point the elderly lord of the manor, forced to entertain tourists to keep the family estate solvent, chimes in: "There's no business like show business; I'm a lumber jack and I'm okay." Responds the American, "Shakespeare wrote that? That guy's a genius!" This reduced Shakespeare, composed of catchphrases made meaningless by their insistent repetition and commodification and functioning in the same manner as snatches from a show tune or a line from a Monty Python routine, reveals the emptiness of heritage. Had Will experienced an engagement with a living Shakespeare unmediated by the embalming tendencies of the heritage industry, he might more readily have rejected his unrealistic dreams to find true happiness with his family. Or at least this is what those who argue for Shakespeare's relevance from a humanist perspective would have us believe.

3   Humanist Shakespeare

A heritage Shakespeare is an outmoded Englishman with no great resonance outside his own country; a humanist Shakespeare is a cosmopolitan who speaks to all the world in contemporary terms. As Fiona Shaw says in *Great Britons*, "The problem about being a national icon means that he got trapped into a waxwork identity, where in fact his greatness and uniqueness lies in his ability to write about us as we are now. That's why we still need this 16th-century man today, not for what he says about Britain but for what he says about us." The humanist Shakespeare, set free from the stifling historicism of

a particularly English heritage, is a transcendent genius who wrote of universal themes and emotions and created emblematic characters recognised by
all. Says Shaw, "His plays can be reset in any time and any place because
what we recognise in them isn't the dates and the towns, it's the emotions
and the experiences and the personalities familiar to everyone everywhere."
In *The Genius of Shakespeare*, Richard Eyre speaks of a Shakespeare who has
particular meaning to the British:

> Shakespeare is our icon, our emblem, our logo, our talisman, our secular saint, our
> patriarch, our sage and our national poet. But Shakespeare's importance stems not
> from his Britishness, but from his understanding of the human condition. Shake-
> speare affirms the infinite ambiguity of people and of nature and takes upon him-
> self the mystery of things […].

In *The South Bank Show*, Glenda Jackson makes a similar argument for Shakespeare's continued relevance:

> His great genius was to observe people as they really are and not to be judgmental
> about them. What it is to be a human being really doesn't change very much and
> that is why he is as contemporary now as he was when those plays were first seen
> and heard on the South Bank.

The fact that his plays are read and performed around the world makes
claims for Shakespeare's universality literal rather than metaphorical. As
Melvyn Bragg says in *The South Bank Show*, "His creations are the best candi-
date we have for a universal literature. Tokyo has its own Globe Theatre,
Germany celebrates his birthday, in Bulgaria he's a set text. There are Shakespeare festivals in New York's Central Park and in the other Stratford in
Ontario." *Great Britons* and *The Genius of Shakespeare* confirm claims to universality with facts and figures. Fiona Shaw says that Shakespeare has been
translated around the world and the image track shows several foreign language editions. Shaw says that Shakespeare is the most filmed author ever
and the image tracks shows shots of Akira Kurosawa's *Ran*. *The Genius of
Shakespeare* contains excerpts from Orson Welles' Voodoo *Macbeth* of 1936, a
Romanian *Hamlet* performed by the Bulandra Theatre Company and a Japanese *Tempest* performed by the Ninagawa Theatre Company. But foreign
appropriations of Shakespeare remain firmly within the constraints of a very
Western liberal humanism. *Great Britons* includes shots of Nicolae Ceaușescu
at a Romania Communist rally (monster portraits, sea of red flags, massed
humanity), as Shaw says, "*Hamlet* still worked perfectly well as a metaphor
for corrupt states in the 20th century." The same programme has an extended
sequence on the infamous Robin Island, the South African prison for protest-
ers of apartheid, the most famous of whom was Nelson Mandela. Shaw tells
us that the prisoners clandestinely passed around a copy of Shakespeare,
writing their names next to the favourite passages. Mandela chose lines from
Julius Caesar: "Cowards die many times before their deaths; The valiant never
taste of death but once." Only Richard Eyre in *Changing Stages* challenges the
humanist vision by acknowledging one of the mechanisms responsible for

Shakespeare's universality. Eyre says, "The Victorians transformed Shakespeare into a secular saint. Shakespeare as national poet was exported to every corner of the empire well into the 20th century. He was used as one of the main props of an imperialist culture." He speaks over newsreel footage from Kenya in which black people watch white people enacting a pageant of Elizabethan England. Eyre continues this is a "pageant that might have taken place on an English village green."

Eyre wishes to replace this particularly bad heritage Shakespeare with the humanist Shakespeare. None of the programmes, however, admits that the humanist Shakespeare is every bit as time-bound and ideologically suspect as the heritage Shakespeare. Humanist Shakespeare can only acknowledge appropriations that accord with the supposedly transcendental and universal values of Western humanism, which, as many within cultural studies have pointed out, have in practice justified Western expansion and domination. *Great Britons*, for example, aligns Shakespeare with liberal democracy, although, as we now see from the example of Russia and other former Soviet bloc states, liberal democracy is not the universal panacea it was once thought to be. The programmes also fail to understand that historical context determines the form taken even by a supposedly trans-historical humanist Shakespeare. Each age uses Shakespeare to construct a Foucauldian formation of the subject particular to its own time. Contrast the stern Victorian Shakespeare with the touchy-feely 21st-century Shakespeare. The Victorians believed in a humanist Shakespeare and made claims for the universal relevance of his themes and characters, but did so in a way that accorded with Victorian didacticism and morality. Reading Shakespeare strengthened the moral fibre. Fiona Shaw argues for Shakespeare's continued relevance in strikingly 21st-century terms, reducing him to the level of a self-help book: "Shakespeare makes us understand our thoughts and our feelings. And what could be more useful in our lives than that?" Reading Shakespeare puts us in touch with our inner child, or actualises our potential or any other number of psycho-babble phrases.

4　Populist Shakespeare

Shakespeare might be cast as a self-help book, but *The Atkins Diet* and similar best-sellers are not written in an iambic pentameter blank verse that intimidates ordinary people and Royal Shakespeare Company actors alike. The different manners in which *The Genius of Shakespeare* and *Great Britons* attempt to demystify the iambic pentameter epitomise the contrast between the programmes' humanist and populist Shakespeares. In *The Genius of Shakespeare*, Peter Hall compares the iambic pentameter rhythm to jazz. He says that the meter is like a "system underneath a piece of jazz. Great Shakespearean playing is like great jazz playing. You keep the beat, you preserve the line, but it's how you nearly break the line which enables you to express the emotion, enables you to actually say what it feels." Hall's metaphor may be apt, but renders the iambic pentameter no less frightening, given that jazz has become a relatively restricted and inaccessible art form. In *Great Britons*, Fiona Shaw, speaking over images of a black rap group, asserts that "the genius of Shakespeare is that the same rhythm connects with us today." Rap is far more today, and hence populist, than jazz and some of the programmes under consideration argue that Shakespeare must be populist to survive.

One way to assert Shakespeare's populism is by harking back to Elizabethan England, as did Laurence Olivier in the famous opening sequence of his *Henry V* (1944), which shows a mixed and rowdy audience of aristocrats and common people assembling in the Globe Theatre. In *Great Britons*, Fiona Shaw draws parallels between the Elizabethan theatre and contemporary rock concert audiences. Over footage of an outdoor rock concert, Shaw says, "Shakespeare wrote for an audience that experienced his plays live — many couldn't read and write." Later she wanders through the crowd saying in voice-over: "This is what theatre was like in Shakespeare's time — like a modern pop concert, raucous, lively, excited. It's so ironic that some people might feel excluded from Shakespeare's plays as if somehow they're slightly highbrow or alienating." *The South Bank Show* invokes the original Globe and its surroundings to attest to Shakespeare's populism. Over footage from *Shakespeare in Love* showing Will running through the London streets, Shakespeare biographer Anthony Holden refers to "the seamier side of life on the South Bank." Mark Rylance talks about the prostitutes in the top gallery of the first Globe, as the camera takes a low angle pan of the galleries of the new Globe. Rylance continues: "The Globe was partly based on bull- and bear-baiting rings. It's into that wild and earthy environment that Shakespeare makes a particular effort to put his plays."

His works, as well as the nature of the original audiences and the South Bank, confirm Shakespeare's populism. The programmes present the plays as the Renaissance *Simpsons*, densely intertextual and polysemic texts with appeal to a wide and diverse audience. In *Great Britons*, Shaw asserts that Shakespeare's "popularity was precisely because he was able to talk to many different types of people. His wit was a mixture of sophistication and vulgarity." The multiple attraction of the plays continues to this day, as Julie Taymor asserts in *The Genius of Shakespeare*, when she speaks of "his ability to write on so many levels that he doesn't play to one audience." But then as now, all appreciate the sex and violence. In a voice-over accompanying an excerpt from her *Titus*, Julie Taymor says, "*Titus* is a play about violence and about violence as entertainment. We are obsessed with sex and violence as entertainment," the implication being that the Elizabethans were similarly obsessed. In a bid to prove Shakespeare's populist credentials, these programmes argue that the desires and responses of the Elizabethan audience would have been the same as today's popular audience. This is consistent with the humanist assumptions about unchanging human nature that these programmes espouse, but, as Douglas Lanier points out, the too easily-drawn Elizabethan/modern parallel erases historical difference:

> This argument assumes that audiences have always found the same things funny, entertaining, tragic or moving [...] But at the very least suggesting that Elizabethan audiences responded to Shakespeare in the same ways that we respond to popular culture risks projecting our own assumptions, preoccupations and emotions onto popular audiences of a demonstrably different past. (Lanier 2002: 96)

This erasing of history can be seen in a Baz Luhrmann quote from *The South Bank Show*: "The Globe Theatre was the television of its time." Just as the Globe permitted Shakespeare to convey his timeless and transcendent truths to an Elizabethan audience, today's dominant popular forms, cinema and television, permit him to do so to a modern audience. Says Melvyn Bragg in *The South Bank Show*, "Over the past ten years we've seen a resurgence of interest in Shakespeare's ability to communicate not just to a highbrow audience but to everyone through the poplar medium of film."

The programmes also present Shakespeare as the precursor of certain contemporary cultural forms, as in the previously drawn parallel with rap. *Great Britons* contains excerpts from and sequences on the set of the most popular of British soap operas, *East Enders*. The programme begins with an intensely dramatic scene from the soap projected onto a screen in an indoor theatre from the Elizabethan period, signified by its ornately painted and panelled ceiling. A younger man with blood on his lip says "I'm sorry, I'm really sorry," to an older man who responds, "Get out!" As two women look on in reaction shots, the older man says "This isn't about you being illegitimate. It's about you being a bastard." Fiona Shaw then talks to camera, establishing the soap's populist credentials by saying that it is watched by over a quarter of the population everyday. She continues, "We see Shakespeare's legacy at work. This fiction is inspired by his great tragedy *King Lear*." Later in the programme, Shaw returns to the *East Enders* set. Speaking once again to camera, she says, "Like soap writers today, Shakespeare realised that there are only a few good stories. The trick is how you tell it." The programme then intercuts an excerpt from Edmund's Act 1, Scene Two speech, with the opening *East Enders'* excerpt, making clear the parallels between soap and Shakespeare.

> As to the legitimate: fine word, — legitimate!
> Well, my legitimate, if this letter speed,
> And my invention thrive, Edmund the base
> Shall top the legitimate. I grow; I prosper:
> Now, gods, stand up for bastards!

Following on from this is a series of shots of *East Enders* scripts, with *King Lear*, *Macbeth* and *Romeo and Juliet* written on the covers. Shaw says in voice-over, "*East Enders* writers sometimes use the titles of Shakespeare's plays to describe the themes in their own scripts."

Drawing facile parallels between cultural forms performs the same historical erasure as does paralleling Elizabethan and contemporary audiences.
As Lanier (2002: 96) says, those who compare the Shakespeare plays to contemporary popular cultural forms assume "deep continuities of theme, character type, plot line and appeal." Such arguments depend upon:

> very general resemblances, so much so that it becomes hard to know whether par-
> allels between *Macbeth* and *The Wolf Man* point to deep continuities between high
> and popular culture [...] or our own interpretative ingenuity. What's more by fo-
> cusing on parallels we tend to distance both Shakespeare and popular culture
> from their specific cultural and historical contexts [...]. (*ibid.*)

Despite their different approaches to shoring up the bardbiz, the heritage,
humanist and populist strategies all seek to erase history. As the presenters
of these programmes themselves say, the heritage approach constructs a
waxwork icon Shakespeare divorced from the vibrancy and brutality of the
popular culture of his own time. Humanism pretends that Shakespeare is
transcendent and trans-historical but still appropriates him in terms of its
own age. Populism blurs distinctions between historical and contemporary
audiences and cultural forms. This erasure of history seems to be a central
tendency of the Shakespeare genre, no matter how reconfigured. Michael
Wood's *In Search of Shakespeare*, which seeks to understand the writer precisely by placing him firmly within his historical period, may be a significant
exception (cf. Pearson & Uricchio, in press).

5   Epilogue: Heritage by Other Means?

The debunking of heritage seen in the programmes under discussion constitutes a major reconfiguration of the Shakespeare genre. Linking Shakespeare's greatness to his Britishness, or, for that matter Britain's greatness to
Shakespeare, can no longer maintain the bardbiz, but the programmes nonetheless retain a certain degree of national pride in the national poet by invoking the dominance of the English language and by reinforcing the dominance
of the British Shakespearean establishment. A sequence in Melvyn Bragg's
The Adventure of English traces how Shakespeare made "his indelible mark on
the English language." It begins with Bragg's claim that Shakespeare is English's biggest export. The image track shows a Stratford tour bus, a book shop
window full of Shakespeare titles, Stratford tourists, a rack of Shakespeare
postcards, Anne Hathaway's cottage, the Shakespeare birthplace, and Shakespeare quote-adorned T-shirts, fridge magnets and chocolates. The programmes discussed above make these objects stand synecdochically for the
despised and rejected heritage Shakespeare, but *The Adventure of English*
equates foreign consumption of bardbiz commodities with foreign consumption of the English language. In keeping with the other programmes, however, *The Adventure of English* traces Shakespeare's global dispersal. Bragg
says "Shakespeare's English has become so quotable that it's come to define

English in the words that we use, the thoughts that we express, be it for native speakers, for students of English or for tourists." The following series of shots features foreign tourists in Stratford reciting remembered Shakespeare quotes, with "to be or not to be" winning handily. Bragg continues, "the Oxford English Dictionary lists 330,000 quotations, his plays have been translated into over 50 languages and at any given moment a Shakespeare play is being read or performed somewhere in the world." *Great Britons'* Fiona Shaw is rather chauvinistic about the English/Shakespeare link: "The language is littered with phrases and words that he invented and that have made English the envy of the world."

Emphasising Shakespeare's contribution to the English language makes him indisputably an Englishman, re-establishing the old heritage link between the poet and English national identity. And, just as in Victorian times, this is an imperialist Shakespeare; he may no longer prop up English hegemony in far flung colonies, but he is at the very heart of the English-language *imperium* of the global knowledge economy. And in true imperial fashion, the programmes under discussion play to the reflex cultural cringe of the former colonies in which they will undoubtedly be aired by drawing their talking heads from the heart of the British theatrical and academic establishment: Ian McKellen, Judi Dench, Peter Brook, Peter Hall, Richard Eyre, Jonathan Miller, Kenneth Branagh and Jonathan Bate. Occasionally a 'colonial' is permitted to speak – Australians Germaine Greer and Baz Luhrmann, Americans Julie Taymor, Harold Bloom and George Wolfe. But for all the talk of Shakespeare's universality, there is not a single non-native English speaker talking head in any one of the programmes. Shakespeare may be read and performed in tens of languages around the world, but to pontificate about him on British television, English must be your mother tongue. This exclusion of the non-native speaker reinforces the link between Shakespeare and the English language, once more casting the poet as an English subject rather than a cosmopolitan citizen.

This heritage by other means is consistent with Shakespeare, PLC, which, just like the English language, is a British product gone global. This globalisation required shedding embarrassing 'ye olde England' heritage connotations and, like most major global brands that exhibit tensions between the local and the global, becoming adapted to the local environment. Glocalisation was further achieved through associations with humanism, making Shakespeare suitable for consumption around the world, and through associations with populism, providing the brand with some badly needed updating. Now all that is needed is a corporate logo. And could anyone ask for a better one than that coined by Ben Jonson almost four hundred years ago? "Shakespeare – not for an age, but for all time."

Bibliography

Bennett, Tony & Janet Woollacott (1987), *Bond and Beyond: the Political Career of a Popular Hero*, Basingstoke : Macmillan Education.

Brooker, Will (2000), *Batman Unmasked; Analyzing a Cultural Icon*, London: Continuum.

Higson, Andrew (1995), *Waving the Flag: Constructing a National Cinema in Britain*, Oxford:Clarendon Press.

Hodgdon, Barbara (1998), *The Shakespeare Trade: Performances and Appropriations*, Philadelphia: University of Pennsylvania Press.

Lanier, Douglas (2002), *Shakespeare and Modern Popular Culture*, Oxford: Oxford University Press.

Pearson, Roberta E. (2002), "Shakespeare's Country: The National Poet, English Identity and the Silent Cinema," in Andrew Higson, ed., *Young and Innocent? The Cinema in Britain, 1896*-1930, Exeter: University of Exeter Press, 176-190.

Pearson, Roberta E. & William Uricchio (in press), "Brushing up Shakespeare: relevance and televisual form in *Great Britons* and *In Search of Shakespeare*", in Diana E. Henderson, ed., *Concise Companion to Shakespeare on Screen*, London: Blackwells.

-----, eds. (1991), *The Many Lives of the Batman: Critical Approaches to a Superhero and His Media*, London – New York: British Film Institute & Routledge, Chapman, Hall.

Samuel, Raphael (1994), *Theatres of Memory: Volume 1, Past and Present in Contemporary Culture*, London: Verso.

Taylor, Gary (1990), *Reinventing Shakespeare: A Cultural History from the Restoration to the Present*, London: The Hogarth Press.

From Auntie's Heritage to Anti-heritage

Sarah Street

"The Mirror Crack'd":
Heritage, History and Self-reflexive Discourse

1   Introduction

Television has long been fascinated with heritage and history. Indeed, historical documentaries and dramas are currently very popular and highly visible in terrestrial and cable schedules. This chapter will examine the extent to which television engages with postmodern approaches to history, in particular in relation to heritage themes and aesthetics, and whether they encourage such developments. While postmodernism and heritage might appear to be contradictory terms, in the sense that constructing the latter can be seen as a reaction to the uncertainties of postmodern society, it is the case that representations of heritage have been dependent on an aesthetics associated with postmodernism. Potentially, television provides an exciting arena for histories that introduce innovative, even challenging propositions about historical events. The self-consciously authorial and reflective stance of historians such as Simon Schama, for example, deploys television as the perfect medium for the presentation of histories that depart from rigid conventions of empiricism, the primacy and implicit authority of the written word, and notions of historical objectivity. In the academy also, new ideas about historiography have emerged, often causing controversy, as postmodern thought challenges historians to develop methodological approaches that equip them to consider new forms of evidence (cf. Jenkins 1997).

At its most ambitious, Robert Rosenstone (1996: 203) summarises the main elements of the postmodern approach as presenting history that

> "problematises the entire notion of historical knowledge." That foregrounds the "usually concealed attitude of historians towards their material." That reeks with "provisionality and undecidability, partisanship and even overt politics...." [...] That "breaks down the convention of historical time ... and substitutes a new convention of temporality ... rhythmic time." That aims not at "integration, synthesis, and totality." That is content with "historical scraps." That is not "the reconstruction of what has happened to us in the various phases of our lives, but a continuous playing with the memory of this." That is expressed not in coherent stories but in fragments and "collage."[1]

---

[1]   Rosenstone quotes Linda Hutcheon, Elizabeth Deeds Ermarth, and F.R. Ankersmit.

Clearly this represents a radical break with ideas about a linear development of knowledge, or of the historian as being impartial or able to deliver 'truthful' accounts of past events. Inspired by Hayden White (1973), this rethinking of historical accounts as narratives with their own agendas, structures and interpretative arenas, has been influential in historical studies and beyond. In its more inclusive criteria as to what might 'count' towards the process of historical enquiry, the postmodern approach takes films and television programmes far more seriously than historians who have traditionally drawn upon 'primary' documentation such as official papers in their research.

The variety of heritage aesthetics described in their most familiar cinematic form as featuring slow-moving episodic narratives, frequently 'stopping' to showcase heritage sites, commodities and stars, as well as the more frenetic but nevertheless spectacular approach of films such as *Elizabeth* (1998), display conventions that can also be seen in television programmes about the past (cf. Higson 2003: 37-42, 220-33). After all, one of the earliest heritage texts identified in the 1980s was Granada Television's *Brideshead Revisited* (1981), and television's episodic nature lends itself very well to the heritage narrative style. The programmes I discuss here, *The Lost Prince* (BBC 1, 2003) by Stephen Poliakoff and *The Other Boleyn Girl* (BBC 2, 2003) by Philippa Lowthorpe, are representative of the broad stylistics of heritage and 'post-heritage': *The Lost Prince* is a long, slow and pictorialist drama, while *The Other Boleyn Girl* features techniques more readily associated with *Dogme*/'reality' television. The term post-heritage has been applied by Claire Monk (1995), who argues that in the early 1990s films such as *Orlando* (1992) and *Carrington* (1995) developed new ways of articulating discourses around the notion of heritage. In this chapter I want to extend discussion of this trend to television. Since heritage and post-heritage aesthetics invite a multiplicity of readings and perspectives, this stylistic choice would appear to be conducive to a destabilisation of conventional historical method, as outlined in Rosenstone's summary. Facets of particular importance are the refusal of a singular point of view; editing that allows 'gaps' to be perceived between narrative trajectory and visual aesthetics and the encouragement of 'outsider' viewpoints. In looking at these two programmes I therefore consider the extent to which heritage television offers a way forward for exciting, postmodern popular histories that offer fresh insights and suggest new approaches.

The two programmes share a common interest in rescuing 'lost' figures of history. *The Lost Prince* focuses on Prince John, the youngest child of Queen Mary and King George V, who was 'hidden from history' because of his epilepsy and learning difficulties. Since he died at the age of thirteen and played no obvious role in 'history' Prince John's existence was only drawn attention to in February 2002, when a family photograph album among the effects of the Duke and Duchess of Windsor was sold at an auction in Paris. The album featured a photograph of John taken in 1915, probably by his eldest brother, later King Edward VIII and afterwards Duke of Windsor. As we shall see, Poliakoff's fascination with photographic evidence, demonstrated in his drama *Shooting the Past* (1999) and featured again in *The Lost Prince*, presents 'traces' of the past which inspire animated scenes. *The Other Boleyn Girl* is about Mary Boleyn, Henry VIII's mistress and mother of his illegitimate daughter Catherine and son Henry Carey, but also sister of the far more famous Anne, Henry VIII's second wife who was later beheaded. In seeking to create a 'voice' for her characters, Lowthorpe draws on televisual aesthetic conventions such as direct address to camera as used in *Big Brother* and *Video Diaries*, creating an intimate space between performer and audience. In their different ways both dramas attempt to offer new perspectives on history, albeit history 'from above', and demonstrate the familiar heritage passion for royalty. Both dramas illuminate the constraints on public figures in their private lives, concentrating on outsider views normally excised from history books. I argue that while these dramas follow the broad approach represented by Simon Schama, their heritage aesthetics assist them in the task of suggesting new ways forward for television drama and indeed benefit from their directors' use of techniques which are concerned with representing alternative perspectives. In their different ways both exercise imagination, and invite audiences also to do so.

An important context for and influence on recent historical television dramas is the plethora of historical documentaries and docu-dramas. Simon Schama's *Murder at Harvard* (BBC 2, 2002) is indicative of a self-conscious attempt to introduce postmodern approaches to history on television. *Murder at Harvard* foregrounds the historical process, the role of the historian and questions of impartiality in an extremely overt manner. Based on the murder of George Parkman by Harvard Professor John Webster in 1849, Schama takes the audience through the process of historical enquiry, stressing the provisional nature of 'the truth', as well as the scope for dramatic, imaginative speculation as a legitimate activity for a historian who seeks to read between the lines of conventional documentation. He examines alternative scenarios from those handed down by history – in this case that Webster was murdered by Parkman when he went to collect a debt from him in his rooms. Schama speculates that Ephraim Littlefield, a janitor at the Medical College, who was instrumental in convicting Webster when he discovered dismembered body parts in Webster's privy, might also have had a motive to murder Parkman. Schama proceeds to examine the notorious case from a variety of perspectives, assisted by dramatic re-enactments that he scripted, illustrating how little can be concluded about 'the facts' of the past, whereas these can be used as an inspiration for creative interpretation. In particular, he considers lowly janitor Littlefield's resentment of Parkman, claiming it as representative of more extensive class tension in Boston between the poor and the élite. He is seeking to rescue the 'history from below' perspective not foregrounded in previous accounts. Schama first published an article on the case, "Death of a Harvard Man" in *Granta* (1990) and his book *Dead Certainties*

(1998) also uses the case as a basis for exploring questions of historical method.

Schama concludes, however, that Webster did murder Parkman, but he also demonstrates that this verdict is in itself provisional and simply his own deduction, selected from a number of possible 'truths' about the incident that he has staged during the programme. In foregrounding this approach by speaking direct to camera and taking the audience through the steps of his method, Schama is clearly drawing on the categories outlined by Rosenstone, in particular by highlighting his own self-reflexivity. He has indeed problematised the notion of historical knowledge; foregrounded his own position; stressed that any conclusions are necessarily partial and provisional; pointed out the 'scrappy' nature of evidence and partial nature of deduction; introduced innovative methods of considering multiple viewpoints when there is little conventional historical evidence available, and conveyed the collage-like and fragmentary nature of history. Above all, he shows the contested status of historical knowledge. He ends the programme by being filmed walking through a graveyard, noting that the remains of John Webster are not to be found. He remarks that this is appropriate because

> History is never about resting places, about arrivals, conclusions. It's a long journey through memory... In the end, history isn't written to arrive at a verdict. It's written like poetry, or philosophy or great fiction, to help us explore the nature of the human condition; to understand what we are through what we think we've done.

As a historian he cannot, however, resist the desire to reach a conclusion (that Webster did indeed murder Parkman), albeit one couched in ambivalent terms, indicating that while the postmodern position recognises history as fragmentary and re-presentational, his position as 'auteur' of this particular programme, emphasised by his physical presence and control of the voice-over narration, confers on him a status and authority that is hard to question. I shall return to the issue of authorship, but for now note it as a factor that perhaps works against a complete application of Rosenstone's aspirations for postmodern history on the screen. The historian cannot resist selecting one probability above others, and in this case is assisted by the televisual mode of presentation in emerging as an authoritative voice.

I will now examine the two dramas in more detail, measuring them up against Rosenstone's summary. Unlike *Murder at Harvard* these are dramas, not documentary-dramas, yet they share the same desire to give a voice to hitherto neglected figures in history. As we shall see, both directors of these programmes are, like Schama, self-conscious in their roles as interpreters of events and the work they have produced engages on narrative and aesthetic levels with questions of 'truth', the authorial voice and self-reflexivity. On the other hand, they are more likely to be criticised than Schama because as directors of dramas rather than documentaries they are not able to be as explicit on screen about questions of method and approach. Nor do they possess Schama's academic credentials which, as previously mentioned, grant him the status of 'auteur' – the learned Professor who is in command of his material. Rosenstone's categories will provide an analytical framework within which to examine *The Lost Prince* and *The Other Boleyn Girl*.

2   The Notion of Historical Knowledge

Established historical knowledge is questioned in *The Lost Prince*, in the sense that it shows a well-known narrative (the events leading up to the outbreak of the First World War) from the sidelines. By privileging Prince John's story attention on him becomes the main focus of the drama, becoming more important than detailing the diplomatic events leading up to the war. The idea that historical knowledge is attainable and re-presentable is thus problematised but not refuted: 'history' with a small 'h' replaces any notion of 'History'. Interestingly, between the two parts of Poliakoff's drama the BBC broadcast a documentary, *The King, The Kaiser and the Tsar*, as if to allay fears that people might be confused about the facts behind the 'real' history. This documentary detailed the relationships between the European royal families, as well as the details of diplomatic history that led to the outbreak of war. On the other hand, in Poliakoff's drama several fragments of histories are broached – Johnny's, Lalla's (John's nanny), Georgie's (his brother who became George VI on the abdication of his elder brother Edward VIII), that of the Russian royal family or of Stamfordham, King George's private secretary. Much in the same way that Schama presented enactments of likely scenarios in the Parkman murder, Poliakoff's cast of characters accentuates the experience of people who would normally be considered to be marginal figures during these years.

Similarly, *The Other Boleyn Girl* proposed how it *might* have been in Tudor England by deploying televisual conventions drawn from contemporary programmes: 'these people are being presented to you in a way that you should recognise'. By selecting a particularly controversial aspect of this history – the claim that in desperation to produce a son, Anne slept with her brother George – the drama acknowledges that historical knowledge hitherto gained is indeed a case of one person's interpretation against another's. As Lowthorpe, an award-winning documentary filmmaker, explained: "We are doing history in a completely different way. The improvisation process should bring a freshness and modernity to the production, each actor is able to interpret their own role rather than the script presenting one writer's view of history" (qtd. in BBC press release). Despite these exciting pronouncements that invested *The Other Boleyn Girl* with innovative aspirations, the drama was heavily criticised for taking this route, leaving itself open to charges of sensationalism and being dismissed as 'low-brow' nonsense, not least because of its origins in a bestselling historical romantic novel by Philippa Gregory. In the views of the critics, Lowthorpe had taken a foolish path in diverting her career away from the documentary genre with which she was previously associated. Issues of authorship are again raised when we compare this reception with that for *The Lost Prince*. While some viewers found the drama too slow and were confused by the lack of direction as to who was who in the royal family, Poliakoff's credentials as a dramatist attracted praise and admiration. While Schama and Poliakoff are well-known, Philippa Lowthorpe, the director of *The Other Boleyn Girl*, did not have a reputation for drama, and her 'feminine' subject-matter was considered to be more trivial.

3   The Role of the Historian

In his schema, Rosenstone cites a key aspect of the postmodern approach to history as recognising that the historian is by no means impartial, or that she/he is capable of reaching a definite conclusion about a particular event. Gone is the idea that meticulous empirical research methods can produce 'accurate' accounts of the past; historians ought not to be afraid of being explicit about their own motivation for conducting a particular enquiry, or even confessing that they are not impartial in relation to their subject matter. Similarly, Poliakoff made his attitude towards his material clear in interviews and his views were very evident during pre-publicity. He had a definite perspective to depict – that of Prince John – which allowed him also to comment on events leading up to the outbreak of the First World War in an unusual way. He obviously had sympathy for this 'lost' figure and for Lalla, the nanny who cared for John out of public sight and away from his parents. But he also suggests that John's isolation might have protected him from the pressures put on other royal children, particularly his brother George, who is made to go to naval college even though he hates it. By contrast, John can pursue his interests in music, painting and gardens without disapproval. Poliakoff admits to being far from a royalist, a perspective clearly picked-up by Tom Paulin when the drama was reviewed on BBC's *Newsnight Review*: "What it represents, I think, is the British mixed feelings about the House of Windsor." The royal family is indeed shown to be arrogant but also human and caught in a web of diplomatic moves beyond their control. They are creatures of European dynasties who suddenly find that their family ties require severing, with Russia and Germany in particular.

Lowthorpe also makes no attempt to conceal her views on her subject-matter as a feminist historian. *The Other Boleyn Girl* is an unashamedly popular romantic drama, detailing the sexual politics of the royal court with all its hypocrisies around issues such as virginity and marriage. While Mary is openly encouraged by her family to become Henry VIII's mistress even though she is married, her sister has to insist on her own virginity when she eventually marries Henry. The sexual economy of the Tudor court is exposed as brutal, to be exploited by the ambitious (for example, Anne) but ruthless in its punishment of those considered to be treacherous (Anne and George). While this news is hardly new, in its presentation – aimed at younger audiences than the average costume drama – it is conveyed in an uncompromising way and from a different perspective from that which is usually offered. In this sense Lowthorpe's previous interest in women's history (she directed a highly-regarded television documentary entitled *A Skirt Through History*) is carried on as the female characters are shown to suffer from and be circumscribed by men's political machinations.

4   New Conventions of Temporality

Film and television, with editing and other strategies of time compression or, in the case of the heritage genre, elongation, are excellent media to break down linear conventions of temporality. As in 'classic' heritage dramas, *The Lost Prince* is extremely slow-paced, allowing the camera to linger on details in a pictorialist fashion. As a drama that is, in part, about the events leading up to the First World War, the whole notion of 'war by timetable' is transgressed by this slow-moving meditation on the minutiae of life surrounding Prince John. The fact that viewers were confused because Poliakoff was not concerned to carefully point out who was who, and were critical of the slow pace of the programme, illustrates its different, if frustrating for some, approach to temporal conventions. One viewer, for example, wrote that: "I wonder if it isn't too ponderous. Long drifting scenes can sometimes be dramatic, but they help if one is involved in the characters", while another considered *The Lost Prince* to be "disappointing, spent half the time trying to work out who was who and where the rest of the children had gone. Seemed to charge from 1910 to 1914 and then took best part of an hour to do a couple of months" ("*The Lost Prince*: Your views" 2003).

Poliakoff's use of photographs is particularly interesting as an example of his approach to historical method and temporality. The photograph that is most striking is one of King George V and his cousin Czar Nicholas II, whose mother was a sister of Queen Alexandra of England, George's mother. Poliakoff draws on the original as a 'trace', a memory of the blood ties between two public figures who in many ways represent the closing door on 19th century regimes, attitudes and values, the Edwardian period so beloved of other heritage narratives. (We do not see the original photograph of George V and Czar Nicholas in Poliakoff's drama, but it can be viewed via http://images.google.com, as found at www.firstworldwar.com.) Just as in other families, the far-flung royal family was no exception in seeking to document occasions when they met. Poliakoff animates this knowledge by creating a scene of the taking of the photograph, allowing the moving image to reveal the dramatic conflicts and emotional subtext behind the image. While we see the pair posing for the camera we do not actually see the photograph being taken. Instead, Poliakoff uses the incident to make a point about the Czar being dominated by his wife. After an uneasy positioning for the photographer, the pair of monarchs shift their posture frequently, the Czar seeking constant reassurance from Alexandra and appearing to be completely indecisive. Thus Poliakoff shows us a likely context for the taking of the photograph, rather than the still image itself. In so doing, he refuses the freeze-frame convention whereby the still image is replicated and, by implication, fixed. This choice of scenario is all the more poignant for, as the drama goes on to relate, George V decides against offering the Czar and his family refuge in England, by implication contributing to their deaths in 1918 under the new Bolshevik regime. In this way Poliakoff juxtaposes the private connection between these men with their public personae. This emerges as all the more tragic when we consider the fate of Czar Nicholas, taking the photograph out of time, as it were, as an image that acquires poignancy in retrospect. In this sense, the photograph can be seen as an attempt to conceal a family secret by creating an illusion of solidarity that is about to be shattered. More than most, this photograph performs the function of John Berger's 'radial system' in which its meaning intersects with a myriad of contexts, personal, political, economic, dramatic, everyday and historic (Berger 1980).

By contrast, but in the same spirit of experimentation, *The Other Boleyn Girl* drew on different temporal structures associated with 'reality' television in which different characters were given a space of their own in direct address to the audience. This approach is very evident, for example, in the sequence when Anne is sent away because of her affair with Henry Percy. Mary has told her father of this unsuitable liaison and the family decide Anne must leave court because public knowledge of it might threaten Anne's delicate relationship with Henry VIII. When Anne is told this devastating news – that she must leave her lover – the camera is very mobile, roaming from character to character without cuts between shots; several shots are out of focus and as the emotional tension heightens extreme close-ups are used. Then, in a scene that is reminiscent of *Big Brother*, Mary addresses the camera in a contemplative scene that seeks to explain her position: that she thought she was doing the best for everyone. A lapse-dissolve shot takes us into a moment of even more intimate confession, when she tells us that in addition she has fallen in love with Henry. Instead of being depicted as a distant figure from the past, she emerges as a desirous but vulnerable young woman, whose dilemmas can be related to by contemporary audiences. As well as relating to contemporary television, these techniques can be compared with Peter Watkins' *Culloden* (1964), a film that presented 'interviews' with a range of people involved in the battle of Culloden and its aftermath. Also, a few weeks before *The Other Boleyn Girl* was broadcast television audiences had been exposed to this approach in BBC 2's *Witchcraze*, a programme that also drew on broadcast-news techniques to detail a 17th-century witch-hunt. In this way the programmes' aesthetic structures and formal techniques were key elements in their claims to innovation, but also in their perhaps less immediately evident *homage* to earlier experiments in historical programming.

5   Fragments and 'Collage'

Rosenstone's ideas on the nature of historical evidence are clearly important as a call to historians to be creative in their collection of evidence, and as an inspiration not to be defeated by an apparent lack of 'hard' evidence about an issue, event or problem. From this perspective, 'traces', fragments and even 'scraps' become as important as official papers and diaries in constructing interpretations of the past. Similarly, the approach taken in both dramas by their directors towards the question of historical 'truth' is one that is based on the deployment of fragmentary evidence. In this way *The Other Boleyn Girl* dealt with 'scraps', using these as an incentive to present 'imaginative' history. This approach is always controversial, not least because of its focus on romance and sex, taking Lowthorpe away from her celebrated documentary credentials and into the low-brow territory of melodrama, a genre that has often been dismissed by critics as trivial. Although of course in film and television studies it has been re-evaluated as a significant register of popular desires, contemporary concerns and aesthetic experiment, cf. Landy (1991). While Philippa Gregory's source novel lists a range of respectable academic texts in its bibliography, the text is footnote-free and aimed at a popular historical readership. Low-brow connotations are further emphasised by the cover jacket notes: "Two sisters competing for the greatest prize...the love of a king". Lowthorpe worked with the actors in devising the final script when adapting the novel for television and the structure is relatively loose for a television drama.

This approach, however, clearly encouraged a confused reception. Reviewers (for example, Smith 2003) were frustrated at what they thought was a misguided loss of focus on Mary Boleyn as the drama progresses in favour of the more usual suspect, Anne, despite the expectations conjured up by the title. Reviewing the drama in *The Guardian*, Stuart Jeffries (2003: 16-17) objected to the "stylised cinematography" as "unnecessarily intrusive: it mars the telling of a gripping, well-written narrative, rather than serving it". Some previewers have suggested that the thing has the feel of Peter Greenaway-lite, but that misses the mark: it rather occasionally has the feel of NYPD Blue visits Hampton Court, which is much worse." Jeffries' condemnation of the programme's pretensions to innovation (the refusal of an affinity with Greenaway, but instead a firm comparison with popular television) is further evidence of its low-brow status among critics. Yet the stylistic approach chosen by Lowthorpe arguably assists the drama's ability to convey some of the imponderables of historical knowledge and suggest disturbing links between the past and the present. Like *The Lost Prince*, but by using a different aesthetic approach to issues of heritage, *The Other Boleyn Girl* introduces levels of complexity that a more conventional historical drama would have failed to achieve. While its approach might appear to be a world away from that of Poliakoff, in their aesthetic structures both dramas manage to engage with some of the aspirations of postmodern history. It is perhaps no accident that links have been made between similarly structured heritage films that might on first analysis appear to be disconnected. Examples of this would be 'classic' heritage films such as *Brideshead Revisited* (1981) and *Howards End* (1992) and 'postmodern' or art-house heritage-inspired films such as *The Draughtsman's Contract* (1982) and *Orlando* (1992).

The Lost Prince also presents several narrative strands, associated with different people and events. Poliakoff worked from 'scraps' of evidence regarding Prince John, including the photograph previously mentioned, extracts from Queen Mary's diary and six letters (his access to this material was restricted). Publicity for and discussion of the drama stressed that "Stephen has undergone exhaustive research" (*Guardian*, 1 March 2002), and that "his research was meticulous and included time spent at the Royal Archives at Windsor" (BBC Television Drama press release, 6 June 2002). In a way the paucity of conventional evidence about Prince John assisted Poliakoff in that his account did not contest, or compete with, more established interpretations. Also, the dramatic approach, for all its concern with narrative coherence, in many ways did defy synthesis and closure. Several stories are unfinished – George's and Lalla's, for example – although it could be argued that the narrative strands relating to well-known historical events did not need to be resolved because audiences' familiarity with them provided an assumed notion of closure. Poliakoff's desire to depict the distant relationship between the Queen and her son is exemplified in several scenes in which the Queen seeks to use 'public' duties as a way of refusing intimacy with John, of refusing to allow herself to be as emotionally caught up with his achievements as Lalla. When, for example, the Queen is collecting material for the war effort, John and Lalla are nearby in the woods. When Lalla asks the Queen to speak to John, she is told that she will call the following day, at an appointed time, rather than take pleasure in a spontaneous encounter. In scenes such as this Poliakoff draws out the family's emotional repression, made all the more acute in the case of a mother-child relationship in which it has been decided that the child must be sent away and that any close bonds must be severed.

While I am not claiming that these films deliver all of the aspirations for postmodern history as completely as Rosenstone might wish, it is nevertheless the case that they go far enough to suggest that a productive cycle is occurring in television drama. This draws not only on heritage aesthetics, but also on techniques more often associated with different genres and more contemporary sensibilities. These also can be related back to Peter Watkins' *Culloden*, one of the most daring and innovative historical films ever made but also anticipate a more sustained phase of visual experimentation with historical method. As these two case studies show, considerable variation is possible within hybridised television forms, inviting interesting questions about authorship, shifting paradigms of critical judgement and developments in form introduced by digital imaging and other technical innovations. It is therefore to be hoped that further experiments will be produced, 'cracking' the mirror of history into a fragmented, complex and fascinating phenomenon.

Bibliography

BBC Press Release, *The Other Boleyn Girl* (n.d.) http://www.bbc.co.uk/pressoffice/ pressreleases/stories/2002/10_octob.../other_boleyn.shtm

Berger, John (1980), *About Looking*, New York: Pantheon Books.

Higson, Andrew (2003), *English Heritage, English Cinema: Costume Drama Since 1980*, Oxford: Oxford University Press.

Jeffries, Stuart (2003). Rev. of *The Other Boleyn Girl*, *The Guardian*, 24 March, 16-17.

Jenkins, Keith, ed. (1997), *The Postmodern History Reader*, London: Routledge.

Landy, Marcia, ed. (1991), *Imitations of Life: a Reader on Film and Television Melodrama*, Detroit: Wayne State University Press.

"*The Lost Prince*: Your views" (2003), http://news.bbc.co.uk/1/hi/entertainment /reviews/2669849.stm (2 March 2004).

Monk, Claire (1995), "Sexuality of the Heritage", *Sight and Sound*, 5:10, 32-34.

Rosenstone, Robert A. (1996), "The Future of the Past: Film and the Beginnings of Postmodern History", in Vivian Sobchack, ed., *The Persistence of History: Cinema, Television and the Modern Event*, London – New York: Routledge, 201-218.

Schama, Simon (1990), "Death of a Harvard Man", *Death of a Harvard Man: Granta*, 34.

----- (1991), *Dead Certainties: Unwarranted Speculations*, New York: Granta.

Smith, Jim (2003), "*The Other Boleyn Girl*" http://www.shinyshelf.co.uk/article/3/st/ 568 (2 March 2004).

White, Hayden (1973), *Metahistory*, Baltimore: Johns Hopkins University.

Carolin Held

From 'Heritage Space' to 'Narrative Space' – Anti-heritage Aesthetics in the Classic TV Serials *Our Mutual Friend* and *Vanity Fair*

1   Introduction

The title of this paper is inspired by Andrew Higson's criticism of the heritage film as a cinema of attractions, representing the national past as visually spectacular pastiche with audiovisual strategies that create 'heritage space' for the display of heritage properties rather than 'narrative space' for the enactment of dramas (Higson 1993: 117-118). Higson's argumentation belongs to a critical discourse which has been labelled by Claire Monk as "the anti-heritage position" (Monk 1995: 117), treating heritage films of both cinema and television as a unified entity and thereby ignoring significant differences between them as well as essential aspects of their respective audiovisual language.[1] The essential arguments put forward by critics in rejecting the way space is displayed in heritage films of the last twenty years have been frequently defined in terms of an alleged anti-narrative pictorialism, based on conventional audiovisual devices beyond the experiments of modernism. This means in particular the showcasing of landscapes and costume props by employing formulaic stylistic strategies such as long takes and deep focus (Griem & Voigts-Virchow 2003: 319) which go beyond narrative motivation and thereby creating, on the whole, an emotionally empty space. Claire Monk, however, has argued that

> the mise-en-scène of these films should not be read in terms of heritage display but as expressive of what E.M. Forster would call the 'inner life' […] not […] as a separate discourse of scenic display, in conflict with the narrative, but as expressing the emotional intensity of the scene, props acting not as spokespersons for the heritage industry but as symbolic indications of the inner life of the characters.[2]

---

[1]   In a similar vein, John Caughie argues that in order to achieve a profound analysis of the complex nature of the heritage film "film scholars […] would have to afford to the heritage film and the representations of the national past in both film and television at least the same attention as we used to afford to the Western or the melodrama, discriminating between this Western and that Western, this melodrama and that melodrama, and finding in them, through critical analysis rather than description or cognitive mapping, the secret workings of values, ideologies and contradictions." (Caughie 1998: 61)

[2]   Claire Monk, *Sex, Politics and the Past: Merchant-Ivory, the Heritage Film and its Critics in the 1980s and 1990s Britain*, MA Dissertation, British Film Institute/Birbeck College, 1994, quoted in Higson (1996: 241).

Following Claire Monk's suggestion, this paper will discuss some of the ways in which the two classic TV serials *Our Mutual Friend* (BBC 1998) and *Vanity Fair* (BBC 1998) work in their departure from established conventions against the presumed canon of monolithic generic formula and are proof for the increasingly complex representation of heritage in contemporary British television. More specifically, it will investigate the extent to which space is being used as semantically charged space, hence rejecting the distanced gaze of admiring spectatorship (Higson 1996: 241) inherent in the creation of heritage space.

2   *Our Mutual Friend*

Taking a closer look at the representation of space in *Our Mutual Friend* reveals an aesthetic language which can be characterized along the lines of Claire Monk's argumentation. Sandy Welch's adaptation of Dickens' last completed novel was transmitted as a four-part-serial on BBC-2 in March 1998 and formed part of a mini-boom of Dickens adaptations on the small screen.[3] This version of *Our Mutual Friend* belongs to a canon of Dickens adaptations which deal with "the radical Dickens, the critic, prophet and preacher" of the later, darker novels, with their "angry, unsparing indictment of social injustice, selfishness and greed" (Richards 1997: 349). In a similar vein as Arthur Hopcraft's version of *Bleak House* in 1985,[4] this adaptation meant a departure from the BBC Sunday teatime serial – the flagship of Dickens production in the 1950s and 1960s, with its clear preference for Dickens the family entertainer and its representation as "the epitome of television as an educational, uplifting, socially cohesive force" (*ibid*.: 345) according to the Reithian image of public television. The aesthetics of *Our Mutual Friend* reveal an 'optical' quality of Dickens which can be interpreted as "the visual translation of the plot, making expressionist use of the background to secure stunning dramatic effects" (Samuel 1989: 276) – a quality which has been ascribed by Raphael Samuel to David Lean's cinematic versions of *Great Expectations* (1946) and *Oliver Twist* (1948) (*ibid*.). In this sense, the serial adopts the conventional pathetic fallacy of symbolically equating characters' emotions or mental states with setting. This is particularly evident in the serial's treatment of space in combination with lighting techniques which convey, in their strong imagery, a sense of the urban gothic, and a sinister late-Victorian quality.[5]

---

[3]   Along with Tony Marchant's adaptation of *Great Expectations* (BBC 1999), Adrian Hodges adaptation of *David Copperfield* (BBC 1999) and Alan Bleasdale's adaptation of *Oliver Twist* (ITV, 1999).

[4]   And later BBC's *Martin Chuzzlewit* and *Hard Times*, both produced in 1994.

[5]   This stands in contrast to the picturesque poverty celebrated by Christine Edzard's 1987 adaptation of *Little Dorrit*, often cited as a rather unsuccessful version of a later Dickens novel. "Entirely studio-shot, with static camera, flat lighting, naturalistic acting it has of-

A closer look at the introductory scene of the serial makes the overall dark tone of this adaptation clear at the very outset. What seems to be at first glance a pictorialist setting with the characters' appearance as mere silhouettes set against a background of a moonlit surface of the river, is soon disturbed by the appearance of a dead body which is being dragged behind the boat of Lizzie and Gaffer Hexam.[6] Together with the following dialogue between father and daughter,[7] the river is established as a functionalised setting, representing on a metaphorical level one of the two main paradoxes of the story – the river as the source of both life and death.

The theme of death is further developed in the serial's use of the setting as a symbol for "life amid the debris of the dead" (Giddings & Selby 2001: 163). This is echoed in the visual representation of Mr Venus' Shop, in which this articulator of bones is surrounded by skeletons, skulls and stuffed animals, as well as in Gaffer Hexam's place, in which one of the walls is plastered with police posters informing of dead bodies found in the river. Likewise, the cemetery does not only serve as the scene for the threatening and unsuccessful proposal of marriage by the psychologically obsessive schoolmaster Bradley Headstone to Lizzie Hexam in Part Two of the serial, but also as the trigger mechanism for John Harmon's revelation of his true story to the audience in the same part. At the beginning of this revelation sequence, the sensation of the graveyards leads John Harmon to the remark that he does not belong among the living any more than the buried souls around him. The following visual flashback in conjunction with his voice-over narration[8] reveal the circumstances in which John Harmon lost his true identity in the river – emphasised throughout the serial by the repeated remark "John Harmon has drowned" or "This is John Harmon drowning"[9] – and, at the same time, ex-

---

ten been described as dramatically inert" (Richards 1997: 348). While its primary aim of authenticity as far as furniture and costumes were concerned was used for promoting this film, it was exactly this feature which was put forward by critics as the main objection, applying the term 'heritage film' in its negative sense and claiming that "although large in scale and ambition missed the energy and vitality of Dickens completely" (*ibid.:* 349).

6 The aesthetics of this setting seem to be directly adapted from one of the original illustrations by Marcus Stone, "recapturing exactly the stagey qualities" (Giddings & Selby 2001: 160) which Stone brought to the novel.

7 During this dialogue, it becomes obvious that Lizzie Hexham cannot bear the sight of the corpse and does not approve of her father's profession. Gaffer Hexham reproaches his daughter for her attitude by saying, "As if it wasn't your living! As if it wasn't meat and drink to you!"

8 The sequence opens and ends with a close-up of his face, suggesting that he is the source of the memories the viewer hears represented as voice-over narration and sees as visual flashback. Hence, the viewer is to take the sound as occurring in the present (spoken thoughts) and the images as occurring in the past (visualized memories) (cf. Bordwell & Thompson [5]1997: 338).

9 First articulated in Part One by Mortimer Lightwood, then several times in Part Two by John Harmon himself, and finally by Bella Wilfer in Part Four.

plain why he gained a new identity as Julius Hanford and later as John Rokesmith.

This transformation of identity is presented in visual terms as a series of five shots moving from a medium shot of the dead Radfoot, who has been killed in mistake for Harmon and found in the river, to the 'imagined' dead body of John Harmon, then to a close-up of the real Harmon, back again to the dead Radfoot, and finally dissolve to a shot of Harmon's reflection on the surface of the river. This movement from one image to the next not only places the main protagonist in connection to the river, but also lends the river an increasing narrative significance and dramatic purpose. In addition to its renewed metaphorical establishment as a source of both life and death, the river also provides John Harmon with a new identity and thereby enables him to liberate himself from his father's evil spirit. Furthermore, this sequence illustrates John's description of his state as a limbo between life and death, based on his assumption of various identities and the officially confirmed death of his true self. This finds an additional effective visualisation towards the end of the sequence where he is seen in profile against the background of the surface of the river with its expressionist light reflections, which slowly dissolve to a high-angle shot of Harmon amidst several gravestones.

However, the river, in its function as narrative space, runs through the serial in a sequence of other images, too. Having nearly drowned after Headstone's vicious assault upon his life, Eugene Wrayburn is finally able to liberate himself from his carelessness and arrogance, thus suggesting that the river serves for him as an instrument of purgation. Likewise, Lizzie is purged of her shame at being a boatman's daughter as she puts her skill to powerful use by saving Eugene's life. The death of characters like Bradley Headstone or Riderhood in the last part of *Our Mutual Friend* exemplify a further function of the river as a destructive force for those who are evil (cf. Hobsbaum 1998: 264-65). Clearly, then, the river becomes in its multiple narrative function "the thread on which the narrative is suspended and connected" (Giddings & Selby 2001: 163), thereby attaining in its omnipresence in the serial the status of an almost additional character.

In other exterior scenes, the streets of London, especially the riverside area, become a telling metaphor for imprisonment. In its function as the main setting for the dramatisation of the love triangle plot of Eugene Wrayburn, Bradley Headstone and Lizzie Hexham, the riverside area is established as a signifier of character, a metaphor for the state of mind of the protagonists. This is particularly evident in one of the most expressionistic sequences in the serial – the night chase of Eugene Wrayburn and Bradley Headstone in Part Three. At this point in the story, Lizzie has fled from London to protect herself from an impossible social relationship with Eugene and from Headstone's passionate fixation upon her. In the context of their relationship to each other and to Lizzie, the two deserted men are both presented as being trapped in their feelings and social positions. In narrative terms, the impossibility of the love triangle finds its emotional outlet in the absurd night chases around the riverside area. The dialogue between Eugene and his friend Mortimer Lightwood, who accompanies him in this sequence, makes clear that he is aware of this absurdity and sees the chases in his carelessness and arrogance as his only solace for the loss of Lizzie and a pleasurable way of passing the time.[10] Headstone's psychological state, conversely, has already been developed in previous scenes of the serial, in which he is presented as a dark character who is caught up in a tumultuous state of mind dominated by feelings of inferiority, anger, jealousy and thwarted passion. His helplessness before Eugene's ridicule and humiliation is already evident during his first encounter with Eugene in Part Two and finds a further development in the night chase sequence.

Visual equivalents for this sense of helplessness and emotional imprisonment are created by means of the *mise-en-scène* in this sequence which conveys a labyrinthine, oppressive atmosphere. The setting is correspondingly characterised by narrow alleys enclosed on both sides by high walls, arcades and colonnades, upper and lower levels linked by stairs, tunnels and dark corners. The camerawork, with its tracking and high angle shots in combination with the lighting intensifies the gloomy atmosphere in an expressionistic way. In addition to this, the labyrinthine appearance is effectively illustrated in those instances when the movement of the characters is shown from a high camera angle or presented in a long shot, making their enclosed position inside the surrounding architecture even more vivid. The notion of imprisonment is further supported by the overall combination of shots used for the depiction of space in this sequence. The lack of an establishing shot of the setting at the beginning of the sequence, the lack of any shots which include the sky, and the fact that in every shot only parts of the location are visible onscreen all frame the exterior space in such a way as to lend it the appearance of confined interior space.

At several points in the night chase, the interaction of verbal and visual means effectively illustrate the reversal of the roles of hunter and hunted and the feelings of superiority and inferiority related to it. Towards the middle of the chase, for instance, Eugene explains to his friend why Headstone is of use to him: "I need him, I grind him, I expose him as a favour of fun." At the same time, the image on the screen presents the schoolmaster unsteadily going along a narrow alley in a high angle shot. This does not only signify Eugene's humiliation of him but also his feeling of inferiority. Likewise, the depiction of Headstone pressed against the right wall of a tunnel as Eugene unexpectedly turns back and passes him by appears as a direct visualisation

---

10 Eugene seems to be unaware of Headstone's violent nature and his devouring paranoia that he might track him to Lizzie. Their conflict reaches a climax when Eugene changes the rules of their 'game' by transferring the chase to the countryside and thereby lending it a new purpose. Consequently, as he finds Lizzie and the chase comes to an end, he is almost killed by Headstone.

of Eugene's articulated intention to "refuse to even acknowledge his existence." At the end of the night chase sequence, Eugene's remark, "as you see,
he is undergoing grinding torments. I goad him into madness," is visually
supported by a shot of an ominously appearing, white-faced Headstone. The
camera is moving away from him by means of a tracking shot, thus revealing
the dramatically lit background which appropriately represents Headstone's
imprisonment in his murderous and self-destructive state of mind.[11] Furthermore, the light reflections on the walls, caused by the moving surface of
the water, bring in again the omnipresence of the river and could be taken in
this context as a kind of metaphorical prolepsis hinting at Headstone's suici-
dal drowning in the river at the end of the serial. This night chase sequence,
then, is an excellent example of the way the serial translates physical and
psychological nuances of the characters' complex relationships of dominance
and interdependence into spatial configurations which are created via the use
of certain camera angles, camera movements and lighting.

The visual strategies which are employed in *Our Mutual Friend* to present
some of the interiors also work in accordance with the overall dark atmosphere of the serial and, at the same time, stand in contrast with the lavish
display of interiors with its heritage props and costumes as part of the generic conventions of the heritage film. This does not only apply to the gloomy
interiors of both Mr Venus' shop and Gaffer Hexam's place, but also to the
dwelling house of Old Harmon, a dull and oppressive place, dominated by
dark colours, bare of light, furniture, and signs of human life. Situated amidst
the desert-like landscape of the dust-mounds, it presents in its visual appearance the aspect of desolation. The clouds of dust, undulating throughout the
house, represent in the dramatic context the contaminating bad influence of
dust as part of the serial's second leading line of paradoxical symbolism,
equating dust with money, and the dust-mounds with accumulated wealth
and greed for money.

The lavishness of the serial's society scenes, an essential ingredient of the
heritage formula, stands in a stark contrast to the gloominess of the river
scenes and the dust-mounds scenes. However, these society scenes are
greatly reduced in this serial and presented as functionalised space, working
as "a kind of chorus to the rest of the action" (Giddings & Selby 2001: 163) by
presenting the ridiculing comments of the Voices of Society on the Harmon
Will and its aftermath and on the marriage of Eugene and Lizzie. Their visual
representation from tilted camera angles, especially in Part One, establishes
the *mise-en-scène* as both heritage space and narrative space at the same time.

---

[11] The serial's representation of Headstone's state of mind corresponds with Dickens'
description in the novel: "Looking like the hunted, and not the hunter, worn, with the
exhaustion of deferred hope and consuming hate and anger in his face, white-lipped,
wild-eyed, draggle-haired, seamed with jealousy and anger, and torturing himself with
the conviction that he showed it all and they exulted in it, he went by them in the dark,
like a haggard head suspended in the air: so completely did the force of his expression
cancel his figure." (Dickens 2000: 580-581)

Together with the comments of the Voices of Society, the aesthetics of these scenes reveal on a metaphorical level the moral corruption and superficiality of the upper classes, who are governed solely by money (cf. Hobsbaum 1998: 258-261).

What becomes clear from all these examples is the extent to which *Our Mutual Friend* attempts to find audiovisual and spatial signifiers for the mental states of its characters, creating, by means of semantically charged space, some kind of emotional reality.[12] By using exteriors as well as interiors against the generic representations of heritage film landscapes, the symbolism of the setting, in particular "the sinister, almost threatening, nature of the Thames" (Giddings & Selby 2001: 163), the riverside area of London and the lunar landscape of the dustheaps, becomes an integral part of the plot.

3   Vanity Fair

Andrew Davies' 1998 adaptation of Thackeray's satire on the hypocrisy of English middle-class society is the third BBC adaptation of this novel in thirty years. From the very beginning, it becomes clear that this latest adaptation of *Vanity Fair* resists the obsession with heritage authenticity and ornate backgrounds. Instead the six-part serial is characterized by a disrespectfulness and coarseness rarely seen before in a classic television adaptation. Whereas Becky Sharp as a brilliantly manipulative modern anti-heroine can be interpreted as a departure from the 'conventional' female heroines of the costume film, it is especially the audiovisual language in which the story is told that disrupts the stylistic spectrum of heritage films by using a whole range of almost alienating effects (cf. Whitley 1998). In adopting this language, *Vanity Fair* does not only carry the deft satire inherent in the literary source text with it, but can also be interpreted as a parody or satirical expansion of conventional heritage aesthetics. The grotesque realism and the "in-your-face immediacy" (Durman 1998: 47) of the visual representation of characters and the anti-picturesque settings are pervaded by the imagery of a society in moral decline. The serial's treatment of space is strikingly at odds with the exteriors of other television costume dramas such as the pastoral landscapes in the 1994 BBC adaptation of *Middlemarch* or the picturesque parks and houses in the 1995 BBC adaptation of *Pride and Prejudice*. Nature presented as picturesque country gardens and stately homes in summer with the sole function to serve as visually seductive spectacle (Griem & Voigts-Virchow 2003: 323-324) is turned into a parody in *Vanity Fair*. The first establishing shots of the rural surroundings of Queen's Crawley, the family estate of Sir

---

12 Catherine Wearing, the serial's producer: "What we are aiming at is some kind of emotional reality, using various ways of shooting, using steadicams and moving cameras, not framing everything classically, seeking a kind of energy in film making which will feel very modern and not perioditis (...)," quoted in Giddings & Selby (2001: 162).

Pitt Crawley, which are embedded in the coach ride sequence in Part One of the serial, are a good illustration of this anti-heritage tendency.

In the course of Sir Pitt's and Becky's journey to his country estate, the viewer is confronted with a series of images deviating from "the cultural codes of heritage film landscapes" (*ibid.*: 323), such as his neglected land workers, thieves being flogged for the stealing of rabbits and a number of broken down buildings, including a church half in ruins. The exterior shot of the passing coach reveals a landscape which lacks picturesque ornaments, variety and details, presented from below in a wide-angle long shot from a static camera perspective, showing a panorama of extreme simplicity in two-dimensional minimalism. Queen's Crawley itself is presented as a nasty, gloomy old place, shot from below, overcast by a grey sky and decorated in the foreground with a dark dead tree and two ravens sitting on one of its branches – an image which is later replaced by a grunting swine rooting about in the mud in front of the estate. The atmosphere of rottenness, described later by Becky with the ironic words "Arcadian Simplicity", is taken up in the representation of the dark and gloomy interior of Queen's Crawley, which is in a later scene even extended to the depiction of Lady Crawley, who is shown lying in her bed with a plate of food in front of her which is infested with maggots. These exterior and interior landscapes of *Vanity Fair* are suffused with the idea of a society in decay. They both serve as part of the serial's meta-heritage and as a metaphor for the moral deterioration of the characters.

However, the anti-heritage aesthetics of *Vanity Fair* are not limited to the display of the setting. The representation of food, for example, breaks at several points in the serial with the conventional lavish display of artistically decorated food which is an essential element of the iconographic cliché of the heritage film. In *Vanity Fair*, this element is replaced with the display of abominable innards, a cow head, or a huge ox tongue which are all presented in a grotesquely exaggerated manner in the foreground of the respective scene. Allusions to the grotesque in its broader meaning, in particular in its association with caricature and the accompanying references to animal features, as well as in its combination with the disgusting,[13] can also be detected in the audiovisual representation of several characters. Sir Pitt and Lord Steyne are illuminating examples for the depiction of characters in accordance with the foregrounding of this line of grotesque imagery. Sir Pitt's rottenness and filthiness are at a parodistic level (Parker 1998: 11). One of his characteristic features – his carnal lust for young women – is visualised by his slobbering mouth, the repulsiveness of which is underlined by his extremely yellow teeth, all of which is presented in close-up and accompanied

---

[13]   Cf. Arthur Clayborough (1965), *The Grotesque in English Literature*, Oxford: Clarendon Press and Wolfgang Kayser (1961), *Das Groteske und seine Gestaltung in Malerei und Dichtung*, Oldenburg: G. Stalling.

with the corresponding sounds as he kisses his new sister-in-law in the deathbed scene in Part Four. In a similar way, the implication of the rabbit-like libido of Lord Steyne (Giddings & Selby 2001: 177) is displayed via his enormous caricature-like front teeth which are staged in the foreground by means of a close-up during his first encounter with Becky Sharp in the same part of the serial. The representation of the human body in a distorted manner in combination with the exaggerated visualisation of a person's clumsiness are striking elements in the depiction of short, fat figures like that of Amelia's brother, Joseph Sedley, whose bottom appears twice in extreme close-up while he tries to get off a coach and to get on a horse respectively, or that of Miss Crawley, whose enormous physique hinders her in her ability to move. The close-up of Lord Steyne in Part Four is also an illuminating example for several instances in the serial in which the composition of the frame does not simply serve to direct our attention to foreground elements, but rather to create a dynamic relation between foreground and background, indicating in this case the allocation of roles in the triangle-relationship of Lord Steyne, Becky Sharp and Rawdon Crawley, reducing the latter via his position in the background to an observing bystander.

The predominant modern dynamic camera style in *Vanity Fair* is defined by the use of panning shots, crane shots, unusual camera angles, in combination with the unconventional use of the wide-angle lens, rapid movements as well as a preference for close-ups which is not limited to the faces of the protagonists, but also used for the conveyance of action-laden sequences such as the ball sequence in Part Three or the Waterloo sequence in Part Four. On the whole, this style rejects the 'tourist gaze' – a term used by John Urry with reference to the changes in modern tourism and the growing of the heritage industry, denoting the clear emphasis on tourist consumption as visual, which goes along with the essential significance of buildings as objects upon which the tourist gaze is directed (Urry 2001: 111). In *Vanity Fair*, however, the gaze of the viewer is not directed upon the heritage iconography but upon the physiognomy of the characters, including the "realistically pimply, unmade-up faces of Becky's pupils" (Durman 1998: 47), which lends a suitably immediacy, embracing a more intimate, almost documentary approach to the investigation of the morally corrupt Victorian society.[14]

The overall atmosphere of the serial comes out most immediately in Murray Gold's startling music which Christopher Dunkley has called a "cross between a mariachi and a colliery band" (1998: 18).[15] The music, which

---

[14] This camera style hints at director Marc Munden's track record as a documentary-maker, who also worked with Mike Leigh and Derek Jarman (Whitley 1998).

[15] Whereas critics like Philip Hensher have rejected the music as "appallingly wrong" (1998: 5), Dunkley also praises the excellent narrative use of diegetic on-screen music in the serial, showing how one of the songs performed by Becky Sharp serves as one of her manipulative weapons. As far as its atemporal character with its mixture of modern and period elements is concerned, Murray Gold's score stands in contrast to Carl Davis's music for *Pride and Prejudice* (BBC 1995), acclaimed by Giddings and Selby for its histori-

seems to be at some moments too loud and slightly out of tune, vividly silhouettes the serial's carnivalesque character and serves as an acoustic equivalent to a world which is on the whole presented in a distorted manner.[16] In its departure from the conventional use as 'mood music', it serves the function of a kind of narrator in the serial, constantly making the viewer aware that he is led over a fair of vanities.

Finally, the serial's violation of the heritage formula is even extended to the design of the final credits. The end credits of Part One and Two are flashed on to the screen while a pig munches in front of Queen's Crawley, in Part Four the end credits roll over the ongoing action of a dinner at the city house of the Crawleys, and in Part Five over the most tragic moment in Becky's life, with Becky crying and sobbing because of the break down of her marriage – a formal strategy which gives the impression that the end credits interrupt the ongoing action.

Clearly, then, *Vanity Fair* employs a whole range of strategies which work against the audiovisual language and the iconography of the heritage film, not only in its use of space as anti-heritage space, but also as a satire of conventional heritage aesthetics, conveying ugliness, distortion and decay instead of visual seductiveness and creating, on the whole, a vision of the emotionally empty, morally corrupted, materialistic and vain nature of human society.

4   Conclusion

It is obvious that the expressionist aesthetics of *Our Mutual Friend* and the satirical and grotesque qualities of *Vanity Fair* derive in part from the nature of the respective source novels. But the anti-heritage aesthetics of both television adaptations are also proof of the increasingly complex and varied representation of heritage not only in cinema but also in contemporary British television. Both classic TV serials are examples of how the visual style of 1990s television adaptations departs from canonical movies through social critique, 'gothic' heritage and meta-heritage in the sense of genre-parody or generic satire. Both seek to find visual and spatial signifiers for entrapment, corruption, decay and moral deterioration by opening up new aesthetic dimensions. Such classic TV serials should therefore also be included in the

---

cal appropriateness and its well captured sound texture and style which subtly support and underline action (2001: 113-116).

[16] This carnivalesque character is explicitly depicted in the fair-like Vauxhall Gardens sequence in Part One of the serial. Robert Hanks described this as follows: "(...) the first sight of the pleasure gardens at Vauxhall is of a leering, androgynous face plastered with white make-up, lips painted scarlet, while oompah-ish music played in the background. As a method of signalling decadence and licence, this comes straight out of Bob Fosse's *Cabaret*." (1998: 22)

debate about "regenrification"[17] and "revisionist heritage" (Gibson 2000, Monk 2002) as they bring modern techniques to a tradition-laden genre.[18] Furthermore, their televisual forms, which exhibit highly diverse genre characteristics, are also a justification for Claire Monk's demand, stated towards the end of her historical overview of the heritage debate of the last twenty years (Monk 2002: 192-193), that 'heritage' as a defining feature can only be one amongst several features characterizing the pan-generic range of literary adaptations for the small as well as the big screen.

Bibliography

Bordwell, David & Kristin Thompson (⁵1997), *Film Art: An Introduction*, New York: McGraw-Hill.

Caughie, John (1998), "A Culture of Adaptation. Adaptation and the Past in British Film and Television", *Journal for the Study of British Cultures* 5:1, 55-66.

Dickens, Charles (2000), *Our Mutual Friend*, London: Everyman.

Dunkley, Christopher (1998), "A moving melody in tune with Thackeray's mood", *Financial Times*, 2 December, 18.

Durman, Paul (1998), "A vigorous but slightly coarsened classic", *The Times*, 2 November, 47.

Gibson, Pamela Church (2000), "Fewer Weddings and More Funerals: Changes in the Heritage Film" in Robert Murphy, ed., *British Cinema of the 90s*, London: British Film Institute, 115-124.

Giddings, Robert & Keith Selby, eds. (2001), *The Classic Serial on Television and Radio*, Basingstoke: Palgrave.

Griem, Julika & Eckart Voigts-Virchow (2003), "Trashing and Recycling: Regenrification in British Heritage Movies and Costume Films of the 1990s", in Ewald Mengel, Hans-Jörg Schmid, Michael Steppat, eds., *Proceedings Anglistentag 2002 Bayreuth*, Trier: Wissenschaftlicher Verlag Trier, 319-331.

Hanks, Robert (1998), "Vanity Fair", *The Independent*, 2 November, 22.

Hensher, Philip (1998), "Vanity Fair", *The Independent*, 4 November, 5.

Higson, Andrew (1993), "Representing the National Past: Nostalgia and Pastiche in the Heritage Film", in Lester Friedman, ed., *British Cinema and Thatcherism*, London: University College London Press, 109-129.

----- (1996), "The Heritage Film and British Cinema", in Higson, ed., *Dissolving Views. Key Writings on British Cinema*, London: Cassell, 232-248.

Hobsbaum, Philip (1998), A *Reader's Guide to Charles Dickens*, Syracuse, NY: Syracuse University Press.

---

17 Rick Altman (1999), *Film/Genre*, London: British Film Institute, quoted in Griem & Voigts-Virchow (2003: 321).

18 John Whitley (1998) also sees this modern approach as the linking element between *Vanity Fair* and *Our Mutual Friend*: "Like *Our Mutual Friend*, [...], the serial-makers [of *Vanity Fair*] are concerned less with heritage authenticity than with telling a story in the language of today and that means less ornate backgrounds, fewer peacock feathers and more intimate, expressionistically lit scenes that would be familiar to viewers of Coronation Street or Band of Gold."

Monk, Claire (1995), "The British Heritage Film and Its Critics", *Critical Survey* 7:2, 116-124.

----- (2002), "The British Heritage-film Debate Revisited", in Monk & Amy Sargeant, eds., *British Historical Cinema. The History, Heritage and Costume Film,* London – New York: Routledge, 176-198.

Parker, Ian (1998), "Vanity Fair (BBC1)", *The Observer,* 8 November, 11.

Richards, Jeffrey (1997), *Films and British National Identity. From Dickens to Dad's Army,* Manchester – New York: Manchester University Press.

Samuel, Raphael (1989), "Dockland Dickens", in Samuel ed., *Patriotism – The Making and Unmaking of British National Identity (Vol. III: National Fictions),* London – New York: Routledge, 275-285.

Urry, John (²2001), *The Tourist Gaze,* London: Sage.

Whitley, John (1998), "A new kind of vanity", *The Daily Telegraph,* 3 October.

Barbara Schaff

Still Lifes – *Tableaux Vivants*: Art in British Heritage Films

History films and heritage films share a mutual interest in authentic representations. History films reconstruct documented historical events or lives of real persons. Authenticity is a key concept in historical films: every object, setting and costume must appear true to the historical circumstances.

Heritage films, on the other hand, are mostly based on literary, i.e. purely fictional sources.[1] They are representations of representations of fictional events and persons, which are, however, embedded in a certain historical period. Historical accuracy is a quality which has not always been important in period films — if one compares, for instance, different adaptations of *Pride and Prejudice*, one notices very quickly that the version from the 1940s is totally unconcerned with correct historical costumes. When the new British heritage cinema manifested during the 1980s, this was different: the rules of period fashion, architecture, interior design etc. were meticulously observed and heritage films, such as the numerous BBC adaptations of classic English 19th-century novels which were produced during the 1990s, were especially faithful to the historical contexts. Heritage films now began to emphasise the visual evidence of social practices and behaviour, of domestic rituals and living conditions, of social distinctions in dress, situation and occupation (Sargeant 2000: 304). Or, to put it more concretely, they promoted images of an aristocratic, pastoral and pre-industrial Englishness, in order to recreate and save the past in the cultural memory of contemporary spectators. Part of the ideological function of heritage films, especially the ones produced in the 1980s under the flag of Thatcherism and conservatism, is the reassurance of continuity with a shared past (Corner & Harvey 1991: 72) as well as the representation of this collective national past to corroborate and shape a collective cultural identity.[2] Another aspect is, of course, the particular attractiveness of heritage films to foreign markets and their beneficial influence on British tourism industry (Sargeant 2000: 308). They sell especially well abroad for two reasons: firstly, they show harmonious and elegant stereotypical images of the British geography, past, and people (Higson 2001: 250), and

---

[1] The term heritage film, of course, denotes a hybrid genre, displaying a wide variety of stylistic and aesthetic features, of themes, narratives and forms (cf. Hill 1999). In my paper, I focus on intermediality and therefore deal exclusively with adaptations from literature.

[2] The most recent and famous history film that fulfils this purpose is Simon Schama's epic series *A History of Britain* (2002).

secondly, they deploy aesthetic strategies and cultural referents which distinguish them from mainstream Hollywood (Hill 1999: 79).

Whereas authenticity in history films is labelled quite simply as 'true to historical reality', in heritage films it seems to be a much more complex and multi-facetted concept. Due to the intermediality of literary adaptations, reality in heritage films is always two-faced: it displays the reality of history and the reality of fiction. Many heritage films foreground this consciousness of a double or alternative reality by translating the fictional reality into images that show distinct references to art. Their iconography quotes certain historical modes of representation such as portrait, landscape and genre painting or *tableaux vivants*. Representation in heritage films is very often turned into representation in terms of art. The meticulously displayed visual splendour, the pictorial lushness, aesthetic grandeur and tasteful reconstructions of the British past make many heritage films appear as a chain of carefully composed single shots, each of them a perfect work of art in its own right.

This pictorial quality has led critics to define the heritage film as a hopelessly traditional and conservative genre that answers the spectator's nostalgic needs for the recreation of a stable and glorious past.[3] Many critics have opined that the pictorial representation of the British past in heritage films reflects a general sense of loss and nostalgia of images of an ideal bygone Britain. The visual stock ingredients of classic heritage films, mainly in the adaptations of genteel 19th century novels, are outdoor scenes with pleasurable landscapes, magnificent parks and country houses, and indoor scenes with elegant interiors and well dressed people.[4] The "period spectacle" was said to corroborate elitist ideas of cultural value and satisfy the spectators' emotional and aesthetic needs in a consumerist culture (Sargeant 2000: 302).[5]

In view of this emphasis on historical accuracy and visual splendour, there does not seem to be much critical potential in the films' iconographies, in their images and settings, which could undermine established ideas of heritage and national identity. Critics who were concerned with a potential ideological critique in heritage films, have therefore argued that it is confined to the narrative and the dialogues, and they have noted a tension between the visual work and the narrative work of period dramas (Higson 2001: 256). If the visual quality of a heritage film is only seen as a subsidiary element of the adaptation of prose fiction, this evokes the old Western tradition of

---

[3] Cf. Griem & Voigts-Virchow (2003: 319-322) for a detailed discussion of the development of an early anti-Thatcherite critique of the identity politics in heritage films in the early 1990s to the later more differentiated critique, influenced by gender studies and genre theory.

[4] Andrew Higson (1993: 114) has rightly observed the class bias of many heritage films of the 1980s, where the heritage of the upper classes was represented as the national heritage.

[5] Sargeant explicitly points out the academic aesthetic critique of heritage as an "attractively packaged consumer item" (304).

thought which has always placed words above images. Consequently, if heritage were to be conceptualised in this genre, framed in new terms or even subverted, this would always have to be done in dialogues, whereas the images could only serve the purpose of representing heritage in an iconic mode.

Of course, heritage films operate on a far more complex level than this binary opposition between language and image would suggest. I would like to abandon this concept of an ideological rift between dialogue and the aesthetics of display and ask whether the lavish visual pleasures in heritage films could not be regarded as part of a critical discourse which contests notions of mimetic rendering of history/reality. Higson, although he notes the frequent references to art objects and art forms in heritage films as a distinct stylistic feature, sees no other semantic function here than that of "the added weight to the tasteful production values" (1993: 117). I will argue instead that the function of the frequent reference to art in heritage films, to individual paintings or artists, to historical styles of pictorial representation, or historical modes of performance such as *tableaux vivants* or opera, is not restricted to the aesthetic embellishment of the films. I would like to show that the abundant references in heritage films to British portrait and landscape paintings are more than an attempt at pleasing the spectators with an ample dose of nostalgia. The fact that heritage itself is constructed in terms of art here, implies an important shift of focus, which lessens the importance of authenticity. Heritage films do not recreate or envisage the past, rather they construct the past as a work of art. What follows from this emphasis on art is that heritage films are not authentic in the sense that they present the adaptation of a novel – a fictional construct after all – in realistic terms as historically truthful renderings of events. As truthful to historical fashion and design as these settings may be, they are not iconic representations, but rather symbolic functions and self-referential markers of the films' inherent fictionality and artificiality.

Heritage films refer to art in various ways — in direct and specific, or indirect ways. The most frequent technique of reference is the arrangement of single shots as works of art — either as pictures or portraits. Heritage films often show a series of single, discontinuous and spatially independent shots, of which each can stand on its own as a complete picture. The typical aesthetics of heritage films has been described as characterised by long takes and deep focus, long and medium shots, deliberate crane shots and high-angle shots divorced from any character's point of view, shots that rather follow the view than motivate it (Higson 1993: 117). "Heritage culture appears petrified, frozen in moments that virtually fall out of the narrative" (*ibid.*). Andrew Higson's metaphors of immobility aptly describe these visual techniques which render shots into aesthetically pleasing still lifes, discontinuous with the narrative.

Even more direct reference to art is indicated by methods of framing and editing. James Ivory's method of providing the episodes of *A Room with a*

View (1986) with chapter headings framed with painted ornaments in the Pompeian style is an example of framing the narrative on a non-diegetic level. These captions point not only to literature as the primary source for the film and to the controlling voice of a narrator, but in their ornamental style also revive Florentine art as a means of representation.

Sometimes frames are used as part of the *mise-en-scène* – figures standing in the centre are flanked by others, persons standing in doorways, the use of curtains, windows etc. – all these elements are used to emphasise the single shot in its independent aesthetic value, and to separate it from the narrative sequence. The diegetic function of these markedly single shots is of course less important than their aesthetic, pictorial quality. The absence of action here allows the spectator's vision to linger on the pictorial surface. This editing method of stringing together single shots like beads, or, to use the rhetoric of pictorial art, this sequence of still lifes enhances the visual beauty of heritage films and, above all, in referring to pictorial art as a corresponding medium of representation, it marks the single shot as a work of art. Ang Lee's adaptation of *Sense and Sensibility* is very much informed by traditions of English painting. In many scenes the spectators can get the impression of wandering through a picture gallery of late 18th century landscape paintings. Austen's arrangement of characters is visualized in the film by allusion to two different English schools of portrait painting. Mrs John Dashwood, Sir John and Mrs Jennings, his mother-in-law, come close to caricatures in the Hogarth Style; whereas Mrs Henry Dashwood, her daughters Elinor and Marianne, Edward Ferrars, and Colonel Brandon echo Gainsborough's sensitive portraits of representatives of genteel society. Apart from the recognition effect these references to British painters produce, their message to the spectator is clear. It is not heritage in the sense of a collective historic past this film is concerned with, but rather heritage in the sense of a collective national history of art.

Apart from the allusion to painting, there are also intermedial references to specific genres. The famous view scene in *A Room with a View*, when the party drives out to the Campagna and an overwhelmed George kisses Lucy, is much enhanced by Italian opera music. The non-diegetic sound effects brought about by Puccini's arias not only function as very powerful emotional stimulus, but they evoke another medium which links the budding love story between Lucy and George to the predestined genre for love relations, the Italian opera.

Reference to art is even more explicit when paintings are used as props in the film. There is one scene in *An Ideal Husband*, in which Mabel is waiting for Lord Goring in a picture gallery, looking at an exhibition of contemporary, i.e. late Victorian art. In a medium long shot we see her standing in the gallery, facing the spectator; in the background there are two portraits of ladies with the same slender silhouettes as Mabel's. Now, if we look at Mabel looking at portraits in a film, this analogy makes us aware of the fact that we are also looking at a visual representation, a symbolic construct. This scene

shows how art functions as a metonymical reminder of the film's constructedness and symbolic dimension.

In the examples discussed above, reference to art does not indicate critical
distinction between different, i.e. realistic and non-realistic modes of representation. Sometimes, however, a work of art is used on the diegetic level of
the film to highlight the problematic status of reality in heritage films. Art,
then, is shown as a means of representation that is not opposed to a realistic
mode of representation, but that is essentially the same. A most famous scene
that very cleverly blurs the boundaries between these two modes of representation – a pictorial representation as a work of art and a 'realistic' representation of a 'real man' – is the well-known 'wet-shirt scene' in Andrew
Davies' adaptation of *Pride and Prejudice* from 1995. Into Austen's famous
Pemberley-scene[6] Davies cuts an addition of his own, and that is Darcy div-
ing into the pond. This shot functions as a non-diegetic insert, a symbolic
element which is not part of the narrative, but gives the scene in the portrait
gallery metaphorical value.

The overlap violates the rules of spatial continuity. While Elizabeth is in
the portrait gallery at Pemberley and admires Darcy's life-size portrait, the
man himself rapidly gallops towards the house (and symbolically towards
Elizabeth), then stops his horse, dismounts, and dives into the pond. The way
these two pieces of action are intercut, suggests, however, that Elizabeth
gazes at Darcy's portrait and at the same time imagines Darcy in a kind of
striptease symbolically ridding of his pride and stiffness. In his shirt, he appears to her for the first time as a real human being – and, of course, as a
very attractive man.[7]

What is most important in this scene is the symbolic function of the portrait. The difference between Darcy and his portrait is shown as a very unsta-
ble opposition which collapses in Elizabeth's view because to her the portrait
of Darcy and the man she knows merge into one another. We see her in a
close-up looking at the portrait; the next shot is a medium close-up of the
portrait, which is then followed by a close-up of Darcy himself beginning to
undress. The way these shots are intercut, suggests that the portrait no longer
functions as the pictorial representation of the man. Instead, both are shown
as works of art presented in a synchronic mode. Davies' reference to the art
of portrait painting makes it explicitly clear that the film does not distinguish
between literature and portrait painting as media which construct a fictional
world on the one hand and film as a medium of representation which reflects
an authentic reality on the other hand. Rather, heritage itself is constructed in
terms of art.

---

6   In this scene, Elizabeth Bennet visits Pemberley for the first time, recognizes Darcy's
    personality and falls in love with him merely by looking at his house and portrait.
7   The gender aspects of this scene, the emphasis on the female gaze and the erotic male
    body indicate another aspect of heritage films, which has contributed much to their suc-
    cess: the visual, voyeuristic pleasure particularly female audiences experience. Cf. Mul-
    vey (2000) and Cook (1996).

If one reads this wet-shirt scene symptomatically, one can conclude from it that heritage films do not recreate the past, but self-referentially create the past as a work of art. Rather than confirming images of national history, these films contest the idea of heritage as based on a communal cultural memory, a shared understanding of national history, and a collective cultural core identity, because heritage is shown as a purely aesthetic and pleasurable construct.

Any distinction between art and life (as a point of reference) is even more blurred in Oliver Parker's elegant adaptations of Oscar Wilde's *The Importance of Being Earnest* and *An Ideal Husband*. Here, we find all the characteristics I have mentioned above: The framing of shots, abundant sequences of single shots and the self-referential staging of art as a system of representation. By employing these techniques, Parker, of course, intertextually reflects Wilde's own artistic credo, namely that life imitates art far more than art imitates life. One particular historical art form appears in both films in crucial scenes; it is the living picture or *tableau vivant*. Whereas the single shot and long take in heritage films very often give the impression of a still life, or, if persons are in the picture, of a carefully and elaborately composed constructed grouping, the *tableau vivant* is a much more complex form of representation. It is an art form in its own right; it refers to a historical social practice of a certain class. From the late 18th century, the reenacting of masterpieces of art history became a fashionable party game in bourgeois and aristocratic circles. The *tableau vivant*'s most significant feature is its hybridity and intermediality, because as an art form placed in the liminal space between the pictorial and the theatrical, it translates sculpture or paintings into a theatrical performance. The spontaneous performance of a classical art work sheds light on the complex relation between the "eternity" of the original work of art and the transitoriness of the performance, the intended discrepancy between the immense amount of time, money, and preparations needed for a relatively short-lived silent performative act (cf. Folie & Glasmeier 2002). As a work of art, the *tableau vivant* is the ideal metonymy of the heritage film, because both share many analogies: both are works of art representing another work of art in the disguise of a live performance. Moreover, the still-like quality of the *tableau vivant* mirrors the typical technique of the heritage film, where sequences of single shots and apparently staged images appear to the audience like a *tableau vivant* performance. The silence of the *tableau vivant* is also mirrored in the preponderance of the visual over the dialogue in heritage films. As a live and corporeal appropriation of a painting, it keeps art history alive in the process of transformation — just as the heritage films transform and keep alive their literary sources in the collective cultural memory.

Parker uses the *tableau vivant* in *An Ideal Husband* in one of the most remarkable episodes as a reference to a social practice, as a pictorial embellishment, and as a semantic link between two corresponding scenes. These two temporally parallel scenes are intercut in such a way that each shot mirrors the following. The semiotic and aesthetic link between the two scenes is their construction as *tableaux vivants*. The episode starts with a fencing scene, which establishes the semantic context and the colour scheme (black and white) for the following scenes. Here the heroic theme of the episode — which will be ironically subverted — is introduced. Robert Chiltern is shown as a dynamic fencer, representing the ideal Englishman, the Victorian masculinity model of Muscular Christianity. This scene is followed by a few shots in a kind of Turkish steam bath. Lord Goring and Sir Robert are relaxing in recumbent positions and look like persons posing in a *tableau vivant*. There are many classical allusions. There is a pillar in the centre, and the white towels which are wrapped around the naked men's bodies, have a toga-like, Roman air. In the next four shots, the camera moves closer to Arthur and Robert, up to a close-up of their faces. Then there is an abrupt change of scene, a crosscutting to yet another classical scene. A group of women, among them Mabel and Lady Chiltern as corresponding female figures to Lord Goring and Sir Robert Chiltern, are occupied with the fashionable pastime of a *tableau vivant*. The heroic theme and the colouring of the men's scene are taken up by the ladies' scene. In their reenactment of a classical painting, they are posing as heroic warrior women or antique goddesses with white classical flowing robes, helmets, spears and shields.

The abruptness of the change of scene is very much reduced by the analogous *mise-en-scène*; the semi-nude bodies, the white robes, the classical allusions all belong to the same semantic field of the classical ideal of physical beauty. Also, the visual discontinuity is somewhat reduced by the thematic continuity; the subject of marriage is discussed by the men as well as by the women.

After a couple of shots of the *tableau vivant*, in which a female instructor corrects the ladies' positions, we see Mabel and Gertrude in a close-up, looking into different directions. The next shot takes us back to Arthur and Robert in the bath house, echoing the ladies' poses. The extremely artful arrangement of the ladies' *tableau vivant* is thus taken up in the parallel scene in the bath. The semantic opposition between two entirely different contexts — between ladies performing a *tableau vivant* and gentlemen relaxing in a steaming Turkish bath — collapses, because both scenes are staged as parallel performances, each echoing the other. Here again, art and life are represented as analogies; there is nothing outside artistic performance and no reality or truth outside representation. Just to make this point very clear, this episode is followed by the most theatrical scene in the film, where all protagonists watch Oscar Wilde's *The Importance of Being Earnest*, a play, above all, about truth, and continually gaze at each other from their respective stalls with their opera glasses.

In *The Importance of Being Earnest*, Parker marks the *tableau vivant* even more explicitly, because in those scenes where *tableaux vivants* are arranged, he shows the originals, in both cases prints of romantic Victorian historical paintings. In contrast to *An Ideal Husband*, however, the *tableaux vivants* are not presented in a realistic context, but are highly fictionalized. Both appear to be romantic delusions, daydreams of Cecily's. She looks at two pictures in her journal — one of a knight in armour saving a virgin in chains, the other of a knight lying under a tree, his head in the lap of a virgin, and musicians sitting above on the tree's boughs — and then imagines herself in the position of the virgin and Algernon as the knight. If the two different ontological levels of her daydreams on the one hand and of the plot on the other hand remained separate, one could not classify Cecily's imagination as a *tableau vivant*, because it would not have the same status of reality as the other scenes. Parker, however, cunningly intersects the dream scene with a realistic scene in several short takes, so that the distinction between the two dissolves. Cecily's comic inability to distinguish between her dreams and reality (she tells Algernon, for instance, about her fantasies of their engagement, his letters to her, their breaking up and final reconciliation in a very matter-of-fact tone, as if these imagined events really had taken place) is visually reinforced by the quick change between the reenactment of the painting and the realistic scene. In one take Cecily shows Algernon her album with the picture of the knight and tells him about their engagement; the next take shows Algernon lying on the grass in full armour with his head in her lap. Another switch to the realistic setting, then the next shot takes us back to the medieval scene again. These abrupt changes are counteracted by a coherent dialogue which runs over the semantic breaches of the changing shots, and the positions of the protagonists, which remain exactly the same in both the medieval and the contemporary context: Cecily sitting on the grass with Algernon's head in her lap. As a last device to completely blur the distinction, Parker has the Butler enter the scene. He approaches the couple, who are both in the medieval costume, and we see him enter from the side, virtually breaking into the picture. Thus, the 'frame' of the medieval picture is destroyed by the Butler; the next shot shows Algernon and Cecily back in their normal outfits.

In this episode, Parker uses the *tableau vivant* as a highly self-reflexive art form with regard to the problematic status of reality in order to highlight the inherent artificiality and anti-realism of his Wilde adaptation. If this interpretation of the use of the *tableau vivant* is generalised, one may argue that reference to art in heritage films beyond enhancing the visual effects has a more complex semiotic function. The frequent references to forms and traditions of art in heritage films – to paintings, opera and performative forms of art such as *tableaux vivants* – mark heritage films as a highly self-reflexive genre that foregrounds problems of reality and identity. Rather than confirming images of national history by a mimetic approach, these films contest the idea of heritage as based on a communal cultural memory, a shared understanding of a national history, because heritage is shown as a purely aesthetic construct and a pleasurable commodity which does not exist outside representation — either as a painting, a novel, a performance or a film. The visual splendour and display of period art in heritage films is marked distinctly as mere décor or simulacrum in order to make it clear that what is at stake here is not the relation to any historical reality, but only to the history of art. Through such intermedial reference, heritage films simulate heritage, and they mark this act of simulation by means of constant references to other forms of medial representation. Jean Baudrillard (1988: 167) has said that "To simulate is to feign to have what one hasn't", and this seems to me the very essence of British heritage films. Heritage is constructed and reconstructed again in different forms of medial representation in a self-referential, circular mode, thus signifying a cultural loss of identity, a void of meaning. By means of abundant, gorgeous visual effects and carefully composed scenes heritage films draw upon pictorial art, sculptures, architecture and design in order to make up for this lack as well as to camouflage it.

Bibliography

Ashby, Justine & Andrew Higson, eds. (2000), *British Cinema, Past and Present*, London: Routledge.

Baudrillard, Jean (1988), "Simulacra and Simulation", in Baudrillard, *Selected Writings*, Stanford: Stanford UP, 166-184.

Church Gibson, Pamela (2000), "Fewer Weddings and More Funerals: Changes in the Heritage Film", in Robert Murphy, ed., *British Cinema of the 90s*, London: British Film Institute, 115-124.

Cook, Pam (1996), *Fashioning the Nation. Costume and Identity in British Cinema*, London: British Film Institute.

Corner, John & Sylvia Harvey, eds. (1991), "Mediating Tradition and Modernity: The Heritage/Enterprise Couplet", in Corner & Harvey, eds., *Enterprise and Heritage. Crosscurrents of national Culture*, London: Routledge, 45-75.

Dalle Vacche, Angela (1996), *Cinema and Painting. How Art is Used in Film*, Austin: University of Texas Press.

Easthope, Antony (1998), *Englishness and National Culture*, London – New York: Routledge.

Folie, Sabine & Michael Glasmeier, eds. (2002), *Tableaux Vivants. Lebende Bilder und Attitüden in Fotografie, Film und Video* (exhibition catalogue), Wien: Eigenverlag der Kunsthalle Wien.

Giddings, Robert & Erica Sheen, eds. (2000), *The Classic Novel from Page to Screen*, Manchester, Manchester University Press.

Gutberlet, Kerstin (2001), *The State of the Nation. Das britische Kino der Neunziger Jahre*, St. Augustin: Gardez!.

Griem, Julika & Eckart Voigts-Virchow (2003), "Trashing and Recycling: Regenrification in British Heritage Movies and Costume Films of the 1990s", in Ewald Mengel, Hans-Jörg Schmid, Michael Steppat, eds., *Proceedings Anglistentag 2002 Bayreuth*, Trier: Wissenschaftlicher Verlag Trier, 319-331.

Higson, Andrew (1993), "Re-presenting the National Past: Nostalgia and Pastiche in the Heritage Film", in Lester Friedman, ed., *Fires Were Started: British Cinema and Thatcherism*, Minneapolis: University of Minnesota Press and London: UCL Press, 109-129.

----- (1996), "The Heritage Film and British Cinema", in Higson, ed., *Dissolving Views. Key Writings on British Cinema*, London: Cassell, 232-248.

----- (2001), "Heritage Film and Television", in David Morley & Kevin Robins, eds., *British Cultural Studies. Geography, Nationality and Identity*, Oxford: Oxford University Press, 249-260.

----- (2003), *English Heritage, English Cinema. Costume Drama since 1980*, Oxford: Oxford University Press.

Hill, John (1999), *British Cinema in the 1980s. Issues and Themes*, Oxford: Clarendon.

McFarlane, Brian (1996), *Novel into Film. An Introduction to the Theory of Adaptation*, Oxford: Clarendon.

Monk, Claire & Amy Sargeant, eds. (2002), *British Historical Cinema. The History, Heritage and Costume Film*, London & New York: Routledge.

Monk, Claire (2002), "The British Heritage-film Debate Revisited", in Monk & Sargeant, eds., 176-198.

Mulvey, Laura (2000), "Visual Pleasure and Narrative Cinema" ([1]1975), in Robert Stam & Toby Miller, eds., *Film and Theory. An Anthology*, Oxford: Blackwell, 483-494.

Sargeant, Amy (2000), "Making and Selling Heritage Culture. Style and Authenticity in Historical Fictions on Film and Television", in Ashby & Higson, eds., 301-315.

Lucia Krämer

Subversion in Disguise:
Oliver Parker's Adaptations of Oscar Wilde's *An Ideal Husband* and *The Importance of Being Earnest*

Oscar Wilde has lately joined authors like E.M. Forster, Jane Austen, Henry James and Thomas Hardy as a source of inspiration for a series of recent film adaptations of his life and works. Two of these, Oliver Parker's adaptations of Wilde's society comedies *An Ideal Husband* (1999) and *The Importance of Being Earnest* (2002), form the main subject of this paper. While the following interpretation of these two films puts more emphasis on the relationship between work, author and adaptation than most other papers in this volume, the intention is not to discuss the films according to a specific typology of adaptations, to elaborate on the medial differences between the films and Wilde's plays, or to judge their possible 'fidelity' to the source texts.[1] The aim of the paper is instead a description, based on a close textual analysis of the films, of the strategies employed by Parker to emphasise specific aspects of Wilde's works. His ways of fleshing out and opening up the dramatic texts particularly show affinities to Wilde, since Parker's main interpretative devices are the introduction of a homosexual subtext, the play with intertextuality and reality levels, and the conscious use of the theme of theatricality.[2]

As several of these devices are related to the aspect of authenticity, and thus to a topic that sits at the very heart of the discussions about the so-called 'heritage cultures'[3] and 'heritage films',[4] *An Ideal Husband* and *The Importance of Being Earnest* might be considered self-reflexive comments on these phenomena. Yet in the light of Claire Monk's warnings that the predominance of

---

[1] See Eckart Voigts-Virchow's introduction to this compilation for a summary of recent trends in adaptation studies.

[2] My view of Parker as the creative agent of *An Ideal Husband* and *The Importance of Being Earnest* is based on his double credit as writer and director. It is not meant as a denial of the collective production process, nor necessarily as a characterisation of Parker as a film *auteur* as defined by the *politique des auteurs*.

[3] The plural is used to indicate the heterogeneity of heritage phenomena, which concern in particular the aspects of region and class. For a critique of the history re-presented by heritage sites, its 'authenticity' and commercialisation, cf., for example, Wright (1985) and Hewison, who complains that the heritage industry offers "a contemporary creation, more costume drama and re-enactment than critical discourse" (1987: 135). Both fear that the accumulation of details from the past creates a surface look that actually separates the spectator from history.

[4] See Higson for a discussion of the term 'heritage film' (1996: 232-237; 2003: 9-13) and of the role of authorship and 'authenticity' for this kind of film (1993: 119; 2003: 42, 63-66).

the heritage framework in the critical discussion of recent British period films has meanwhile become anachronistic (2002), the heritage aspect of Parker's two films should not be over-emphasised. *An Ideal Husband* and *The Importance of Being Earnest* do have obvious aesthetic parallels to recent British period films which have been termed heritage films. Whether their presentation of the past is meant as a comment on the reworking of history as heritage remains an open question.

It seems more rewarding to regard the two adaptations as reflections of Wilde's own creative use of history and the literary tradition. Wilde himself had, after all, quite specific ideas about the creative and original potential of appropriating history and art. He considered the first duty of the critic as artist to be the creation of something new out of given historical or artistic material, and Höfele defines Wilde's position thus: "It is only such 'critical', meta-textual, art which possesses the potential for innovation." (1999: 155) This tendency is most obvious in Wilde's *Poems*, in his recycling of epigrams and indeed in his constant re-invention of his public image.

The production of Parker's two films should therefore not only be seen in the light of the international crossover successes of British period films in the past two decades, although this trend has certainly played a major role in their realisation. *An Ideal Husband* and *The Importance of Being Earnest* must also be regarded as the result of a visibly increased interest in Wilde which began around 1995, the centenary of both the first night of *The Importance of Being Earnest* and of the Wilde trials, which ended with the author's imprisonment for 'gross indecency'. Since then, Wilde has been the subject of various official honours (e.g. the erection of statues in London and Dublin, the installation of a window in Poets' Corner in Westminster Abbey) and of several biographical plays (cf. Krämer 2003: 86-89, 111-114). The centenary of his death in 2000, moreover, caused a flood of new books about him and saw several major exhibitions.[5] Unsurprisingly, the British canonisation of Wilde as a writer of national importance and his strong presence have also resulted in a growing commercialisation of his person. We can now buy pictures and quotes of Wilde on mugs, magnets and mouse pads, which necessarily convey a rather simplified image of the man and writer. From a negative point of view such objects propagate the stereotyped views of Wilde as either effete aestheticist or decadent dandy; they reduce the subversive potential of his life and works to mere ornament. On a more positive note, however, they may be said to reproduce an image of Wilde that he himself already propagated in his lifetime. By offering us only certain bits of Wilde, these objects ultimately retain his mercurial personality.

Whatever our view of this development may be, it is proof of the fact that Wilde has increasingly become an object of what Hewison (1985) has called

---

[5]   The two most important ones in London were "Oscar Wilde: A Life in Six Acts" at the British Library and "The Wilde Years: Oscar Wilde and the Art of His Time" at the Barbican Centre.

the English 'heritage industry'. Three recent film appropriations of Wilde are also generally labelled 'heritage'. The first is the extremely reverential bio-pic *Wilde* (1997), a traditional dramatisation of Wilde's life with special emphasis on his family and male lovers. As adaptations of canonical works of English Literature, Oliver Parker's *An Ideal Husband* and *The Importance of Being Earnest* are also generally considered heritage films.[6] I will suggest that the two films make an artistic whole in their emphasis on the subversive aspects of Wilde's plays. Through their different treatment of the conventions of recent classic period films they moreover mirror Wilde's own varying use of the melodrama in *An Ideal Husband* and *The Importance of Being Earnest*.

In Wilde's *An Ideal Husband* (1895) a traditional melodramatic plot still forms the backbone of the play. It revolves around Sir Robert Chiltern, a rising politician, who is adored and idealised for his noble character by his wife Gertrude. Yet Chiltern has a black spot in his past because his career and fortune are based on the fact that he once sold a cabinet secret to a financier, Baron Arnheim. The play thus contains one of Wilde's favourite motifs: the double life. In Mrs Cheveley, the scheming villainess, we also find the typical melodramatic character of the woman with a past. She tries to blackmail Chiltern and puts him in danger of losing not only his social and professional position but also the esteem of his wife. The fact that ultimately all turns out well is in no small measure due to chance, another important element in the implausible plots of many Victorian melodramas. Not only does it lead to mix-ups and suspense, but it also enables Lord Goring, the dandy of the play, to force Mrs Cheveley to abandon her plot against Robert Chiltern. In the happy ending the Chilterns are re-united and Lord Goring finds a wife in Robert Chiltern's sister Mabel.

Wilde manages to relieve this melodramatic plot by ridiculing pretentious members of society and by devising extremely witty (and wise) dialogue based on his outstanding mastery of the epigram and the paradox. Yet in *An Ideal Husband* he does not go as far as in *The Importance of Being Earnest* (1895), his last comedy, where he satirises the melodrama almost beyond recognition (cf. Foster 1956-57). As in the earlier play, Wilde, in the tradition of the comedy of manners, ridicules the behaviour of people in the upper levels of society and in order to do so employs even more outrageous dialogue than in *An Ideal Husband*. To this 'high-comedy' aspect, however, he adds farcical, that is, supposedly 'low-comedy' elements, which serve to underline and thus undermine the constructedness of Victorian melodrama. The improbable situations the characters find themselves in are ultimately only an extension of the many coincidences in melodramatic plots. Similarly, the implausible characterisations in *The Importance of Being Earnest* – for example Gwendo-

---

6   Another recent film with strong references to Wilde is Todd Haynes' glam-rock spectacle *Velvet Goldmine* (1998), a period film mainly set in the 1970s. Not only are many of its dialogues taken from or modelled on Wilde's aphorisms, Wilde is also evoked as a homosexual icon and as the otherworldly spiritual father of pop stardom.

len's and Cecily's obsession with the name Ernest – differ only in degree
from the often type-like characterisations in melodrama.[7]

In *The Importance of Being Earnest* Wilde also takes up specific melodramatic plot elements and ridicules them by trivialising them. Thus there is
once again a woman with a past, Miss Prism, whose fault, however, consists
in having mixed up a baby and the manuscript of a three-decker novel (i.e. in
absentmindedness instead of a moral lapse). The double life is also handled
in a much more playful manner than in *An Ideal Husband*, where it was a
threat. In *The Importance of Being Earnest* it is something to be played with and
can be discarded by Jack and Algernon as they wish: Bunbury, for example,
is simply "exploded" (Wilde 1966: 372) when it seems necessary. Melodramatic speeches are rendered ridiculous by their context, and the play ends
not only with the restoration of a foundling to his rightful (aristocratic) identity, but also with a tableau of not one or two but three deliriously embracing
couples. Excess thus contradicts Victorian moderation and earnestness,
which the pun on 'Ernest' has reduced to a mere tag anyway.

Just as Wilde retains the melodrama in *An Ideal Husband* as the backbone
of his comedy and spices the play up with witty language, Oliver Parker in
his adaptation retains the aesthetics of what Andrew Higson once termed the
'bourgeois heritage film' (1996: 236)[8] but also goes beyond that model. *An
Ideal Husband* corresponds to many earlier heritage films, for example, in its
foregrounding or even fetishising of the male body. One instance would be a
scene which shows off the naked torso of Rupert Everett, who plays Lord
Goring, in a Turkish Bath. Moreover, the film harks back to the strong homo-
social or homoerotic element in films like *Chariots of Fire, Another Country* or
Maurice (cf. Higson 2003: 24). Despite the fact that unlike in films like *Maurice*
or *Another Country* homosexuality is not actually part of the original story of
An Ideal Husband, Parker has created a homosexual subtext that runs through
the entire film. This is achieved by deliberate additions to the source text.
Thus, Parker has inserted a conversation between Baron Arnheim and a very
young Robert Chiltern. This conversation works as a seduction scene in the
sense that it shows Arnheim, the experienced older man, seducing Chiltern
into accepting his doctrine of "power over other men". It gains homoerotic
connotations from the fact that Chiltern's giving in is symbolised by his acceptance of a cigar.

---

[7] As a case in point we might think of Wilde's own characterisation of Sybil Vane in *The
Picture of Dorian Gray* or, indeed, that of Gertrude Chiltern in *An Ideal Husband*.
[8] For a description of the formal features of this kind of film, the most prominent representatives of which are the three Merchant-Ivory adaptations of novels by E.M. Forster
(*A Room With a View, Maurice, Howards End*), see Higson (1993) and Hill (1999). Higson's
attempt at a terminological sub-classification of period films must be seen in the context
of other recently coined terms like 'post-heritage' (Monk 1995) or 'alternative heritage'
(Powrie 2000), and of descriptions of recent changes in the heritage film (cf. e.g. Church
Gibson 2000 and the contributions of Pamela Church Gibson, Carolin Held, Andrew
Higson and Sarah Street to this book).

The dominant heterosexual discourse of the film, which centres on the Chilterns' marriage and on Lord Goring's way towards marriage, is further subverted by the casting of Everett, whose public image as a homosexual contradicts his role of a philandering (heterosexual) bachelor.[9] If *An Ideal Husband* ends with Lord Goring's marriage to Mabel Chiltern, this therefore ultimately underlines the artificiality of the characterisation and the plot conventions of the film (and its source text).

Another aspect of recent classic period films Parker engages with is the topic of authenticity. Critics have repeatedly commented – positively or negatively – on the tendency in heritage films to reconstruct the historical period in which they are set as accurately as possible – a quality which is also used as a selling point in the marketing of the films. That this authenticity is actually only a construct is emphasised in *An Ideal Husband* in various ways, most prominently by the art direction. Like many other period films *An Ideal Husband* has lavish and carefully researched costumes and décors, and a *mise-en-scène* that underlines the visual splendour of the settings. Some details, however, are displayed in such an excessively exhibitionist way that the settings no longer seem like habitable but rather museal spaces. A copy of *The Yellow Book* and Beardsley prints in Lord Goring's apartment are particularly obvious examples of this phenomenon, which includes a tendency towards self-parody.

The resulting artificiality goes hand in hand with several other elements that underline the theatricality of the film, for example the ever-present music and the overacting in the scenes between Rupert Everett and Minnie Driver, who plays Mabel Chiltern. The topic of theatricality is further emphasised on the level of the story when we see people playing a role. Again, Parker has added to Wilde's text. He has, for example, inserted a scene in which Mabel and Gertrude Chiltern pose for a *tableau vivant*. Even more striking, though, is a scene in which all the main characters attend a theatre performance, and where the actors on stage are not the only ones who play a part. The audience, for whom the auditorium is a stage in the public sphere, also act. Just like the actors, they are the subject of another's gaze through opera glasses and react in a theatrical manner when they realise that they are being watched.

Moreover, not only in the public sphere but also in the private sphere almost all characters play a role. Thus, Mrs Cheveley and Lord Goring act when, from different motives, they try to seduce each other. Not only Lord Goring's apartment with its *fin-de-siècle* decoration is obviously a stage, but also the Chilterns' house, where characters are often theatrically framed by curtains. Sir Robert acts the ideal husband with the perfect past for his wife, and Mabel and Lord Goring not only playfully act a part for each other but at

---

9   Everett's image ultimately goes back to his breakthrough role in *Another Country*. In *An Ideal Husband* the continuity casting typical of heritage films (cf. Higson 2003: 30-31) is therefore used disruptively.

the end of the film also improvise a scene around a stolen letter to appease Sir Robert – again a scene that is not in the source text.

By means of such additions Parker puts special emphasis on a topic that is already prominent in Wilde's comedy, the topic of acting. Especially in Parker's adaptation, it points to a more general engagement with the themes of seeming and being and of the relationship of reality and fiction. This is evident from the way in which the film plays with and transgresses reality levels. In the theatre scene mentioned above, for example, the play that is performed is Wilde's *The Importance of Being Earnest*, as anybody who knows the comedy can deduce from the dialogue. The dramatist addressing the audience after the performance is therefore none other than Oscar Wilde. Moreover, the snatches of the dramatist's speech that are audible over a conversation between Robert and Gertrude Chiltern are taken from a curtain speech that the real Oscar Wilde delivered on the first night of his play *Lady Windermere's Fan* (Ellmann 1988: 346). Fittingly, it plays with the notion of the audience as actors.

Sir Robert Chiltern's situation is reflected by the intertextual allusion to *The Importance of Being Earnest*, where at least Algernon and Jack lead a double life, and by the allusion to Wilde, who, as a homosexual, was also forced to lead a double life. Fiction and reality, the difference between which Wilde himself liked to question, interact and create what McHale calls an "ontological scandal" (1987: 85). This is also the case with other intertextual references to fictional works by Wilde and to his life. Lord Goring, for example, wears a green carnation just as Wilde himself used to do; at a reception in the Chilterns' house at the beginning of the film a 'Lord Windermere' is announced; and in Lord Goring's club somebody addresses another character as 'Bunbury', who, according to the credits, is impersonated by director Oliver Parker himself.

While this play with reality levels has a special affinity to Wilde's own aestheticist reflections about the relationship of art and life, it also serves the purpose of bringing the film up to date. *An Ideal Husband* contains two scenes with specific references to a reality beyond the historical setting of the film that are again not in Wilde's play. They are obviously addressed to a contemporary audience. The first is the seduction scene between Sir Robert Chiltern and Baron Arnheim, where Arnheim talks about information as "the modern commodity; it can shake the world." The second is a speech delivered by Robert Chiltern in the House of Commons, where he demands that society act against the "growing compulsion to use power merely to beget more power, money merely to beget more money, [...] commerce without conscience, which threatens to strike at the very soul of this nation." In our time of globalisation, "this nation" designates all the countries of the West and the United States in particular. *An Ideal Husband* should therefore not be regarded as a kind of elegy which, by dwelling on period décor and costume, nostalgically laments the passing of a former age of glory (cf. Higson 1993:

122-125). Through its references to today's world it achieves a deliberate topicality which is as international as it is national.

This may be one reason why *An Ideal Husband*, a US/UK co-production, was quite a success on the international market. At production costs of $14 million it may have grossed 'only' £2.9 million in the UK, but it made $18.5 million in the USA,[10] the most important market for the kind of specialised crossover film that *An Ideal Husband* represents.[11] It was therefore only logical that an attempt was made to repeat this success. The packet of talent that Fragile Films, Miramax – both of whom had already played a role in the production of *An Ideal Husband* – and Ealing Studios assembled for *The Importance of Being Earnest* included once more Wilde as the author of the source text, director (and screenwriter) Oliver Parker and actor Rupert Everett in a leading role. Again this was spiced up with young as well as established British acting talent and an American actress in one of the leading roles (Julianne Moore in *An Ideal Husband*, Reese Witherspoon in *The Importance of Being Earnest*). Nonetheless, *The Importance of Being Earnest* was far less successful in theatrical release than its predecessor. Despite a UK gross of £3.5 million, which was a better result than that of the earlier film, the US gross of $8.4 million must, at production costs of $15 million,[12] be regarded as relatively disappointing. I would suggest that one reason for this result was a disruption of audience expectations, due to an even stronger tendency than in *An Ideal Husband* to bring things up to date.

Many of Parker's interpretative strategies in *The Importance of Being Earnest* are very similar to those in *An Ideal Husband*. Thus, he emphasises the topics of performance or theatricality, and he plays with reality levels.[13] The first conversation between Jack and Algy, for example, does not take place in Algy's morning-room but starts in the theatrical setting of a music hall. A mirror motif associated with Jack throughout the film supports the theme of the double life, the mirror serving on the one hand as a rehearsal aid for Jack's performance in society, on the other hand as a confidante for his secret emotions. Moreover, just as in *An Ideal Husband* the characters are wary of being observed. As soon as they feel the gaze of another person they modify their behaviour to correspond to the role that they are expected to play in

---

[10] http://www.imdb.com/title/tt0122541/business (17 January 2004); http://www.bfi.org.uk/facts/stats/1999/ukfeatures_boxoffice.html (17 January 2004).

[11] See Higson for an analysis of the role of American companies for British heritage films at the levels of production and, more importantly, distribution (2003: 119-141).

[12] http://www.imdb.com/title/tt0278500/business (17 January 2004); http://www.bfi.org.uk/facts/stats/2002/ukfeatures_boxoffice.html (17 January 2004).

[13] Instead of the homosexual subtext of *Husband*, however, the topic of sexual identity and gender roles is dealt with in a more general way. Women, who are dressed as men, for example, perform in a small theatrical interlude at the beginning of the film. More importantly, Parker takes up the fact that Wilde's women characters in *The Importance of Being Earnest* are very domineering. He therefore supplies Gwendolen with cigarettes, a car and a tattoo, i.e. attributes with strong masculine connotations; he even has her enter a pub.

society. Algernon and Jack, for example, disguise a fight as a hearty embrace when they find that they are being observed by Cecily, Miss Prism and Dr. Chasuble, and they stop fighting over the muffins when they realise that Gwendolen is watching them through a pair of binoculars.

Once again the theme of acting and performance is taken up in a play with reality levels. Thus, just as we found an Oscar Wilde figure in *An Ideal Husband*, there is an Aubrey Beardsley look-alike in *The Importance of Being Earnest*. That it is indeed his purpose to evoke the theme of acting in the widest sense is obvious from the context in which he is placed: he is visible in the background of the scene in which Jack confesses his double life as Jack and Ernest. This self-exposure moreover takes place in front of an audience of female and male prostitutes in a setting that is a mixture of a bordello lounge and a casino. This shadow society also points to the themes of acting and the double life. Ironically, it is an almost theatrical environment where for the first time the truth is told.

As in *An Ideal Husband* the settings and costumes veer on self-parody because they constitute a pastiche which not only reproduces but even exceeds the museum aesthetics of many period films (cf. Higson 2003: 63-67). *The Importance of Being Earnest* thus not only contains the obligatory country house, landscape garden, steam train and oldtimer car; it also has Beerbohm drawings and William Morris paper on the walls, ties with the classic Burlington pattern, and houses that are simply too large for the characters to inhabit and are therefore obviously stages.

While the strategies mentioned so far are very similar to those Parker used in *An Ideal Husband*, he also takes several steps beyond this film in *The Importance of Being Earnest*, thus mirroring Wilde's own more liberal and disruptive treatment of the melodrama in the source play. By doing so, Parker serves the implicit discussion of ideas in Wilde's play, which are first and foremost concerned with the topic of being and seeming. Since they also relate to the topics of authenticity and representation, they may be said to add an implicitly self-reflexive quality to the film.

One field in which Parker creates a deliberate break with the seamless aesthetics apparently expected from period films is the camera work, which in *The Importance of Being Earnest* is often highly visible. On the one hand there are very obvious camera movements (e.g. in the interrogation scene between Lady Bracknell and Jack) or zooms (e.g. in a scene where Jack and Algernon are observed by Cecily, Ms Prism and Dr Chasuble); on the other hand, the camera work is sometimes pictorialist to the extreme, especially when the visual style is recognisably modelled on actual paintings (e.g. in the wooing scenes between Cecily and Algernon).

Parker has also made additions to Wilde's text that are obviously meant to disrupt the expectations of the audience in the 'fidelity' or 'authenticity' of a period film or of an adaptation of a canonical text. In many of these additions, which in contrast to those in *An Ideal Husband* are clearly recognizable as such, Parker follows Wilde's own strategies in his 'trivial comedy for serious people': he draws on both popular or 'low' culture and serious or 'high' culture and trivialises the serious while treating the trivial with seriousness. The result is a film which highlights its own constructedness and artificiality and refuses to be "the kind of glorious period piece the British do so well, with sumptuous settings and costumes" (Thomas 1999).

That many spectators did not approve of this strategy at all is evident from a large number of negative comments on the film, both from professional and amateur critics. Thus, in *The Guardian* Peter Bradshaw (2002) complained of "some wacky stand-alone inventions". Ann Hornaday (2002) wrote in the *Washington Post* of "annoyingly distracting gimmicks" and entirely unnecessary "frippery", while Henry Baker, a user of the internet movie database, criticised "a lot of stupid, incongruous, and/or anachronistic elements".[14]

Parker's disorienting approach is already obvious in the title sequence, which sets the tone of the film. Thus, unlike the play, the film does not start in Algernon's flat but in a dark alley. There we see a man in late Victorian evening dress, who is being chased and threatened with the words, "Time to pay your debts." He manages to escape by a ruse, jumping onto a carriage that happens to be passing by. The carriage is occupied by a single lady, who, after getting over her first fright and after being offered a cigarette by our hero, gives him a flirtatious glance. He, however, jumps out of the carriage and alights right outside his home, unmolested by his pursuers. *The Importance of Being Earnest* thus starts with a very common sequence in films, a chase, but a sequence that has more affinities to the action and gangster film than to the heritage film. This impression is reinforced by the rather high frequency of cuts and the dynamic music in the scene.

Parker's references to canonical art in *The Importance of Being Earnest* also differ markedly from most other films which are commonly regarded as heritage films. Not only are many of these based on a well known work of literature; very often they also contain references to elements of highbrow culture.[15] In *The Importance of Being Earnest* Parker takes up this tendency by incorporating Pre-Raphaelite art, and more particularly Millais' painting *Knight Errant*, as a leitmotif into Cecily's love to Algernon. Cecily models her romantic and sexual fantasies on this picture in all stages of the relationship, thus creating her own personal variations on it. This fantasy world is sometimes invaded by the outside (e.g. in the shape of Jack's butler) in such a manner as to make the clash of reality and imagination (and of the realms of reality and art) very evident. Moreover, despite its affinities with the period represented in the film, Pre-Raphaelite art in *The Importance of Being Earnest* is

---

14 http://www.imdb.com/title/tt0278500/usercomments-71 (16 April 2003).

15 Even in a film like *Jude* by Michael Winterbottom, which breaks with the bourgeois heritage film in many respects, the main intertextual references may be to films and thus to a popular medium, but the *nouvelle vague* or Ingmar Bergman (cf. Church Gibson 2000: 119) are certainly not part of popular culture. See also Barbara Schaff's contribution to this volume for an interpretation of the references to art in heritage films.

not at all contained within the background of the action. It comically exceeds its filmic context and therefore serves to underline the artificiality of Parker's film.

The same is true of specific references to recent classic period films, which go beyond the simple fact that *The Importance of Being Earnest* shares with them an iconography of stately homes and picturesque landscapes or gardens. Thus, Algernon dressed for tennis or Gwendolen doing archery must not necessarily be interpreted as references to *A Room with a View* or *The Age of Innocence*. Yet a field of bluebells and a punt that ends its journey under a willow tree are more specific nods to *Howards End*. Moreover, the fact that Algernon's luggage is brought to "the blue room" and a shot of a figure near a lake at night are highly reminiscent of *Maurice*. Similarly, the 1930s tune of the song with which Algy and Jack serenade their lovers was already used in the Loncraine/McKellen *Richard III*, and the treatment of Jack's servants as an audience of the love play unfolding under their eyes both underlines the theme of theatricality and is reminiscent of Kenneth Branagh's *Much Ado About Nothing*. What such references emphasise is the degree to which our expectations of what a period film or an adaptation of a literary work should be is determined by the films that are already there. We are therefore faced with questions about originality and representation.

Another interesting case of intertextuality in *The Importance of Being Earnest* is that Parker not only draws on the commonly known three-act version of Wilde's play but also on the little known four-act version. This raises the topic of authenticity because the four-act version is actually the 'original' version of Wilde's play, although it was already altered in 1895 by actor-manager George Alexander during rehearsals and early performances into the form in which it is known today (Ellmann 1988: 406, Kohl 1980: 415/6). The most important difference from the three-act version is the addition of a scene in which Algernon, who lives notoriously beyond his means, is threatened with imprisonment for not paying his bills at the Savoy Hotel. Parker changes even this passage to emphasise the motif of the double life because in the film it is not Algernon but Jack who runs up the bill at the Savoy while pretending to be Ernest in town. Moreover, Algernon is threatened with imprisonment while posing as Ernest in the country.

However, Algernon in the film has accumulated quite enough debt for himself to be pursued by creditors. This leads to a running gag in the literal sense of the word, which starts in the title sequence mentioned above. What is striking about this opening scene is, of course, first and foremost that the situation does not at all correspond to the polite behaviour and morning-room setting we would expect from our knowledge of the play. Instead of witty but genteel conversation we find a chase with a suave hero, who is obviously a natural favourite with the ladies. Together with the Swinging-Sixties-style music, all this is not a little reminiscent of James Bond, and it is only one of several references that confer a touch of hybridity to *The Importance of Being Earnest* by hinting at popular films that today are received as peculiarly British. Thus the fact that the film was made by Ealing studios places it in a long tradition of English film comedies, albeit of quite a different nature. There is also a reference to cinematic adaptations of English detective novels in the style of the Agatha Christie films when Jack enumerates and brings evidence for all of Algy's lies. Even the period or heritage films mentioned above can be considered popular films to a certain degree. The Bond connection, however, is the most obvious and is emphasised by the casting of Dame Judi Dench, who has played 'M' in the latest Bond films, as Lady Bracknell. It also occurs when Algernon arrives at Jack's country estate by hot-air balloon – a situation which has been criticised as a gimmick by several reviewers, although this is exactly the point: James Bond's gimmicks are among the highlights of each Bond adventure. Ironically, of course, in *The Importance of Being Earnest*, the most masculine of all action film heroes is imitated by Rupert Everett, an open homosexual, so that once again we are faced with a playful interaction of reality levels.

While Parker in *The Importance of Being Earnest* certainly goes beyond *An Ideal Husband* as far as the visuals and the more unconventional use of intertextuality are concerned (with references to popular culture that often smack of anachronism), the most relevant step beyond the earlier film occurs on the theoretical level. Parker achieves a general problematisation of the nature of representation or the relationship of sign and meaning, a fundamental topic in Wilde's play, where the wordplay and the problem of naming in particular point to the problematic relationship of sign and reality.

Again, Parker puts particular emphasis on this aspect by extending Wilde's text, for example in a scene between Miss Prism and Dr. Chasuble. Here Parker takes up the fact that in the play the two characters unintentionally use sexual innuendos and then have to explain to each other that they have spoken metaphorically. The whole scene in the film elaborates on this theme of the ambiguity of language, with Chasuble even asking: "Isn't language a curious thing?" It thus points to the arbitrary relation between the sign and its referent.

Parker also elaborates on the fact that in Wilde's play the sign precedes, and has actually become more important than, its meaning (cf. Höfele 1999: 161, 164); this is particularly obvious when Gwendolen and Cecily insist that their fiancés must be called Ernest, the name being more important than the person's character. Parker catches this in a nutshell in the film when Gwendolen has the name 'Ernest' tattooed on her bottom. In the tattoo the sign may be only skin-deep but it is also ineradicable, and ultimately reality is changed in order to correspond to it. In the film, when Jack looks through the army lists to hunt for his father's name, which is also his own, the name he finds is, after all, not "Ernest John" as in Wilde's source text; it is only "John". Thus, whereas in Wilde's play Jack's name "naturally is Ernest" (Wilde 1966: 383) and Jack's lie has unwittingly become the truth, in Parker's film 'Jack' is indeed Jack, but he deliberately assumes a false name to fulfil the expectations of a world where the label is more important than the content.

Jack's self-reinvention as Ernest, just like Cecily's mental variations on Millais' painting *Knight Errant*, may be compared to what Wilde himself regarded as the first duty of the critic as artist, namely to create something new out of given historical or artistic material. It is also something that Oliver Parker has clearly attempted in his adaptations of *An Ideal Husband* and *The Importance of Being Earnest*. The result may be called 'subversion in disguise', a phrase that not only refers to Wilde's own strategies of hiding social critique behind the mask of comedy and of showing his audience that they live in a world of theatricality, uncertain (sexual) identities and indefinite signification. The phrase also refers to Parker's films, which despite the strategies explored above are first and foremost entertainment films with splendid visual assets. It is telling, for example, that even the anachronistic elements in *The Importance of Being Earnest* are perceived as elements from the past by the audience and thus figure as potential objects of nostalgic longing. Yet, since Parker retains and partly even emphasises Wilde's criticism and proto-postmodernist (Höfele 1999) ideas, he certainly also achieves something else. Despite the historicising appeal of gorgeous costumes and settings, *An Ideal Husband* and *The Importance of Being Earnest* are not only Wildean in the sense that they transport us back to Wilde's time and social environment; they are also Wildean in the sense that they work against received ideas by ultimately questioning the process of representation and signification.

Bibliography

Bradshaw, Peter (2002), "The Importance of Being Earnest", *The Guardian*, 6 September.

Church Gibson, Pamela (2000), "Fewer Weddings and More Funerals. Changes in the Heritage Film", in Robert Murphy, ed., *British Cinema of the 90s*, London: British Film Institute, 115-124.

Ellmann, Richard (1988), *Oscar Wilde*, London: Penguin.

Foster, Richard (1956-57), "Wilde as Parodist. A Second Look at *The Importance of Being Earnest*", *College English*, 18, 18-23.

Hewison, Robert (1987), *The Heritage Industry. Britain in a Climate of Decline*, London: Methuen.

Higson, Andrew (1993), "Re-presenting the National Past. Nostalgia and Pastiche in the Heritage Film", in Lester Friedman, ed., *Fires Were Started. British Cinema and Thatcherism*, Minneapolis – London: University of Minnesota Press/UCL Press, 109-129.

----- (1996), "The Heritage Film and British Cinema", in Higson, ed., *Dissolving Views. Key Writings on British Cinema*, London: Cassell, 232-248.

----- (2003), *English Heritage, English Cinema. Costume Drama Since 1980*, Oxford: Oxford University Press.

Hill, John (1999), *British Cinema in the 1980s: Issues and Themes*, Oxford: Clarendon.

Höfele, Andreas (1999), "Oscar Wilde, or, The Prehistory of Postmodern Parody", *European Journal of English Studies*, 3:2, 138-166.

Hornaday, Ann (2002), "Fussy 'Earnest' Is Wilde at Heart", Special to *The Washington Post*, 24 May.

Kohl, Norbert (1980), *Oscar Wilde. Das literarische Werk zwischen Provokation und Anpassung*, Heidelberg: Winter.

Krämer, Lucia (2003), *Oscar Wilde in Roman, Drama und Film: Eine medienkomparatistische Analyse fiktionaler Biographien*, Frankfurt/Main: Lang.

McHale, Brian (1987), *Postmodernist Fiction*, London – New York: Methuen.

Monk, Claire (1995), "Sexuality and Heritage", *Sight and Sound*, NS 5:10, 32-34. Repr. in Ginette Vincendeau, ed., *Film/Literature/Heritage. A Sight and Sound Reader*, London: British Film Institute, 2001, 6-11.

----- (2002), "The British Heritage-film Debate Revisited", in Monk & Amy Sargeant, eds., *British Historical Cinema. The History, Heritage and Costume Film*, London – New York: Routledge, 176-198.

Powrie, Phil (2000), "On the Threshold Between Past and Present. 'Alternative Heritage'", in Justine Ashby & Andrew Higson, eds., *British Cinema, Past and Present*, London: Routlege, 316-326.

Thomas, Kevin (1999), "'An Ideal Husband' Withstands Test of Time", *Los Angeles Times*, 18 June.

Wilde, Oscar (1966), *The Complete Works*, London – Glasgow: Collins.

Wright, Patrick (1985), *On Living in an Old Country. The National Past in Contemporary Britain*, London: Verso.

Stefani Brusberg-Kiermeier

Stormy Novel, Thorny Adaptation:
Recent Appropriations of *Wuthering Heights*

In contrast to film versions of novels that are not so well known to a film audience, film versions of strongly canonised texts continue to confront us with the question of how faithful a film version is to the original literary text. However, even literary film critics for whom artistic fidelity is still a central category do not automatically imply that they wish for scrupulous transfer of every character or scene. Brian McFarlane suggests that what fidelity critics have in mind is that the illusion of the reality created by the text and the illusion of reality created by the film should coincide (McFarlane 1996: 164). As Erica Sheen argues, fidelity criticism can clearly be understood as a rhetoric of possession and as the articulation of a loss (Sheen 2000a: 3). The literary texts are institutionalised in the academic field, and transferring them to another context threatens the relative autonomy of academia. Sheen proposes that the literary academics provide the "changing frames of reference for critical perceptions of textual integrity" and can thus be regarded as guardians of humanist values. But which values are these and what is their relation to the commercial market of film production? Sheen seems to imply that the ideological background of academic institutions is more conservative than that of film-makers who are not regarded as intellectuals. But interestingly enough the most successful literary adaptations are products of traditionally organised film-making institutions, like BBC versions or Merchant-Ivory films. And many crucial members of the production process can certainly be more adequately described as intellectuals or artists than as technicians.

Although I clearly see how problematic the criterion of artistic fidelity has become, I propose not to completely renounce the term as obsolete, but open it up to a much wider understanding that is no longer hierarchical concerning the 'original medium' and the 'adapting medium'. Like Sarah Cardwell I opt for a discussion of medium-specific issues with as little "gut feelings" as possible (Cardwell 2002: 31). Furthermore, I would like to suggest that the two central values of fidelity criticism are subtlety and authenticity. Both subtlety and authenticity do not only refer to the linguistic medium but to the cinematic as well. In contrast to McFarlane I would argue that film is absolutely capable of conveying subtleties as well, even though it is difficult to adapt the discourse level of a narrative text. As Imelda Whelehan states, certain features of novelistic expression must be retained in an adaptation, but the idea of which features are essential to a reproduction varies largely (Whelehan 1999: 7). I would argue that the question of literary genre comes into play here, since for a drama not only film versions but every stage production as well can be regarded as an adaptation of the 'original' text, whereas for a novel the filming constitutes a much greater media shift. Therefore considerations about the appropriate setting, realism and historical verisimilitude or the problem of nostalgia are so much more dominant in the case of a novel adaptation.

In my view, not the illusion of reality has to coincide in both media – novel and film – but the emotional and intellectual experience when watching the film should be comparable to the emotional and intellectual experience when reading the novel. The audio-visual medium has means – though different, just as subtle – as literature to create a strong and authentic impression. To describe the effects of a novel or a film I find the idea of 'interactivity', very helpful. When Espen J. Aarseth claims that successful fiction must be interactive (Aarseth 1997: 50), this clearly applies to novel and film at the same time. For a novel or a film to become 'important' to an audience, this audience must get involved mentally and emotionally during the reception, constructing 'meaning' while reading or watching (cf. Griem & Voigts-Virchow 2002: 159). This process is usually based on the medium's coherent narrative and especially on key moments of great intensity and stimulation.

Instead of confronting a legal body of literary academia with a legal body of film-makers, I would like film adaptation of literary texts to be understood as a process of transmission which starts with the subjective interpretation of the literary text and ends with the subjective reception of the film. In terms of stimulation of feeling and thought the intermedial process can even be reversed: More and more frequently popular novels have been written *after* a film's success showed that it is worth turning the film-script into a novel. Also, nowadays novels are sometimes made into films so quickly that the film reaches an international audience faster than the novel does. In contrast to the long reception history of canonised texts, a short reception period of a novel creates fewer problems for the film-maker and also assimilates the two intermedial processes and their hierarchies: it does not matter so much any longer whether we deal with novel-into-film or film-into-novel. To my mind, it is a strong emotional and mental involvement in one of the media that can make the audience turn its attention to the other medium as well: if you enjoyed reading the novel you might want to see the film, too, and vice versa.

I suppose that – besides basic marketing considerations – the decision which classical text should be adapted has to do with the special literary features of the original text and also with processes of literary canonisation. The popularity of a novel, its love story or certain strong female figures is closely connected to its canonisation. Just think of the hundreds of Victorian novels, whose heroines used to be highly popular, which have only gradually been reprinted during the last decade or still stay out of print. Concerning the criteria of the final reception I find it important to stress that the popularity with the general audience and commercial success might even correspond with academic approval. And even if they do not approve of certain features, academic film critics have no difficulties whatsoever to explain, e.g., why the 1995 BBC version of *Pride and Prejudice* could create 'Darcymania' or why the film version of *The Remains of the Day* (1993) was nominated for eight Oscars. Criteria like the films' visual perfectionism and fetishization of landscapes, gardens and other period details come into play here. The processes and techniques of transferring a text to an audio-visual product are at least as complex and amorphous as literary criticism and audience reception themselves. All that film criticism of classical adaptations can therefore do is try to describe these processes and techniques as soberly and accurately as possible.

It is certainly generally true that – as Foucault says – a highly creative author is an "initiator of discursive practices" and that the author is paradoxically reinforced by the historical supersession of her work. This is obviously more correct for film versions of classical, canonised texts than for those of more recent texts. Most viewers who recollect a positive impression of seeing *The Remains of the Day* or *The English Patient* certainly remember the titles of the films and the names of some actors. But they will most probably not remember the names of the authors of the books the films are based on nor will they read any (other) of their novels. Teachers of English might, however, choose novels that were great successes on screen in order to make their classes read them. Therefore it would be a worthy endeavour to analyse whether successful film versions of more recent literary works do in turn influence the academic teaching syllabus and the literary canon likewise.

There are many imponderabilities of filming novels that are situated in the past. One of them is getting the historical setting and visual register right. Georgian or Victorian houses, for instance, might have to look new, as they have just been built – like in the BBC *Middlemarch* – but because of horses and carriages they should not be without any dirt in front of them – as they are in the 1996 *Emma* directed by Douglas McGrath. Another imponderability is the actor's or actress's ability to act period drama. The body language of, e.g., Joaquin Phoenix in *Gladiator* or of Richard Gere in *First Knight* gives the audience not a historical, 'past times', but a 20th century fitness studio feel. Such imponderabilities make obvious how difficult it is to find the appropriate visual mode that is able to combine historical realism and authenticity with the idea of a cinema of attractions (Tom Gunning).

Erica Sheen claims that the novels of the Brontës are "infinitely less adaptable" than Jane Austen's, especially because of their opening up "the abyss of marital failure" (Sheen 2000b: 18). The depiction of three unhappy marriages has certainly a great potential for an anti-heritage production. Other criteria mentioned by Sarah Cardwell are the "rustic" aspects and the appearance of "if not working-class [...] at least 'workers'" (Cardwell 2002: 162). I would like to suggest that *Wuthering Heights* is "infinitely less adaptable" than a Jane Austen novel because it is so difficult (1) to portray the relationships of its passionate characters convincingly, (2) to appropriate their complex moral values and aestheticism and (3) to reproduce the novel's multiple narration (cf. Holderness 1985: 5). I will in the following investigate these claims in the two most recent film versions of Emily Brontë's novel: the cinematic version of 1992 and the television version of 1998.

The version of 1992, directed by Peter Kosminsky, is a British-American co-production, obviously aiming at becoming the 'new definite version' in terms of cinematic greatness and thus attributing the status of 'old definite version' to William Wyler's version of 1939. Like in the American black-and-white film Heathcliff is played by a 'classic', Shakespearean actor – Ralph Fiennes – and Cathy by a movie-starlet – Juliette Binoche –, which creates strong effects as well as weaknesses for the film. The two weaknesses most frequently mentioned with regard to Binoche are her strong French accent as well as her difficulties in handling her doubling as Cathy and Catherine (cf. Francke 1992: 60). One weakness with regard to Fiennes is obviously the whig that he is wearing, which seems like an unintended meta-heritage comment.

One of the greatest difficulties for a director who wants to film *Wuthering Heights* is to decide which narrative perspective she is going to choose. In the novel, Mr Lockwood, the new tenant of Thrushcross Grange, is the first main narrator and the nurse, friend, and servant Ellen Dean, called Nelly, is the second, narrating the longest passages of the story by far. Whereas the 1939 film version adheres quite closely to these points of narrative – it even places Nelly in an armchair in front of the fireplace – the version of 1992 introduces Emily Brontë in person as the narrator. We see Emily Brontë (played by Sinéad O'Connor) on a walk over the moors and hear her voice (as voice-over) first talk about her plans to write a story and later comment on time shifts. This peculiar narrative structure provides a frame which stresses the story told as a fictitious product and implies that the film does not claim historical verisimilitude. In my opinion, the introduction of Emily Brontë as narrator reinforces the author as initiator of discursive practises and helps spreading the so-called 'Brontë myth' and the literary industry linked to it, which has been persuasively described by Lucasta Miller in her book *The Brontë Myth* (2002). By stressing the fictitious character of the story depicted, the film tries to bestow a special status to itself, which I think is the status of a 'Hollywood romance'. Together with what Lizzie Francke calls the film's "Gainsborough-nesque splendour" (Francke 1992: 60), the film's self-referentiality has the object of establishing the film as the new and contemporary version of William Wyler's film and therefore as the more appropriate Hollywood version of *Wuthering Heights*.

The British ITV television version of 1998, directed by David Skynner,[1] is a low-key, 'no frills', anti-heritage production which concentrates on social realism instead of Hollywood glamour. While the 1992 version fetishises costumes, especially the dresses worn by Binoche, the 1998 version tones

---

[1]   In typical heritage style it was co-produced by London Weekend Television and WBGH from Boston.

down visual pleasure, which furthers the concentration on the inner strug-
gles of the characters and the film's social critique. Following a "politically
correct" approach in terms of social politics, it shows Heathcliff's badness as
a product of social circumstances. Interestingly, the film eliminates Nelly
Dean as the main narrator and mostly adheres to traditional, realist techniques of filming, e.g. to the general viewpoint of the camera as the invisible
and inaudible omniscient narrator. This viewpoint also removes aspects of
unreliability, for instance in Lockwood's narration, as well as the multiple-
voice narration and the multiple chronologies of the book and claims that this
is an authentic, a 'true' representation, e.g. by inserting time shifts in print or
by extreme close-ups. This style of filming, which sometimes reminds of a
documentary film, is quite appropriate for many scenes, since it not only
offers a feeling for a 'past time' but also allows the audience to distance themselves from the 'romantic' aspects of the love story that can so easily become
overwhelming as earlier film versions have shown. The 1998 version makes
clear that different visual registers are helpful for filming this novel, e.g., to
display the contrast between the carefree childhood that Heathcliff and
Cathy enjoy as long as Mr Earnshaw is alive with the cruelty that Hindley
exerts after Mr Earnshaw's death.

The departure from the female point of narration is understandable as
Nelly's presence in many scenes in the book may be found unrealistic or
disturbing in a film, especially as the audience might want to concentrate on
the dialogue of the lovers. From a feminist point of view, however, it is dis-
satisfying in at least two respects. Firstly, it underrates the important role that
Nelly plays for Heathcliff as well as for Cathy and her daughter Catherine as
a friend, mother substitute and even confidante in these motherless house-
holds. And secondly, it deprives the film-maker of interesting possibilities of
presenting the story as a complex multiple-voice narration, in which positions of minor female characters like Isabella can be taken into account. The
film-makers thus forfeit chances for "a feminist revision of the past" (cf.
Cartmell & Whelehan 1998: 5) that are offered by the book through its female
point of narration as well as implications concerning the unreliability of special narrators in certain situations. By stressing Heathcliff's point of view the
film constructs a kind of 'Northern Englishness' as a 'masculine Englishness'
in contrast to the 'Southern' and 'feminine Englishness' of most heritage
films.

Both the 1992 and the 1998 film versions keep the plot of the text and display both generations of the book, which no other film version before has
done. The sequence of events naturally becomes more rapid in each film
because of the necessary cuts, jumping quickly, e.g., from Cathy's and Heathcliff's childhood to their adulthood. This jump has been described by reviewers as too sudden and confusing in both versions. This jump is especially
problematic in the 1998 version, as Robert Cavanah, who plays Heathcliff,
looks like he is in his forties throughout the film but has to show youthful,
adolescent behaviour in most scenes. He is often shown in extremely close

shots, for instance when he shouts for the dead Cathy as an older man. These
takes are obviously meant to be emotionally disturbing, but are in fact exaggerated, over-dramatic and therefore distancing, partly due to Cavanah's
heavy make-up and his shiny dentures. As the juvenile Heathcliff he looks
nearly the same age. Again, scenes of conflicts that he has with Cathy (played
by Orla Brady) are shown with lots of shouting and extreme close-ups. Meant
to be artistic, these takes look artful and tiring. In such scenes the film's visual code seems too clever for its own good and poses the question of how far
one can go within 'realist' representation. It becomes clear that historical
authenticity in film-versions of realist novels has to be brought into accord
with an audience's viewing habits as well: less polished or blackened teeth
might be helpful, e.g, but too perfect dentures or missing teeth might over-
step such boundaries.

Still, both films also use their film techniques to achieve artistic effects,
e.g. concerning the role that letters play in the book. After Cathy is dead and
the children of the second generation are grown up, many letters go forth
and back between the Heights and the Grange. In the book, Nelly comments
on the influence that Heathcliff takes on the correspondence between his son
Linton and the young Catherine: "That part of his letter was simple, and
probably [Linton's] own. Heathcliff knew he could plead eloquently enough
for Catherine's company [...]". "[Heathcliff] kept a sharp watch over [Lin-
ton]; and, of course insisted on every line [...] being shown [...]" (Brontë
1976: 314-315). Both film versions represent this correspondence in a scene in
which Heathcliff dictates a letter to his son. The 1992 version creates an especially clever point of narration here by representing this dictation as a formu-
lation of Heathcliff's longing addressed to the dead Cathy. After a shot of the
painting of the dead Cathy we see Heathcliff through a window, saying
"dearest Catherine". Only after the film cuts first to Cathy's daughter Catherine reading the letter in bed and then to Linton writing the letter do we
realise that Heathcliff has not (only) been talking to himself, but has (primarily) been dictating a letter to Linton. The powerful impression that remains
with the viewer, however, is Heathcliff's yearning for a reunion with his
beloved Cathy.

Both film versions follow the natural symbolism of the text and try to
transport the passionate emotions of the characters through the image of the
bleak, uninhabitable landscape of the Yorkshire moors. Also, the weather
persuasively mirrors the characters' feelings like it does in the text. The scene
in which Nelly tells Heathcliff about Cathy's death and Heathcliff curses the
dead Cathy is very close to the book in both film versions and reproduced
with Nelly and her comments. This scene is certainly one of those key moments of great intensity and stimulation that stay in the audience's memory
irrespective of the medium. The 1992 version sets this scene and another
crucial scene at the impressive Malham Rocks in North Yorkshire. In my
view, this location creates an astonishing effect as the Malham Rocks seem to
symbolise the love that Cathy feels for Heathcliff, which she earlier describes:

"My love for Linton is like the foliage in the woods. Time will change it [...] as winter changes the trees—my love for Heathcliff resembles the eternal rocks beneath—a source of little visible delight, but necessary." (Brontë 1976: 101-102) To witness Heathcliff's curse in such a striking setting has a strong effect that can be better described in terms of *excess* than *lack* of meaning, which makes clear that Imelda Whelehan is completely right in arguing that it is not fruitful to regard adaptations of literary texts as necessarily lacking the complexity, substance or force of its original (cf. Whelehan 1999: 16) – an argument still brought forward by some critics (cf. Faulstich 2003: 139).

The image of a rural England presented here is not so much a pastoral one, but that of a bleak country that defies cultivation. As we see, the 1992 version concentrates on Heathcliff's desire for Cathy and relies very much on Ralph Fiennes's smouldering eyes (cf. Haughton). Fiennes's ability to portray desire and despair is also important for the scene in which he comes to see the dead Cathy. In the book, Nelly narrates this incident as follows:

> [...] Heathcliff spent his nights [...] outside [...].
> I was conscious of his design to enter, if he could; [...] I went and opened one of the windows, moved by his perseverance to give him a chance of bestowing on the fading image of his idol one final adieu.
> He did not omit to avail himself of the opportunity, cautiously and briefly: too cautiously to betray his presence by the slightest noise. Indeed, I shouldn't have discovered that he had been there, except for the disarrangement of the drapery about the corpse's face, and for observing on the floor a curl of light hair, fastened with a silver thread, which, on examination, I ascertained to have been taken from a locket hung round Catherine's neck. Heathcliff had opened the trinket and cast out its contents, replacing them by a black lock of his own. I twisted the two, and enclosed them together. (Brontë 1976: 205)

As the film version abstains from Nelly as narrator in this as in most scenes, Heathcliff has to enter himself and break into the Grange, which he does neither cautiously nor briefly. He cuts his hand when he smashes the window, throws away the locket and grabs the body of his dead beloved with his bleeding hand. This scene certainly creates a strong emotional impact and, in retrospect, gains interesting intertextual cinematic features as Ralph Fiennes's outburst and violent crying in this scene are very close to those in *The English Patient* (1996) when he carries the dead body of Katherine Clifton (played by Kristin Scott Thomas) from the cave to the aeroplane. The touching effect of Heathcliff's complex emotions is heightened by the strangely atmospheric music composed by Ryuichi Sakamoto.

Whereas the 1992 version makes the female dead body its fetish, the 1998 version mainly concentrates on the abuse of Heathcliff's body. When Heathcliff is brought from Liverpool to the Heights as a child we see bruises and scars on his body. He is shown as thankful and devoted to old Mr Earnshaw who saved him. After Mr Earnshaw's death Heathcliff is continuously abused by Hindley and as an adult beaten by Hindley and Joseph. Cathy suffers with Heathcliff, who she feels attracted to in physical as well as in spiritual terms. The social realism of the 1998 version especially helps in providing a strong motivation for Cathy to marry Edgar. Cathy's acceptance of Edgar's offer of marriage is shown as a result of the insufferable circumstances under which she has to live with Hindley and Heathcliff, because Hindley is always drunk and Heathcliff's sexual advances get more and more explicit. Her social status allows for hardly any self-empowerment with respect to her own body as well as to her financial situation. By cutting from Heathcliff's sexual harassment to Hindley's alcoholism and then to Edgar's kind treatment the film makes clear how difficult Cathy's situation is and impressively represents her subjectivity and thought processes. However, by presenting Heathcliff's villainy entirely as a product of social circumstances and maltreatment the film ignores important character traits of Heathcliff and also creates scenes that are highly ambiguous in their political correctness in terms of gender politics. The scene of Cathy's madness, confinement and death is cut to show that it happens parallel to Heathcliff's rape of Isabella. This cutting of the takes has the effect that Cathy's affliction and Heathcliff's behaviour are portrayed as connected with the Lintons and even as partly caused by Edgar Linton. Heathcliff's sexual abuse of Isabella is thus shown in a 'sensitive' light, playing down the brutality of the rape. The parallelism with the sad vision of the mad, pale, dying Cathy conceals the actual harm that Heathcliff has done not only to Edgar, but even more so to Isabella. Still, the film's realist design to be historically authentic makes obvious how conservative, nostalgic, and 'cleansed' all earlier film versions of *Wuthering Heights* are: the portrayal of issues like poverty and starvation, cruelty and ethnicity, have long had to make way for a one-sided reading of the novel as a great love story. Many of these aspects offered by the novel still remain to be tackled by future film versions.

As I have shown, both film versions can boast scenes that are subtle in many respects and succeed in transferring an authentic impression. Several key moments have been transported from the novel into the films, sometimes by close representation of setting and dialogue, sometimes more freely with impressive usage of cinematic means. Quite a few scenes create a strong emotional or intellectual impact comparable to or even exceeding that of the original text even if they do not follow it scrupulously. What seems central to me is the aesthetic presentation in the films which is so closely linked to the moral ideas. As I made clear, *Wuthering Heights* is "infinitely less adaptable" than a Jane Austen novel because it is so difficult to appropriate the novel's multiple narration as well as its great variety of passionate characters. The documentary style of filming of *The Other Boleyn Girl* or the *Dogme95* style of Mike Mundell's *Hamlet* of 2000 (cf. Brusberg-Kiermeier 2003: 340-341) in combination with other new or non-realist filming techniques might well prove suitable for filming *Wuthering Heights* in future, because the traditional heritage film of the 'Janespotting' type can hardly represent the novel's special aesthetics and metaphysical aspects or its social criticism and complex moral values.

Bibliography

Aarseth, J. Espen (1997), *Cybertext: Perspectives on Ergodic Literature*, Baltimore: Johns Hopkins University Press.

Brontë, Emily (1976), *Wuthering Heights*, ed. Hilda Marsden & Ian Jack. Oxford: Clarendon.

Brusberg-Kiermeier, Stefani (2003), "'God has given you one face, and you make yourselves another': Recent Film-versions of Shakespeare's *Hamlet*", in Ewald Mengel, Hans-Jörg Schmid & Michael Steppat, eds., *Proceedings Anglistentag 2002 Bayreuth*, Trier: Wissenschaftlicher Verlag Trier, 333-342.

Cardwell, Sarah (2002), *Adaptation Revisited. Television and the Classic Novel*, Manchester – New York: Manchester University Press.

Cartmell, Deborah & Imelda Whelehan (1998), "Introduction – Sisterhoods: Across the Literature/Media Divide", in Deborah Cartmell, I.Q. Hunter, Heidi Kaye & Imelda Whelehan, eds., *Sisterhoods: Across the Literature/Media Divide*, London – Sterling, VA: Pluto Press, 1-15.

-----, eds. (1999), *Adaptations. From Text to Screen, Screen to Text*, London – New York: Routledge.

Cartmell, Deborah (1999), "Introduction", in Cartmell & Whelehan, eds., 23-28.

Faulstich, Werner (2003), "Versionen von *Wuthering Heights*: Zur transmedialen Rezeptionsgeschichte eines Romanklassikers", *Sprache und Literatur* 92, 118-140.

Francke, Lizzie (1992), "*Wuthering Heights*", *Sight and Sound*, 2:6, 60.

Giddings, Robert & Erica Sheen, eds. (2000), *The Classic Novel from Page to Screen*, Manchester: Manchester University Press.

Griem, Julika & Eckart Voigts-Virchow (2002), "Filmnarratologie: Grundlagen, Tendenzen und Beispielanalysen", in Vera & Ansgar Nünning, eds., *Erzähltheorie transgenerisch, intermedial, interdisziplinär*, Trier: Wissenschaftlicher Verlag Trier, 155-183.

Haugthon, Elspeth, "Apollo Movie Guide's Review of *Wuthering Heights*", http://apolloguide.com/mov_fullrev.asp?CID=509&RID=1453

Holderness, Graham (1985), *Wuthering Heights*, Milton Keynes – Philadelphia: Open University Press.

McFarlane, Brian (1996), *Novel into Film. An Introduction to the Theory of Adaptation*, Oxford: Clarendon.

Miller, Lucasta (2002), *The Brontë Myth*, London: Vintage.

Rauth, Heidemarie (1974), *Emily Brontës Roman "Wuthering Heights" als Quelle für Bühnen- und Filmversionen*, Innsbruck: Kommissionsverlag.

Sheen, Erica (2000a), "Introduction", in Giddings & Sheen, eds., 2-13.

----- (2000b), "'Where the garment gapes': faithfulness and promiscuity in the 1995 BBC *Pride and Prejudice*", in Giddings & Sheen, eds., 14-30.

Whelehan, Imelda (1999), "Adaptations: The contemporary dilemmas", in Cartmell & Whelehan, eds., 3-19.

Transnational Productions
–
Transnational Classrooms

Angela Krewani

Heritage as International Film Format

My paper will trace the international developments of British heritage drama and especially the alliances it has formed with Hollywood culture. My first thesis is that heritage culture facilitated the transformation of a televisual aesthetics into film production and into the cinema. In view of this development, I want to focus on the economic structure of contemporary Hollywood production which has definitely turned away from exclusive film production in favour of a production and distribution of visual merchandise for a variety of different screen technologies such as cinema, video, CD and DVD. Thus, my second thesis understands the conversion of televisual forms into Hollywood cinema as the expression of a change within film production and its underlying organisational and economic structures. The system 'Hollywood' has stepped back from the production of film as film (for the mass audience) into distributing manifold products which vaguely refer to the filmic tradition.

One of the important aspects of heritage is the genre's origin in television, namely as episode drama. Productions such as Granada's *Brideshead Revisited (1981)* and *The Jewel in the Crown* (1984) convey an elite literary tradition into televisual, serial form, at enormous production cost. At £4.5 million, *Brideshead Revisited* still figures as one of the most expensive television productions to date (Roddick 1985). This genre clearly camouflages its origins within television. Instead, it revolves around literary traditions which it reformulates on the screen. Especially credits, titles and intertitles voice the intermedial relationship.[1]

Looking at the 1970s and 1980s, we discover a variety of literary productions within British Television: For instance, Charles Dickens' *Our Mutual Friend* (BBC 1976), Jane Austen's *Sense and Sensibility* (BBC 1971), *Pride and Prejudice* (BBC 1979) with the script by Fay Weldon. These works clearly carry on the BBC's impulse to broadcast adaptations based on the English literary tradition. The same impulse has guided the BBC's adaptations of Shakespeare since the 1950s.

After the general acceptance of the literary adaptation as television drama within the structure of public broadcasting, commercial television stepped in. Granada's *Brideshead Revisited* (1981) and *The Jewel in the Crown* (1984), both having been produced with impressive financial backup, represent the first

---

[1] Compare this camouflage aesthetics with, for instance, Dennis Potter's *The Singing Detective,* which unquestionably points to its origins within television and sets up an intermedial reflection between the respective media of literature, film and television.

steps towards the internationalisation and commercialisation of the form. *Brideshead Revisited* was produced by Granada TV and was distributed by ITV for the UK market and by PBS for the American market. *The Jewel in the Crown* follows the same pattern. Once again it is produced by Granada and distributed by PBS for the American market. The first step towards an internationalisation of a national television production has been taken. And one of the needs of this development is the commercialisation of the form.

One could speculate about PBS's motives to enter the fray. One of its intents may be the wish to confirm an image as television for the educated classes by referring to high-brow productions such as English literary adaptations.

A further step towards the hybridization of the respective media took place with the launch of Channel Four in 1982. Since Channel Four had no production facilities of its own, film production was outsourced to private production units – and distributed in cinema and on television nearly simultaneously. Now the weak British film production was taken over by a television station and labelled 'New British Cinema'. In the wake of this development the double faced, Dr. Jekyll and Mr Hyde imagery of the New British Cinema was completely established, as Thomas Elsaesser (1993: 53) states:

> On one side: home counties, country houses, public schools, sports, white flannel, rules and games; Edwardian England, Decline of the Empire, Privilege and Treason, male bonding, female hysteria. On the side of the counter myth: Scotland, Liverpool, London, dockland, clubland, disco, football, punk, race riots, National Front, working-class males, violent and articulate, working-class women, sexy, and self-confident.

Within this set of oppositional norms, heritage films have experienced a further commercial upgrade and consequently a first encounter between British television and American film production has taken place. Having focussed on literary adaptations, the American producer Merchant-Ivory co-produced some of the most successful British heritage feature films for the time being such as *Heat and Dust* (1983), *Howards End* (1992) and *Room with a View* (1986).

Especially *Room with a View* figures as co-production between the broadcasting station Channel Four, the British National Film Finance Corporation and the American based producer Merchant-Ivory. This kind of financial structure encourages the development outlined above: An original television production – we have a BBC production of *Room with a View* dating from 1973 – is restaged as film – with the cooperation of a television station, in this case Channel Four. Throughout the eighties, the British-American, television-film hybrid gained international recognition and some success at the box office. Within American cinema culture, the elite literary adaptation could figure as 'high-brow entertainment': it drew an audience into the cinema, which usually bypassed the more popular blockbuster. Restricting these productions to a small screen, the multiplex cinemas nevertheless could establish an art house charm within American cinema culture (cf. Hipsky 1994).

Thus, heritage films, in the first place literary adaptations, made their way into American cinemas. After this ground-breaking passage, there was no stopping them. Heritage style literary adaptations are usually produced as co-productions to enter the American market as television drama. We find *Pride and Prejudice* (1995) as co-production between the BBC and the US Arts & Entertainment Channel, *Mansfield Park* (1983), co-produced by the BBC and the US Lionheart Television, and *Sense and Sensibility* (1985), a BBC production with American distribution by CBS/Fox.

Hollywood had smelled blood – the British television productions were successful on the American market, by the mid-1990s there had been a test period of more than ten years. Hollywood was ready to adopt this recipe of literary adaptation, heritage film and televisual aesthetics.

This step from British television into Hollywood film production is not only due to a hostile takeover from Hollywood but it is also a consequence of the massive conflation of film and television in Great Britain. In the wake of Channel Four's film policy, a variety of small production companies were set up in order to produce film for television stations. This example was followed by the BBC with its production policy in 1993, which stated that from now on, 25% of the broadcasting station's production was to be delivered to independent production companies. The BBC re-named its 'drama' department (drama was a term which had always referred to television production) the 'film' department.

Owing to the initiation of broadcasting stations into film production and Hollywood's growing interest in heritage literary screen culture, the door to British-American co-production has been opened. In the wake of this development, we encounter film production taking over the well-tried televisual recipe of heritage literary adaptation with its references to literary culture and a lavish *mise-en-scène*. Under a new label, these television productions were released as film within the traditional 90 minutes length: Television drama was shortened, given a film director, for instance Patricia Rozema, the Canadian director with *Mansfield Park* in 1999 and Ang Lee from Taiwan who directed *Sense and Sensibility* in 1995. The 1990s were dominated by heritage as film production. The label 'film' (rather than 'TV play' or 'TV drama') is supported by a film director and some famous actors. There is usually a combination of American movie actors such as, for instance, Gwyneth Paltrow, cast with notoriously 'English' actors such as Hugh Grant and Colin Firth, who moved from television series (such as the 1995 *Pride and Prejudice* 1995) into film.

As far as the production policies of these films are concerned, we still find the participation of television on the British side. The 1999 version of *Mansfield Park*, instructed by the Canadian director Patricia Rozema, is a co-production of the BBC, the Arts Council and Miramax, representing the traditional formula. In some other instances, however, this kind of production has been completely taken over by Hollywood. This is the case with *Emma* (1996), directed by Douglas McGrath, a minor American director, starring

Gwyneth Paltrow, who has come to be almost synonymous with British heritage since *Shakespeare in Love*. In a similar way, the Ang Lee version of *Sense and Sensibility* (1995) is a complete American production, with Columbia and Mirage as production companies.

Having been produced at the end of the 1990s, both adaptations of Jane Austen's novel stand at the far end of a development that was spawned by British television: the televisual literary adaptation, having once been produced as mini-series, has now become a genre within Hollywood film production. Britishness is now achieved by actors such as Hugh Grant and Emma Thompson. But the excessive *mise-en-scène* does not differ from the original televisual production in any aspect. Since these films originate in television and carry the dramatic legacy of the theatre, they are – compared to a Hollywood production – extremely cheap, as the $6 million production cost of *Emma* proves.

Besides the economic facts, another important aspect of these film products can be found in the development of their genre. In literary theory, Jane Austen's novels tend to be categorised as 'comedy of manners', the behaviour of a small set of middle class individuals is reflected upon, either in literature or in the televisual or filmic adaptation.

Having established the 'comedy of manners' as a filmic genre within Hollywood and the international film market, the genre can be transferred to a contemporary setting, as productions like *Four Weddings and a Funeral* (1994), *French Kiss* (1995), *Clueless* (1995), *Notting Hill* (1999), *Chocolat* (2000), and *Bridget Jones's Diary* (2001) amply demonstrate.

Interestingly enough, apart from having established Hugh Grant's fame as the 'icon of Britishness', *Four Weddings and a Funeral* was produced in the wake of Channel Four's success as a cinema producer. *Four Weddings and a Funeral* is a co-production of Channel Four Films, Working Title, and the American company Polygram. With Andie McDowell as Grant's American romantic interest, it sports a team of British/American actors, in the same way as *Notting Hill* (1999) does with Hugh Grant and Julia Roberts. *Notting Hill* is also of mixed origins, with Working Title as the English, and PolyGram the American Partner. This transatlantic alliance is once again mirrored on the screen with Hugh Grant and Andie McDowell. Both *Notting Hill* and *Four Weddings and a Funeral* feed on the Austen 'comedy of manners' tradition: we find impaired lovers, social mismatches, inadequate behaviour, misunderstandings, overheard dialogues, inhibitions, critical financial situations, etc. Thus the original televisual literary adaptation is re-written within contemporary societies and their manners. Englishness – or heritage – is delivered through 'genre'.

The film *Bridget Jones's Diary* goes even further within establishing heritage as a transnational category. The film was produced with a minimum of English money from Working Title. The largest share came from Studio Canal, a subsidiary of the media company Vivendi Universal, which is part of the French conglomerate Vivendi. The copyright is owned by the American independent Miramax.

The actors Colin Firth and Hugh Grant guarantee Britishness; both are well known from Jane Austen films – Hugh Grant from *Sense and Sensibility* and Colin Firth from the 1995 version of *Pride and Prejudice*. The main character, played by Colin Firth, is even named after Mr Darcy in *Pride and Prejudice*, where the role was played by the same actor. The liner notes in the DVD version quote Helen Fielding's remark about having modelled the story on Jane Austen's *Pride and Prejudice* and the miniseries' leading actor.

As such, Jane Austen's English 'comedy of manners' has been abstracted, transferred to current circumstances and has been constantly re-written in the no man's land of international co-productions. In this sense, English heritage culture has become an open sign that can be applied to a variety of cultural situations, providing that the genre guarantees the origins and the casting brings in actors who can function as icons for national stereotypes.

One of the most interesting examples in this context is the film *Chocolat* (2000), which I would label French heritage – a formidable example of the transnational qualities of heritage culture, since there is no French participation in the movie: Heritage – in this regard 'Frenchness' – is established through casting, with Juliette Binoche in a key role. Interestingly enough, the British production company Working Title dominates this kind of contemporary heritage. It has participated in the production of *Four Weddings and a Funeral*, *Bridget Jones's Diary* and *French Kiss* (1995). The latter is another contemporary heritage 'comedy of manners', which is set in France and which trades images of 'Paris' and 'Frenchness', in this context contrasting with the American identity. Thus Working Title, having started with working class images of Great Britain in Stephen Frears' *My Beautiful Laundrette* and *Sammie and Rosie Get Laid*, or, less well known, Hanif Kureishi's *London Kills Me* or Derek Jarman's *Edward II*, has transferred its activities towards the transnational output of contemporary heritage.

The internationalisation and the abstraction of genre points to the second thesis of this paper: the change within Hollywood film production. Contemporary, international heritage productions underline the changed economic structure of Hollywood film production.

This essay does not allow for a detailed history of the studios and production companies involved, but a few points should be highlighted. As mentioned above, Working Title has developed from a company involved in British film production in co-operation with a broadcasting station, towards a transatlantic co-operation partner. On the other side we find Miramax, the former small independent studio that became part of the Disney Company. The history of Miramax can be regarded as prototypical for the development from a more independent production company into a viable part of a diversified production system with flexible production structures, usually labelled 'New Hollywood'. Having started as a small company in 1979, Miramax became better known with the release of Errol Morris' documentary *The Thin*

Blue Line (1988). The breakthrough came with Neil Jordan's *The Crying Game* (1992), which received $26.6 million in North American rentals.[2]

When independent production and distribution had reached its lowest point, there were several bankruptcies. At the same time, as the 1990s took shape, the Walt Disney Company feature film division was losing steam, Touchstone and Hollywood, their distribution arms, were failing. By the spring of 1993, the Weinstein brothers agreed to bring Miramax into the Disney camp, the executive team stayed – the company received distribution power. (Wasser 2001: 180-183). As such, Miramax could distribute videos through Disney's Buena Vista, the top home video distributor. (Please note how many films have been produced and distributed through Miramax since then.)

Video is the dominant revenue within 'New Hollywood'. Film merely functions as a representative sales label. It may suffice in the context of this paper to provide only some figures that compare the major studio's revenues from film and video release for the year 2000: within the American market it is 21% is generated from cinema and 51% from video (the rest are several forms of TV sales.) Worldwide, it is: 24% cinema 46% video (Wasser 2001: 182-83).

In conclusion, it can be surmised that British heritage films developed within British television, and entered the Anglo-American market through commercial television's enterprises. After having proved their value for an educated audience, either in art-house cinema or for video sale or rental, Hollywood studios came in: But not in the form of the traditional Hollywood major (which has not existed since the 1950s), but as part of a major company that holds a variety of media branches. Heritage – as genre and visual structure – comes in very handy for this kind of business dominated by video release, since it is a thoroughly televisual form – which means, it is the perfect aesthetic experience for the small screen.

Bibliography

Elsaesser, Thomas (1993), "Images for Sale: The 'New' British Cinema", in Lester Friedman, ed., *British Cinema and Thatcherism. Fires Were Started*, London: UCL Press, 52–69.

Higson, Andrew (2003), *English Heritage, English Cinema*, Oxford: Oxford University Press.

Hipsky, Martin A. (1994), "Anglophil(m)ia. Why does America watch Merchant-Ivory Movies?", *Journal of Popular Film and Television*, 22:3, 98-107.

Roddick, Nick (1985), "New audiences, new films", in Nick Roddick & Martin Auty, eds., *British Cinema Now*, London: British Film Institute, 19–30.

Wasser, Frederick (2001), *Veni, Vidi, Video. The Hollywood Empire and the VCR*, Austin: University of Texas Press.

---

[2] Incidentally, this is another British product, which was financed through Channel Four and British Screen.

Carola Surkamp

A Plea for Varied Readings: Teaching British Heritage Films to German Students[1]

1 The Potential Role of Heritage Films in the Foreign Language Classroom

Most books and articles in the field of British heritage films, costume dramas and classic TV serials deal with the audiovisual texts themselves and/or their specific context of production. In particular, questions of adaptation and genre, of the construction of national and gender identities, of a distinct heritage aesthetics, as well as of the films' role within the British heritage industry have been under constant and intense discussion since the 1990s. Of much lesser interest, however, have been the various facets of the reception of heritage films. Therefore, I would like to focus on the context of their reception – more specifically, the potential role of British heritage films in the foreign language classroom. I will explore questions that arise when one teaches English literature and culture through films such as *A Passage to India*, *Howards End*, *Sense and Sensibility*, *The Remains of the Day*, or *Elizabeth* at German schools and universities.

In general, films constitute an important field in the foreign language classroom for various reasons (cf. also Surkamp 2004a). Because of the impact of the visualization of characters and events, learners tend to respond more strongly to a story when seeing a film than when reading a book; films provoke viewers to react emotionally and comment on the story. Therefore, films provide occasions for discussions in class and they incite learners to talk and write in the foreign language. Films are also analyzed on the discourse level in order to make learners aware of the specific cinematic (i.e. audio-visual) means of story-telling and to enable them to develop what is referred to as film or media literacy.[2] And last but not least, since foreign language films present fictitious stories and human experiences in a foreign cultural environment, they enable learners to gain an insight into other ways of life and

---

1 I would like to thank Marc Colavincenzo, Sandra Heistrüvers, and Ellen Surkamp for their very helpful comments on an earlier version of this article.
2 Cf. also the increasing relevance of visual studies, which emphasize the growing importance of a visual mediation of knowledge and a visual construction of world models in our media age today.

into values, norms, and world views different from their own, thus contributing to the important goal of intercultural learning.

When using a specific film genre in the foreign language classroom – such as, for example, the heritage film if we regard it as being a genre – one can consider further in what way this genre can be useful in the teaching of English Literature and Culture. Why should we make use of heritage films in the foreign language classroom at all? One reason for using heritage films is that many of these films are adaptations of canonic novels and plays which are often dealt with at German schools and universities, so one can work with the book and the film. The use of heritage films might even be a way of inciting students to read longer texts, thus running counter to the tendency to deal mainly with short texts in the foreign language classroom. But heritage films are also interesting from the point of view of cultural studies because through heritage films, both in the conventional format of the 1980s and the alternative, revisionist shape of the 1990s, students can learn a great deal about different aspects of English life – about concepts of Englishness and national identity, of class and gender, as well as about British cinema. It is this cultural aspect of heritage films that will be placed in the foreground of my article. I will begin by outlining the problem of different readings of heritage films and seeking answers to the question of how they come into being. I will then illustrate in what way we can deal with different readings of heritage films in the foreign language classroom if we want to interpret them from a cultural perspective.

2   The Problem of Different Readings of Heritage Films and How They Come into Being

How precisely we should read heritage films in class is a very controversial issue. Heritage films have been subject to a number of different and often conflicting interpretations over the last few years. This raises the question of which reading should be preferred when dealing with these films in the foreign language classroom and why? Should heritage films of the 1980s, for example, be read as celebrations of a conservative vision of the national past, as projections of a 'country house' version of Englishness, or as women's pictures and presentations of personal stories?

In order to answer these questions, one has first to explain how different readings of one and the same heritage film come into being. These are not only the result of textual ambiguities or due to the fact that the heritage film is quite a hybrid genre, but rather depend on a number of different factors, for example on the questions and aims of individual interpretations. The focus of interest can be the film itself, i.e. the story (characters, events, settings) or the discourse (field sizes, points of view, camera angles and movements, camera speed, editing); the costumes, the actors and actresses, intertextual references to other films or issues such as class, gender, or race; the relation between a film and its various contexts, such as the circumstances of production, promotion, and reception. The reading of a film also depends on the method of interpretation (close reading, discourse analysis, etc.), on the literary and cultural theories that are used explicitly or implicitly when approaching a film (film theory, reception theory, intertextual theory, etc.), on the historical context of the reception, and on the interpreter's individual set of preconditions, which includes, for example, his or her ideological position, nationality, and background (is she or he a common viewer, the producer or promoter of a certain film, a professional film critic, a cultural commentator, an academic, a German student?).

To illustrate how these factors influence the reading of a film, I will briefly turn to the major ways of reading films such as *Chariots of Fire, Maurice* or *Howards End* which critics have provided in the last ten years.[3] An important framework for studying films like these has been offered by the heritage industry. Andrew Higson (1995), for example, contextualized the work of Merchant-Ivory by situating their films within the broader field of heritage discourses, which constituted an important part of life in England in the 1980s and 1990s and which played a dominant role in public discussions of these films. For him, as for many other critics, films such as *Howards End* played an active role in celebrating the culture, the values, and the lifestyle of the privileged classes through their artful and spectacular projection of the picturesque green landscapes of southern England, of luxurious country-house settings, gardens, interior designs, décor, furnishings, and period costumes. Heritage films were thus conceived of as projecting a conventional vision of the national past and as articulating a nostalgic, conservative, upper-class version of Englishness. From a traditional, conservative perspective, the films, naturally, seemed charming (cf. Higson 2003: 46-47); in addition, they were conducive to a new boom of historical tourism. Within leftist cultural critique, however, the same films have been dismissed, precisely because of their traditional, conservative, elite and narrow concept of Englishness which does not allow for regional and social diversity or hybrid identities, and which seemed to transform the select heritage of the most privileged social strata into a national heritage (cf. Higson 1993: 114, Monk 2002: 179).[4]

A more positive evaluation of heritage films can be found in the works of feminist and gay critics. Whereas Higson's early interpretation focuses on the complex interplay between the films and contemporary heritage discourses, Claire Monk treats heritage films in terms of sexual and gender politics. She bases her interpretation on the fact that many of these films present personal

---

[3] For a summary of the debate about different readings, cf. Hill (1999: 73-99). Cf. also Higson (2003: chap. 5), who compares different readings of *Howards End*.

[4] Cf. also Parker (1994), who considers heritage films as cinematic equivalents of Laura Ashley. For the role of films in the constitution of a national identity, cf. Richards (1997) and Street (1997).

stories with a central romance plot and an emphasis on friendships and domestic life.[5] In this way, they do not offer a view of history from above, but
rather move to the centre of interest characters that are often marginalized in
mainstream cinema – such as women, gays and lesbians, or the lower classes
– thus giving space to the articulation of their concerns. From this perspective
heritage films "provide a critique of social repression and sexual politics
which can be seen as progressive" (cf. Church Gibson 2000: 115) – above all
in the Edwardian context, in which many of the stories are situated – even if
the films are quite chaste compared with the sexual explicitness of mainstream cinema. Precisely for this reason, however, critics on the left see the
films as "sexually repressive, 'body-hating', and incapable of addressing
popular sensibilities" (Higson 2003: 47).

Apart from the different focus which results from the critics' interests and
ideological positions, divergent readings of heritage films have emerged
because of the tension between stabilizing images and destabilizing narratives. Whereas the plots, the conceptualizations of the characters and the
relationships between them often point to a quite liberal world view by, for
example, making social transgression possible,[6] the visual display of heritage
property seems to suggest a much more conservative perspective:

> At the level of the *image* [...] an exclusive, elite, English version of national heritage
> is displayed in all its well-tended finery. Visually, the impression is that England is
> a wonderful, desirable place of tradition and privilege. At the level of the *narrative*
> [...] that heritage is often unstable, at risk, in disarray; social and cultural tradi-
> tions are exposed as repressive; privilege is revealed as exploitation. So many of
> the films insistently scratch away at the idea of an essential England, noting the in-
> stability, the flux in identity, the hybrid quality of Englishness. Many of the films
> also dramatize the dissolution of a particular version of England and Englishness,
> the decay and the decadence of aristocratic life and its hold on the reins of power,
> or the loss of inheritance. In this sense, the narratives of the films seem much more
> radical, questioning the desirability of the lifestyle of those who inhabit these
> spaces. (*Ibid.: 77*)

Therefore, the manner in which heritage films visualize the past produces a
nostalgic viewing position that stands in stark contrast to the irony and the
social criticism so often evoked by the narrative. Depending on which textual
level an interpretation focuses upon – on the visual track or on the level of
the story – heritage films can thus be read "*both* as conservative, nostalgic,
escapist texts, *and* as much more liberal dramas" (*ibid.: 75*).

But one and the same image can be read quite differently, one and the
same form can fulfil contrasting functions in the eyes of different recipients.
Narrative modes and cinematic means are not meaning-producing in and of

---

[5]   Cf. also Dyer (1994), who argues that the films display the emotionalism of repressed
      feelings.
[6]   A case in point is *Howards End*, in which the illegitimate child of Leonard Bast and Helen
      Schlegel inherits Howards End and, thus, on a symbolic level, England (cf. Higson 1996:
      239 and Church Gibson 2000: 116).

themselves. From the point of view of cognitive narratology, it is rather the individual recipient's focus of interest, ideological orientation, and theoretical background which leads him or her to assign meaning and coherence to narrative structures and visual techniques.[7] This is obvious with regard to the narrative style and the visual presentation of many heritage films which have been interpreted quite differently. The narrative style of heritage films is generally described as slow-paced, episodic and de-dramatized, emphasizing character, place, atmosphere and milieu (cf. *ibid.*: 37). As far as the visual presentation is concerned, there is a preference for long takes and deep staging, and for long and medium shots (rather than for close-ups and rapid or dramatic cutting), as well as for camera movements around period settings and props (cf. *ibid.*: 38). Both the narrative style and the visual presentation have thus been interpreted as offering the spectator splendid views of the grandeur of the past with the result of transforming narrative space into heritage space – "a space for the display of heritage properties rather than for the enactment of dramas" (*ibid.*: 39). From this perspective, narrative style and visual techniques of heritage films can be seen to indicate a certain kind of 'artistry' (cf. Hill 1999: 81), fulfilling an aesthetic function rather than a narrative one: they are often not employed to support the causal development of the story, but "in ways which are ostentatious [...] or just visually pleasing in themselves" (*ibid.*: 80-81).

The display of heritage, however, is not the only way of making sense of the images in so-called heritage films. As Monk shows, the same images can be read for their narrative symbolism. Far from being narratively meaningless, the slow-moving narrative style and the episodic plot in many heritage films, for example, can provide space for conversational exchange and for the detailed exploration of character traits and feelings. The specific visual presentation of a certain scene can function as the *mise-en-scène* of intense emotion and desire, of romance and repression (cf. Higson 2003: 40). From this point of view, "props act not as spokespersons for the heritage industry but as symbolic indications of the inner life of the characters" (*ibid.*: 85). In a similar way, the picturesque gardens in many heritage films can be semanticized in that they contribute to the expression of the characters' feelings and moods.[8]

---

7 Cognitive narratology analyzes the cognitive processes that take place within the reader's mind when he or she is trying to make sense of a text. In contrast to constructivist approaches, which have been criticized for overemphasizing the role of the reader, cognitive narratology takes into account the fact that the process of constructing meaning is also guided by a text's formal and structural features. This insight into the complex interplay between so-called bottom-up (i.e., data-driven) and top-down (i.e., conceptually driven) reading processes makes students aware of the fact that every understanding of texts depends both on cognitive processes that are triggered by the text itself and on the readers' individual frames of reception. For an overview of the main concepts of cognitive narratology, cf. Zerweck (2002).

8 For an analysis of the picturesque garden in heritage films, cf. the article by Raimund Borgmeier in this volume.

To illustrate that one and the same image can be read differently depending on the interpretative judgement of the viewer, Higson refers to a scene from *Howards End*. In this scene, Henry Wilcox is showing Margaret Schlegel round his London house and proposes to her on the stairs. Higson describes in what way the images in this scene can be interpreted both as heritage display and as an expression of the characters' emotional lives:

> It is a wonderful scene, perfectly capturing the emotional turmoil of the characters, their propriety and their repressiveness. And it also has some magnificent decor, furnishings and interior designs on display. The space and the props are clearly used expressively, with the emotional distance between the characters conveyed by the distance between them on the stairs, with the staircase and the props literally overwhelming them. But there can be no denying that the scene also makes the most of the opportunity to display some fine authentic period properties, which are of course the properties of a very privileged class. (Higson 1996: 241-42)

3 How to Deal with Different Readings of Heritage Films in Class

In the context of teaching heritage films to foreign students, one has to decide how to deal with these variant readings in class. One of the first tasks of the teacher is to make his or her students realize that there is no clear form-to-function mapping in fictional texts. When I use the term 'function', I do not mean the author's or producer's intended effect or a film's actual historical effect, but rather the potential effect of a film's formal features which structure and organize the content and which, therefore, are relevant to its meaning (cf. Sommer 2000). Since films are open to different, even contradictory interpretations, and since functions are not essential traits of a film, but categories of observation, it is only in the viewing process that a specific segment of a film's potential effect is selected. According to Fluck (2002: 267) the only way to make sense of a text

> is to assume that the text is designed to do something and that the various textual elements have been arranged in the way they are in order to achieve this goal. We can only make sense of them on the assumption that they are 'functional' in relation to a particular effect they are supposed to achieve. Or, to put it differently: It is our hypothesis about the text's function that makes a text coherent and its structure 'readable'.

Thus, depending on the viewer's set of preconditions and the context of reception, one possible interpretation is chosen whereas others are rejected (Sommer 2000: 330). It is precisely because of this complex interplay between textual features and the interpretative choices and strategies involved in the viewing process that the same narrative form or visual technique can convey a number of different meanings and functions, while different forms can fulfil similar functions.[9]

As there are different ways of engaging with one and the same film, the reading of a heritage film in the foreign language classroom depends, above all, on the teaching goals that are pursued by the teacher. In German schools, films are usually used as screen adaptations of literary texts to augment the work on a novel or a play. Questions that are in the foreground of classroom discussions refer for the most part to the content of the film: are there any scenes in the book that have been left out in the film? Are there any new scenes, characters, or events in the film that are not part of the literary work? What about the beginning and the end of the film – are they similar to those in the book? This is, however, clearly not the only possible way of dealing with a film. Therefore, I would like to plead for different approaches, which take also the formal features and the context of production and reception of a film into account.

When dealing with a heritage film as a screen adaptation of a novel, one could, for example, analyze whether, and in what way the narrative style – above all the point of view and the temporal structure – of the literary work with its specific effects on the reader has been conveyed by cinematic means. In order to answer this question, students can fall back partly on their (unconsciously developed) film literacy, but they also need to acquire special knowledge in narratology and film analysis, because "[s]tudying film language makes explicit the techniques for telling a story visually, heightens students' appreciation for the art of film, and increases their awareness of how subtle cues can shade meaning" (Teasley & Wilder 1997: 26).[10]

A close reading of *The Remains of the Day* as book and film, for example, reveals that the irony of Ishiguro's novel, which is evoked by the technique of unreliable narration and the protagonist's/narrator's ongoing process of remembering the past glories of Darlington Hall (which were not exactly glories since the late Lord Darlington was deeply involved in collaboration with the Nazis), is lost to a large extent in the film version.[11] The book accen-

---

[9]   Cf. Sternberg (1982: 112), who introduced the notion of the 'Proteus Principle' to describe the "many-to-many correspondences between linguistic form and representational function".

[10] On the importance of developing specific reading (and viewing) skills, cf. also Campbell (1996: 108): "Learners cannot enjoy texts unless they possess the necessary reading skills, and by helping our students to develop these skills we can empower them to form their own interpretations of texts rather than forcing them to rely passively on works of criticism or on ready-made interpretations provided by teachers."

[11] On unreliable narration in *The Remains of the Day*, cf. Wall (1994), Phelan & Martin (1999), and Lang (2000). On unreliability in literature and film, cf. Currie (1995). Chatman (1978: 235) stresses that unreliable narration *can* become relevant in films: "Unreliable narration is a lovely effect in films, since a voice-over depicting events and existents in the story may be belied by what we see so clearly for ourselves." Cf. also: "Visuals are no more sacrosanct than words. The cinema caught up [...] with a fashion established in verbal narratives well before the turn of the century." (*Ibid.*: 237)

tuates Stevens's fears, emotions, and needs in his attempt to come to terms with his past, not least through the novel's analytical time structure, the temporal distance between the narrating I and the experiencing I, and the resulting tension between the different time levels. The film, however, focuses on the actual events and the interaction of the characters in Darlington Hall, and "through visual excess and a focus on thwarted romance" (Church Gibson 2000: 116) neuters the exposure of Stevens's self-deception and of the subjectivity of his attempts to give meaning to past events that can be ascribed to the narrative strategies of Ishiguro's novel. Therefore, when comparing a novel with its screen adaptation at the level of discourse, students can become aware of the interplay between formal features and potential effects of a novel or a film, and they can perhaps understand that heritage films have been criticized because of their insufficient reproduction of the often subversive potential of the narrative style of their literary source.[12] There is, however, sometimes a tendency in the film *The Remains of the Day* to draw the viewer's attention to Stevens's subjective viewpoint: "[O]n a couple of occasions, we find ourselves looking at events through windows and keyholes – ploys that suggest that our point of view is not omniscient but intertwined, to some extent, with Stevens's. So the film scores a limited success in suggesting that the world we see is the world as it is experienced by the central character." (Parkes 2001: 79) In addition to that, Stevens is exposed as quite an unreliable character on the story level of the film, because very often he behaves and reacts differently to what he says and thinks.[13]

Besides the analysis of heritage films as adaptations of a literary text, another possible use of heritage films in the foreign language classroom is their interpretation under the heading of *Landeskunde* (or: area studies), which constitutes an integral part of the English syllabus in Germany. Such an approach goes beyond the close reading of a film: it implies a conceptualization of films as authentic cultural products and the inclusion of their contexts of production and reception, which means, in our case, above all contemporary heritage discourses. German students, however, are normally not aware of the prominence of the heritage impulse in England in the 1980s and 1990s, which has had significant influence on the reading of, for example, the Mer-

---

[12] Cf. Higson (1993: 120): "The films [...] construct such a delightfully glossy visual surface that the ironic perspective and the narrative of social criticism diminish in their appeal for the spectator." Cf. also Higson (2003: 80). Church Gibson (2000: 116) argues with regard to the film version of *Howards End* in a similar way that its "palpable pleasure in parading the visual splendour of the past undermines the social criticism of Forster's novel". The film version of E.M. Forster's novel *A Passage to India* is a further case in point. Whereas the multiperspectivity of the book, i.e. the presentation of the fictional world from different points of view, is used for the juxtaposition of different views on British imperialism, taking also critical Indian voices into account and resulting in a rather revisionist picture of the British *Raj* (cf. Surkamp 2003), the film by Merchant-Ivory does not challenge the imperialist world view in the same way but rather takes the political dimension out of Forster's story.

[13] I am grateful to Stefani Brusberg-Kiermeier for pointing this out.

chant-Ivory films as heritage display. As there is no real equivalent to the heritage subject in Germany (there is, for example, no real translation for the notion 'heritage') and as Germans have a fractured relationship to their own past,[14] German students very often focus on the plot of these films, and this is why they generally read them as love stories.[15] In order to be able to relate the films to the world views and ideologies of the culture from which they originated, students need specific reading skills and background knowledge.

First of all, students have to be introduced to a cultural approach to literary texts and films.[16] Contrary to structuralist theories, fictional texts are not seen as closed systems and static products within culture-oriented and context-sensitive literary studies. They are rather conceptualized as being closely related to extratextual reality. This relationship between fictional texts and reality, however, is not based on mimesis: fictional texts are not documents of historical events, social facts, or cultural developments. On the contrary, a novel or a film is seen as being "an active force in its own right which is involved in the actual generation of ways of thinking and of attitudes" (Nünning 2000: 360) in so far as its formal properties not only reflect, but also influence the cultural issues of a given period (cf. *ibid.*). This insight is one of the reasons why – after the so-called communicative phase in foreign language didactics – literary texts and films have once more gained importance for the teaching of English language and culture in Germany. They are no longer seen only as objects of interpretation, which represent a foreign culture, but as cultural manifestations in their own right and as 'objects of cultural self-perception and self-reflection' (cf. Voßkamp 1999: 190). A case in point for the assumption that films play an active and constructive role "in the process of forming institutions and shaping mentalities" (Nünning 2000: 360) are heritage films. They engage in heritage discourses in that they offer a specific version of the English past and play an important role in maintaining certain images of Englishness in the public consciousness. Beyond that they are also a vital part of the heritage and tourism industry providing "what often seems to be tailor-made promotional material for attracting visitors to heritage sites" (Higson 2003: 48).

A cultural approach to films implies that the analysis of the features of a film has to be combined with cultural history, i.e. when teaching heritage films in the foreign language classroom we have to move from a description of textual phenomena to broader cultural questions and various contexts. That means students need knowledge of the context of reception, contempo-

---

[14] Cf. also Otten (1979: 96), who points out on a general level that a sense of the past is much more prominent in England than in Germany.

[15] This has been found out with the help of a questionnaire on the films *Pride and Prejudice* and *Bridget Jones's Diary* in several senior classes in a German grammar school. Although this was no representative statistical investigation, I am very grateful to Ralph Seibel and his students for taking part in my study.

[16] For the development of a cultural approach to films in the foreign language classroom, cf. Surkamp (2004b).

rary discourses of heritage, the National Trust, and the National Heritage
Acts of 1980 and 1983, which established the National Heritage Memorial
Fund and an organization to oversee the state's interests in the past, English
Heritage (established in 1984). The students have to explore the ways in
which ideas of national heritage were produced and circulated. Therefore,
the work with the films has to be supplemented by non-fictional material,
such as history texts, newspaper articles, film ads and posters, etc., which
inform the learners about the cultural climate of the period, about the English
class system, about the consolidation of the heritage industry, about the marketing campaign for a film, and about a film's actual reception. An inquiry
into the contexts of production and reception (for example, on the basis of
interviews with film directors or of film reviews) can above all provide insights into the aims of certain film versions of classic English novels and into
the actual effects they had on viewers.[17] It is only on the basis of this knowledge that German students are able to view British heritage films from a
cultural perspective.[18]

As a second step, students have to analyze the formal techniques of the
film not just as structural features, "but as narrative modes which are highly
semantized and engaged in the process of cultural construction" (Nünning
2000: 360). Some elements and formal techniques of many Merchant-Ivory
films to which the function of heritage display can be ascribed are the setting
and décor, the costumes, the camerawork, and the editing, as has been illustrated above. Therefore, possible tasks and questions in class might be: *Describe the costumes and the décor. In what way are these elements of the film's design
significant? What is the function of the sets and props? Does the movie stand out in
terms of photography or visual effects? Describe the camera movements. What did
you notice about the film's editing?* In order to go beyond a mere description of
these cinematic techniques, students have to further analyze their meanings
and potential effects: *Identify the field sizes used in scene x and comment on their
significance. What is the effect of long and medium shots only? What is achieved by
using long takes and deep staging? What might have induced the filmmaker to
choose the camera movements for the situations in which they occur? What impressions can camera movements impose upon the viewer, especially if the camera mainly
moves around settings and objects?* (cf. Liebelt 2002: 9)

The third step of the film analysis consists of an investigation into possible social functions of the cinematic heritage display. It is quite obvious that
heritage films promote certain images of Englishness, but do they give insights into the time in which their stories take place – i.e. into the early dec-

---

[17] For empirical research on viewers' reactions to heritage films, cf. Higson (2003).
[18] This does not imply that the cultural information is less important than the films themselves. In contrast to the tendency to restrict culture to the status of supplementary,
background information as it used to be the case in the EFL (English as a Foreign Language) curriculum in Great Britain (cf. Pulverness 1995), the teaching of heritage films
and heritage culture as I understand it is a means of revealing the close relationship between films as cultural products of a society and the cultural climate of a given period.

ades of the twentieth century with their sense of loss and nostalgia because the coming to an end of the culture of the country house was near – or do they rather reveal something about the time of their origin? In any case, students should be aware of the constructed nature of representations of Englishness and the English national past in heritage films. It has to be clear that the mediated image is *not* (a true image of) England. Therefore, a question that should be highlighted in class is why such a nostalgic and conservative concept of Englishness was conveyed in the 1980s. Critics 'from the Left' have claimed that the return to a past version of Englishness, which is associated with the privileged lifestyle of the upper class, the country, and the ex-colonies (cf. Hill 1999: 77), represents a nostalgic escape, offering images of stability and grandeur in the face of the troubled present with its economic decline, loss of international standing, and increasing multicultural nature of British society, which queried traditional homogenous notions of national identity (cf. Higson 2003: 51). A more positive reading is that nostalgia is used as criticism of the Thatcherite present and its individualistic and materialistic values by contrasting them with "the values of the liberal consensus, making connections across social boundaries of class, gender, sexuality, nationality, etc." (Higson 1996: 239).

With regard to the social functions of heritage films, it might be quite a productive task in class to compare different heritage films – above all to contrast heritage movies of the 1980s with contemporary heritage and costume films, such as *The Wings of the Dove*, *Billy Elliot*, *The Full Monty*, *Jude*, *Shakespeare in Love*, *Elizabeth*, or *Orlando*. These so-called alternative or revisionist heritage films depart from 'classic' heritage movies through their dramatis personae, presentation of characters, social critique, depiction of sexuality, and crossing or blurring of social, national, and gender boundaries.[19] They can, thus, "no longer be said to convey one specific version of nostalgic Englishness, but rather offer different variations of [...] not only national but also regionalized and gendered identities" (Griem & Voigts-Virchow 2003: 320). A case in point is the screen adaptation of Helen Fielding's novel *Bridget Jones's Diary*, in which many intertextual and intermedial allusions to the BBC version of Jane Austen's *Pride and Prejudice* can be found. These do not only produce comic effects, but also reveal that identities are no longer stable but rather fluid (cf. *ibid.*).[20]

The text-centred and the context-oriented approach as described above have one thing in common. In both cases, the teacher leads the students through a guided analysis to a specific reading of the film: in other words, the interpretation was determined more or less beforehand. In this way, the

---

[19] For revisionist heritage films, cf. Church Gibson (2000), Monk (2002), and Griem & Voigts-Virchow (2003).

[20] Another interesting aspect that should be discussed in class in this connection is the German 'Heimatfilm'. In particular with regard to a student-centred approach to films which takes the students' world outside the foreign language classroom into consideration, it is important to ask them about their own national heritage in German films.

subjective reactions of the students to the film, their individual interests, experiences, and needs often go unnoticed, and there is the risk of a one-sided development of cognitive abilities at the expense of affective educational goals. To prevent this and to ensure that the reception of a film is also an active process on the part of the viewer who tries to give sense to the sign system of the film on the basis of his/her individual set of preconditions, a more student-centred und process-oriented approach has to be pursued. This can be achieved by the use of action- and production-oriented tasks as these stimulate the students' creativity and make them develop and express their own ideas. A German student audience might bring values and interests into play when reading a heritage film that are different from those of the intended middle-class female audience of the typical Merchant-Ivory production. To give the students the opportunity to describe their individual impressions, one could begin discussion in class with some 'open questions': *What struck you while viewing the film? What did(n't) you like about the film? What is for you the most important aspect of this film?* Another innovative approach would be to ask students to take over the role of film-makers whose task it is to prepare the filming of a novel, for example of Ishiguro's *The Remains of the Day*. Such a task would require that the students

- examine problems that might arise with the filming of the novel and search for solutions;
- discuss which scenes are especially suited to filming and which ones have to be modified, supplemented, or left out altogether;
- decide which actress/actor they would choose for a certain role and why;
- think about the beginning of the film, about establishing shots and the introduction of the characters;
- consider the number of shots needed for the filming and think about field sizes, points of view, and camera movements, as well as about their respective potential effects;
- convert some scenes of the novel to a shooting script or a story-board.[21]

A comparison of the students' works with the original film draws their attention to the making of the film, to its formal features and visual presentation. It can also reveal what the students accentuated – for example, whether they were interested in a display of settings and props (houses, furnishings, décor, costumes), in the depiction of the relationships between the characters and of the characters' inner lives, or in the transformation of the novel's specific narrative situation with cinematic means. In any case, the students' reading of the original will be heavily influenced by their own ideas and approaches to the film.

---

[21]   Cf. Teasley & Wilder (1997: 69), Stempleski & Tomalin (2001: 63f., 74), and Fiedler (1990).

4   Conclusion

I hope to have been able to show that heritage films can be used in different ways and for different purposes when teaching foreign students English literature and culture. As the reading of a heritage film in class depends on the educational goals pursued by the teacher and on the individual perspectives of the students, there is, in my view, no question of validating one reading over another. It is surely more productive to plead for a diversity of possible readings in class and to make learners recognize "that all these views are simply interpretations, that all interpretations betray the interests and perspective of the interpreter, and that the variety of interpretations is indicative of the vitality of the reception process and the richness of the films themselves" (Higson 2003: 48). This does not mean that I am pleading for a postmodern 'anything goes' approach in the foreign language classroom. In order to help students develop into mature interpreters of cultural products, they rather have to be made aware of how different readings come about, and they have to learn to give reasons for their interpretations by referring to the film, its formal features and its cultural context, and by disclosing their individual points of view. Therefore, the use of heritage films in the foreign language classroom can contribute to the development of the students' analytical skills, media literacy, and cultural competence in both cultures.

Bibliography

Campbell, Nancy (1996), "Narration and Narrators: How Learners Perceive Speakers in Narrative Texts", in Lothar Bredella & Werner Delanoy, eds., *Challenges of Literary Texts in the Foreign Language Classroom*, Tübingen: Narr, 108-124.

Chatman, Seymour (1978), *Story and Discourse: Narrative Structure in Fiction and Film*, Ithaca – London: Cornell University Press.

Church Gibson, Pamela (2000), "Fewer Weddings and More Funerals: Changes in the Heritage Film", in Robert Murphy, ed., *British Cinema of the 90s*, London: British Film Institute, 115-124.

Currie, Gregory (1995), "Unreliability Refigured: Narrative in Literature and Film", *The Journal of Aesthetics and Art Criticism* 53:1, 19-29.

Dyer, Richard (1994), "Feeling English", *Sight and Sound* 4:3 (March, New Series), 16-19.

Fiedler, Eckhard (1990), "Die Umsetzung eines Romanauszugs in ein Filmskript", *Praxis des neusprachlichen Unterrichts* 37:4, 384-393.

Fluck, Winfried (2002), "The Role of the Reader and the Changing Functions of Literature: Reception Aesthetics, Literary Anthropology, *Funktionsgeschichte*", *European Journal of English Studies* 6:3, 253-271.

Griem, Julika & Eckart Voigts-Virchow (2003), "Trashing and Recycling: Regenrification in British Heritage Movies and Costume Films of the 1990s", in Ewald Mengel, Hans-Jörg Schmid & Michael Steppat, eds., *Proceedings Anglistentag 2002 Bayreuth*, Trier: Wissenschaftlicher Verlag Trier, 319-331.

Higson, Andrew (1993), "Re-presenting the National Past: Nostalgia and Pastiche in the Heritage Film", in Lester Friedman, ed., *British Cinema and Thatcherism: Fires Were Started*, London: UCL Press, 109-129.

----- (1995), *Waving the Flag: Constructing a National Cinema in Britain*, Oxford: Oxford University Press.

----- (1996), "The Heritage Film and British Cinema", in Higson, ed., *Dissolving Views: Key Writings on British Cinema*, London – New York: Cassell, 232-248.

----- (2003), *English Heritage, English Cinema: Costume Drama since 1980*, Oxford: Oxford University Press.

Hill, John (1999), *British Cinema in the 1980s: Issues and Themes*, Oxford: Clarendon Press.

Lang, James M. (2000), "Public Memory, Private History: Kazuo Ishiguro's *The Remains of the Day*", *Clio* 29,2: 143-166.

Liebelt, Wolf (2002), *The Language of Film: Fachausdrücke, Interpretationsfragen und Redemittellisten für die Arbeit mit Filmen im Englischunterricht*. Tips für die Medienkunde 6, Niedersächsisches Landesinstitut für Schulentwicklung und Bildung (NLI).

Monk, Claire (2002), "The British Heritage-Film Debate Revisited", in Claire Monk & Amy Sargeant, eds., *British Historical Cinema: The History, Heritage and Costume Film*, London – New York: Routledge, 176-198.

Nünning, Ansgar (2000), "Towards a Cultural and Historical Narratology: A Survey of Diachronic Approaches, Concepts, and Research Projects", in Bernhard Reitz & Sigrid Rieuwerts, eds., *Anglistentag 1999 Mainz – Proceedings*, Trier: Wissenschaftlicher Verlag Trier, 345-373.

Otten, Kurt (1979), "'Kulturelle Kompetenz' im Englischunterricht", in Hans Weber, ed. *Aufforderungen zum literaturdidaktischen Dialog*, Paderborn *et al.*: Schöningh, 88-102.

Parker, Alan (1994), Interview cited in "Realisme uit Groot-Brittanië", *Film Krant*, http://www.filmkrant.nl/av/org/filmkran/archief/fk142/grtbritt.html (March 2004).

Parkes, Adam (2001), *Kazuo Ishiguro's The Remains of the Day: A Reader's Guide*, New York – London: Continuum.

Phelan, James & Mary Patricia Martin (1999), "The Lessons of 'Weymouth': Homodiegesis, Unreliability, Ethics, and *The Remains of the Day*", in David Herman, ed., *Narratologies: New Perspectives on Narrative Analysis*, Columbus: Ohio State University Press, 88-109.

Pulverness, Alan (1995), "Cultural Studies, British Studies and EFL", *Modern English Teacher* 4:2, http://elt.britcoun.org.pl/forum/bsandefl.htm (March 2004).

Richards, Jeffrey (1997), *Films and British National Identity. From Dickens to Dad's Army*, Manchester – New York: Manchester University Press.

Sommer, Roy (2000), "Funktionsgeschichten: Überlegungen zur Verwendung des Funktionsbegriffs in der Literaturwissenschaft und Anregungen zu seiner terminologischen Differenzierung", *Literaturwissenschaftliches Jahrbuch* 41, 319-341.

Stempleski, Susan & Barry Tomalin (2001), *Film: Resource Books for Teachers*, Oxford: Oxford University Press.

Sternberg, Meir (1982), "Proteus in Quotation-Land: Mimesis and the Forms of Reported Discourse", *Poetics Today* 3:2, 107-156.

Street, Sarah (1997), *British National Cinema*, London *et al.*: Routledge.

Surkamp, Carola (2003), "'Alas, the two nations cannot be friends': Imperialismuskritik durch die Aufwertung der indischen Sichtweise, die multiperspektivische Entlarvung stereotypisierender Fremdbilder und die Unvereinbarkeit britischer und indischer Perspektiven in E.M. Forsters *A Passage to India* (1924)", in Surkamp, *Die Perspektivenstruktur narrativer Texte: Zu ihrer Theorie und Geschichte im englischen Roman zwischen Viktorianismus und Moderne*, Trier: Wissenschaftlicher Verlag Trier, 276-283.

----- (2004a), "Teaching Films: Von der Filmanalyse zu handlungs- und prozessorientierten Formen der filmischen Textarbeit", *Der fremdsprachliche Unterricht Englisch* 38:68, 2-11.

----- (2004b), "Spielfilme im fremdsprachlichen Literaturunterricht: Beitrag zu einer kulturwissenschaftlichen Filmdidaktik", in Lothar Bredella, Werner Delanoy & Carola Surkamp, eds., *Literaturdidaktik im Dialog*, Tübingen: Narr.

Teasley, Alan B. & Ann Wilder (1997), *Reel Conversations: Reading Films with Young Adults*, Portsmouth: Heinemann.

Voßkamp, Wilhelm (1999), "Literaturwissenschaft und Kulturwissenschaften", in Henk de Berg & Matthias Prangel, eds., *Interpretation 2000: Positionen und Kontroversen. Festschrift zum 65. Geburtstag von Horst Steinmetz*, Heidelberg: Winter, 183-199.

Wall, Kathleen (1994), "*The Remains of the Day* and its Challenges to Theories of Unreliable Narration", *The Journal of Narrative Technique* 24:1, 18-42.

Zerweck, Bruno (2002), "Der *cognitive turn* in der Erzähltheorie: Kognitive und 'Natürliche' Narratologie", in Ansgar Nünning & Vera Nünning, eds., *Neue Ansätze in der Erzähltheorie*, Trier: Wissenschaftlicher Verlag Trier, 219-242.

Monika Seidl

Kommissar Rex Meets Mr Darcy: Pedagogical Approaches to Visualising the Past and Literary Classics

The 'Janespotters' in this article come from Vienna. That is the perspective from which this article is written and it characterises the pedagogical approaches to the heritage and the literary classics presented. The ways into the classics proposed take as their starting point literary adaptations and the manner in which classics are appropriated for a present-day audience. What are the connections between heritage and classics, adaptation and appropriation? Classics are part of the heritage of an imagined community.[1] Heritage is for its consumers a way of appropriating an imagined community's past, be it one's own or someone else's. Filmic adaptations revisit classics; they adapt them within their respective context of production and thus appropriate them within contingent historical moments.

In what follows, I will describe some strategies used to help students of English in Vienna to find their way into British heritage in the context of filmic adaptations of British literary classics. The perspective is that of a teacher of English as a foreign language, who is also in charge of a mini-module 'Cultural Studies' for first-year students, which has a strong theoretical orientation. The module is based on the proposition that theories are something well worth understanding, as students are encouraged to see theory as an ongoing process and a reflective practice. Ideally, we aim at enabling our students to respond – thus turning them into responsible people who learn to master interpersonal "response-ability", as Bakhtin[2] once put it.

Thus, in this article, heritage and adaptation are not treated within a framework of 'Literature'-courses. Heritage and the adaptation of literary classics are topics dealt with in connection with language acquisition, and in connection with cultural theory, cultural analysis and cultural awareness in the broadest sense.

What are the parameters within the teaching of literary classics as part of heritage in Austria? On closer inspection of the Austrian curricula for secondary or tertiary education it becomes obvious that the teaching of literature in Austria, be it written in German or in a foreign language, to a great extent follows a fact-based transmission model. Emphasis is placed on comprehensively covering historical periods in lecture courses with little attention paid

---

[1] The notion is adopted from Anderson (1983).
[2] Cf. Pope (2002: 261) and Bakhtin (1996 [¹1981]).

to exemplary learning. Austrian curricula favour diachronic surveys, as do the lecture courses offered at the English Department of Vienna University. For secondary schools, this means the Middle Ages up to the 18th century for 16-year-olds, the French Revolution until the Great War for 17-year-olds and the Great War until the present for 18-year-olds. The literature component at university treats students, for example, to *English Literature 1550-1700: A Survey* or *From the Renaissance to the Restoration: A Brief Survey*.[3]

In the Vienna English Department's 'blurb' text concerning literature studies there is a definition of the possible texts that will be covered. The passage tellingly talks of "texts and media products", thus revealing traces of a notion of texts as unmediated products contrary to mediated ones, or more simply a narrow notion of text in the sense of signifying systems made up of language. A wide notion of text is fairly contested within literature in the Austrian scholarly tradition, as is evidenced in wide-ranging terminological and heuristic debates such as the one about the merits of 'intermediality' as a concept alongside 'intertextuality' (cf., for example, Wolf 2002). As a language and cultural studies teacher who prefers a content-based foreign language teaching framework, I have for my purposes always endorsed an extremely wide notion of text, which then goes hand in hand with a wide notion of intertextuality.

This wide notion of text is closely connected with the metaphor that speaks of 'culture and text' and the 'textuality of culture' and which regards language as a hermeneutical device when it comes to the analysis of culture. The advantages as well as disadvantages of the linguistic turn within the Humanities are well known and need no further rehashing.[4]

The language metaphor is frequently used in connection with film studies, as is demonstrated by titles such as James Monaco's film studies classic, *How to Read a Film*, or Cherry Potter's *Screen Language*. These titles mirror Christian Metz's assertion that "film says things that could be conveyed also in the language of words; yet it says them differently" (Metz 1974: 44). Adaptation theory generally relies upon comparative and semiotic approaches (cf. McFarlane 1996), which work best if both the written and the visual text are analysed utilising a linguistic model of description. Following this model, all texts work according to signifying practices so that via semiotics non-linguistic filmic elements such as lighting or *mise-en-scène* can also be conceptualised as signs conveying meaning. Some theorists, such as Metz, draw very close analogies between verbal language and 'film language'; other theorists, such as Bordwell (1997) do not extend the parallels beyond an assumption that both 'languages' signify and communicate. The present article leans towards the latter approach.

---

[3] For more detailed information, cf. http://www.schule.at and http:// www.univie.ac.at/ Anglistik/.

[4] For the linguistic turn, cf. Reckwitz (2000). For the visual turn as a first pointer, cf. Dalle Vacche (2003).

Staying within the language metaphor implies that knowledge about film is conveyed via language, not via the visual channel. Within the language metaphor, the use of the word 'reading' implicitly suggests that the visual is always on display, as a screen and as a spectacle and that the visual channel conveys no knowledge on its own. In order to raise awareness of these shortcomings when mobilising the language metaphor in areas such as film studies, the pedagogical approaches presented are inspired by an interest in "Visual Knowledges",[5] that is, in the role of the visual in creating knowledge. The status of knowledge gained through images versus know-ledge gained through verbal texts has been extensively debated by historians.[6] These discussions have led to the conclusion that visual-auditory media such as films are signifying practices different from verbal media in mode and manner. Adaptations of classics, therefore, never illustrate a novel or a drama, but re-tell the respective text differently and in addition say something other than the source text, thus adding new meaning to it.

My interest in the hermeneutical aspect of the visual inspired me to choose *Pride and Prejudice* and its various re-creations as the 'source text' for my pedagogical approaches, as knowledge and the visual are important for the plot of *Pride and Prejudice*. Understanding and misunderstanding someone or something by, as well as despite, close observation play important roles in the novel. In order to stay within the language metaphor, reading and misreading one another is crucial to the complications caused in the novel, such as those caused by Mr Darcy's misinterpretation of Jane Bennett's countenance. Practices of reading and misreading one another are closely related to projections, to desires attributed to others. Projections in the more narrowly Freudian sense of attributing to others what we ourselves feel and desire is a theme very well known from *Pride and Prejudice*, as the two character traits mentioned in the novel's title first and foremost refer to projections ascribed to each other by the novel's protagonists.

Introducing Freudian concepts reflects the particular Viennese perspective this article is grounded in. As the topics introduced are tackled within the context of EFL, it seems important to stress this position outside the target culture. Such a position turns teachers into mediators, who are a little ahead of their students in appropriating the target culture for the respective purposes of an EFL environment. EFL teachers are therefore facilitators who share with their students the perspective from outside the target culture, which is their greatest disadvantage and at the same time their greatest asset. Thus, non-native teachers of foreign languages are liminal people, mediators who linger in interstices, or third spaces, as Claire Kramsch (1993; 1998) among other EFL theorists who adapted work in postcolonial studies (cf.

---

5 This was the title of a conference held at the University of Edinburgh in September 2003. (Cf. http://www.ed.ac.uk/iash/vkconf.html for more detailed information).

6 Cf. Samuel (1994) and especially White (1988), who introduced the term historiophoty alongside historiography.

Bhabha 1990; 1994) has called the place of the non-native teacher of a foreign language.

This in-between perspective has also informed the pedagogical approaches proposed. Both heritage and literary classics on a general level, and *Pride and Prejudice* more specifically are well-worn topics. What will be new is the view on these matters from an in-between perspective. The Viennese considers the heritage debate from the perspective of someone coming from a city whose historic centre was put on the World Heritage list in 2001. This fact has allegedly not drawn any more tourists to the city as they keep coming anyway, and the Viennese themselves have hardly become aware of the honour yet. Vienna's status as a listed city, however, keeps the heritage debate going. The re-opening in 2003 of an early 19th-century palace, the Albertina, housing one of the world's biggest collections of the graphic arts, was good for a couple of days' headlines. Vienna's status has furthermore fuelled a lively debate about the efforts that have to be made to protect the historic city. Only recently new developments near the city centre have been officially stopped so as not to impair the visual integrity of the historic town. This aspect of tourism and the visual resonates with the theme of visuality and knowledge mentioned above.

For the present line of argument it is worth taking into consideration the fact that heritage, the preservation and presentation of heritage for consumption, is part of Austrian and specifically Viennese cultural identity. The Viennese, and by implication students at the University of Vienna, live and work within a continuously mediated space. Vienna's imperial splendour is annually televised all over the world in the form of the Vienna Philharmonic New Year's Concert. These are the lenses through which the heritage debate is seen, namely from the privileged vantage point of living within what Andrew Higson has called 'heritage space', a label which he used in opposition to 'narrative space' (cf. Higson 1993).

From this it follows that the activation of learners' resources, in the sense of their background within heritage space, is a key feature of the pedagogical approaches proposed towards heritage cinema and adaptations of classics. Adaptation is furthermore a topic that simply must attract any teacher of a foreign language as it has at its core a process that is easily transferable to foreign-language learning, namely the process of appropriation. Adapters, like learners of a foreign language, make things their own. Both adopt and adapt and thus appropriate their respective objects of desire to their own needs and interests.

Appropriation is furthermore a familiar concept against a cultural-studies background, which forms the backdrop of the approaches presented. Cultural studies must be seen as a continuation of a British tradition whose founding fathers were all keen educationalists (cf. Turner 1990). This educationalist aspect of cultural studies is very appealing from a teacher's point of view as is the commitment to popular culture and, consequently, an interest in the affective potential of any text. The popular can be described as bodily practice; the popular is inscribed upon the body as tears, laughter, screams or other symptoms of the fan's devotion. The affective potential of the popular makes popular texts such a valid resource for language learning, as affect can be utilised to aid the language learning process.[7]

Curricula in Austria, as mentioned above, rely very much on the transmission model when it comes to teaching literature. Therefore, pedagogical pointers in the English National Curriculum English[8] in key stages 3 & 4 were explored to find evidence of the use of the approaches proposed. In the section dealing with reading the "Knowledge, Skills and Understanding" parts contain a number of learning objectives that are of interest in the present context. "Understanding texts" includes "Reading for meaning". "To develop understanding and appreciation of texts, pupils should be taught" various abilities, one of which is most relevant for the present purposes, namely "to consider how meanings are changed when texts are adapted to different media". This emphasis on meaning making is worthy of consideration as it offers scope for looking at adaptation from a constructivist perspective. This view re-positions a text within a dynamic framework of repetitive meaning making, which emerges from the constant interaction with a text over time. This approach is underscored by the inclusion of another ability to be taught: "to analyse and discuss alternative interpretations, ambiguity and allusion".

Another point of relevance is the English National Curriculum's use of the word 'heritage' to refer to literary history, as "English literary heritage" is another item in the "Knowledge, Skills and Understanding" part for key stage 3 and key stage 4. The national curriculum has thus inscribed into its agenda the past as a heritage commodity and prescribes introducing pupils to "the appeal and importance of these texts over time".

This agenda opens up new approaches to the classics, as the very notion of heritage, especially English heritage, is, as is well known, somewhat contested. The arguments put forward against heritage condemn the idea of representations of the past as they can be found in heritage centres, National Trust properties, or BBC novel adaptations as an approach to the past based on entertainment and leisure pursuits, and thus based on shallow and passive consumption. What should be supported according to this view is a more active engagement with one's own past. Titles of books such as Robert Hewison's *The Heritage Industry. Britain in a Climate of Decline* (1987) or Patrick Wright's *On Living in an Old Country* (1985) which have negative connotations and the works of Andrew Higson on heritage cinema from the 1990s[9] mark this side of the debate. Raphael Samuel's *Theatres of Memory* (1994),

---

7 Cf. Themenheft „Emotionen" in *Der Fremdsprachliche Unterricht Englisch* and here specifically Kieweg (2003).

8 Cf. http://www.nc.uk.net/index.html.

9 Cf. Higson (1993). Higson has reconsidered his stance towards heritage in Higson (2003), where he leaves more room for polysemous audience reception, while closely analyzing conditions of production.

however, provocatively defends the commodification of the past as heritage when he puts more emphasis on the aspect of re-creating the past starting from the pleasures of the gaze, which he sees as an active and not as a passive form of consumption. Endorsing, as Samuel does, a wider notion of heritage is of interest here, as it helps to understand the negative feelings and regrets that go along with a notion of heritage as myth. (Here, myth is understood in Roland Barthes's sense as a loss of the historical and material qualities of things.) A wider notion of heritage also helps to understand the almost fanatic devotion that people show when it comes to heritage items such as the immensely popular BBC adaptation of *Pride and Prejudice* from 1995.

The approaches-cum-case studies that follow focus on Jane Austen and heritage cinema, specifically on the 1995 BBC *Pride and Prejudice* adaptation and the free-floating signifier Mr Darcy (as impersonated by Colin Firth) that emerged from the mini-series. This meanwhile iconic Mr Darcy found himself inscribed into the modern re-creation of *Pride and Prejudice* plus an extra Darcy, namely the one in *Bridget Jones's Diary* (1996). In the filmed version to follow in 2001, Firth plays the character named Mark Darcy, thus embodying a perfect example of what Fredric Jameson calls the "auto-referentiality" (Jameson 1998) of post-modern culture and what trendy cybernetics would call a self-organising system.

In the examples of the pedagogical approaches presented here, two aspects of such post-modern re-creation-mania and adaptation-mania are highlighted: First, there is the iconicity of Mr Darcy as a male heritage hero of a constructed version of Englishness, which students are encouraged to see in contrast to constructions of stereotypically Austrian male heritage heroes. Second, a trajectory will be drawn from 18th-century versions of the touristic commodifying and fetishising gaze as exemplified in *Pride and Prejudice*, the novel, to a similar construction of looking that Andrew Higson has established as a key feature of the heritage cinema, which is familiar to Austrian students. The reference is to excessive tracking shots of exteriors and interiors of heritage buildings conveying nothing but the splendour of what is shown. These are amply used when representing Austrian and specifically Viennese heritage on TV and on film.[10]

---

[10] There are other strands of heritage cinema of interest in this context which have not been explored any further: the more "painterly" versions of heritage films modelled on Peter Greenaway's explorations the pictorial in *The Draughtsman's Contract* (1982) or in *Prospero's Books* (1991). There is Derek Jarman's tableaux version of the past in *Caravaggio* (1986). Ang Lee's versions of Vermeer's portraits in *Sense and Sensibility* (1995) can be also seen in this context, similar to Shekar Kapur's evocations of Goya in *Elizabeth* (1998). The Dickens, Brontë, or Defoe adaptations of the late 1990s which display a more varied use of settings are not considered. What is also absent is Michael Winterbottom's take on Thomas Hardy, *Jude* (1996), for example, which allegedly set out to "destroy heritage cinema from within", as Hossein Amini, Winterbottom's scriptwriter has put it. In Winterbottom's *Jude* there are startling filmic parallels to Austrian televisual heritage series, set in grim and repressive Alpine farming communities, such as the TV se-

The *Pride and Prejudice* project began with language-based exercises, followed by textual interventionist work in the tradition of Rob Pope (1994) and rounded off by more concept-driven cultural analytical tasks.

The project was started with a fact-finding mission under the cover of a vocabulary exercise, in order to find out how familiar students are with matters to do with Darcy and Bridget Jones. The exercise worked under the assumption that *Bridget Jones's Diary* might be closer to their lived experience than Jane Austen's *Pride and Prejudice*. The two boxes in the task (cf. Appendix 1) contain adjectives which can be variously found in *Bridget Jones's Diary* (the book, film, and director's Sharon Maguire's DVD commentary) as attributes of Mark Darcy and Bridget Jones respectively. First-year students at Vienna University tend to struggle with the words and, when asked which of the words they vaguely remembered from any other context, they said that most of them were unknown to them. Only three of my students out of two different classes of about 15 students each remembered the word "poised" from Bridget Jones's New Year's Resolutions. Students furthermore claimed that there are no proper Austrian celebrities apart from Arnold Schwarzenegger (whom nobody, according to them, identifies as an Austrian) and possibly skiers who win the Olympics. They perceptively observed, however, that the Austrian obsession with mountains, lakes and downhill racing might not travel far beyond the Austrian borders. Therefore, the typically Austrian hero is the sports hero, the Alpine skier, the man whose body represents itself. This Alpine hero fights nature with his body and is himself constructed as a force of Nature. Students struggled a lot in the course of the exercise while trying to use any of the words given for their descriptions of Hermann Maier, the most popular Austrian skier, known as 'Herminator' – the pun intended.

Perhaps unexpectedly, I would like to claim that it is only a small leap from Austrian representations of nature to English representations of heritage culture, as I would like to argue that both representations feed on notions of authenticity. The construction of authenticity is a key feature of the skier as well as the reconstruction of the past in heritage cinema. The BBC mini-series *Pride and Prejudice*, for example, is pre-dominantly shot on various locations, giving the air of authentic representation to the setting and enhancing the series' reality-effect in the context of realist narrative film.

Following the language exercises, students are encouraged to produce more writing, which roughly falls into the category of textual intervention, and which is based on Jane Austen's *Pride and Prejudice*. They are prompted to contract and expand texts, asked to reduce Darcy's letter and expand a passage from the second proposal scene, thus producing dialogue (cf. Appendix 2). They are also encouraged to produce a shooting script for Elizabeth's arrival at Pemberley, which in fact targets the 'heritage shots' and

---

ries *Alpensaga* (1976-1980) or the more recent TV biopic *Andreas Hofer 1809. Die Freiheit des Adlers* (2002), which would provide ample scope for further investigation.

furthermore has them convert written representation of a building and its grounds into filmic representation, that is, into a moving image text (cf. Appendix 3).

In what follows, I will focus on the Pemberley scene. The passage, as is widely known, aims to describe a perfect late 18th-century landscape garden, "where natural beauty had been so little counteracted by an awkward taste", as it says in the novel, and where the house is concealed before it reveals itself as a picturesque landscape and country house. Nature is thus presented as spectacle, a concept not alien to the Austrian perception of a formal garden, although the imperial gardens of the Habsburg family are modelled after the French ideal, where in analogy to the Austen passage "natural beauty has been much counteracted by an awkward taste".

The connection aimed at lies in the factor of middle-class tourism: book and film both display the pleasures of 18th-century tourism, which does not differ a lot from 21st-century tourism. The connection specifically lies in the visual consumption: by looking at land, houses, and, coming to think of it, also at Mr Darcy, spectators gain symbolic ownership of them. By means of visual consumption, a tourist may make land, house, and landowner, her own. The shot sequences employed when visualizing heritage mirror this process, and are interesting especially in terms of genre, as generic markers of cinematic television programmes selling heritage. This is where Vienna, whose heritage buildings are also spectacularly represented on TV, comes in as a valuable learning resource. At this point, the idea of tourism as visual consumption leading to symbolic ownership converges with generic shot features of heritage cinema promoting visual consumption.

A popular programme on Austrian state-owned TV is a prime-time series called *Universum*, which offers natural history documentaries, whose home-made productions more and more devote themselves to Viennese heritage. Surely with a keen eye to tourism and the souvenir market, the first heritage instalment featured St Stephen's Cathedral, with equal weight put on the animals that inhabit this Gothic monument. The second and most recent instalment has the late Sir Peter Ustinov give an introduction to the Habsburg palace of Schönbrunn. As the grounds are also home to the oldest menagerie in the world, the programme also devotes some time to animals, but the main emphasis is clearly on the building and on heritage space.

These *Universum* productions illustrate an interesting detail of Austrian self-fashioning: Austria likes to present itself to others and itself in ways that merge notions of nature and culture. On the national sides of the Austrian euro coins, for example, you find depictions of Alpine flowers alongside depictions of Viennese heritage buildings; and Viennese heritage is presented, as exemplified above, in the nature channel slot.

The *Universum* productions feature unusual and very expensive aerial tracking shots, partly executed with the aid of a balloon as their trademark, and they are extremely popular with people of all ages and from all walks of life, at least within the boundaries of Austria. The point is that generic features listed for heritage cinema by Higson (1993) or Cardwell (2002) are something Austrians are very familiar with as typical features employed to represent Austrian heritage. One generic feature listed by Higson is the extra-diegetic place of the heritage shots within the narrative. This extra-diegetic space, I would like to argue, is the space of the tourist, is the space occupied in *Pride and Prejudice* by Elizabeth Bennett when she does her tour of Derbyshire during which she comes across her main object of desire. Notwithstanding the heritage critics' objections, these extra-diegetic shots offer sheer spectacle because of their affective value.

The Austrians are also familiar with these generic features through a very popular TV drama series, called *Kommissar Rex* (1994 to present), which despite its quick narrative pace relishes long takes of heritage buildings, a form of re-presentation which may be compared to the treatment of heritage in the *Inspector Morse* (1987 to 2000) or the *Inspector Lynley Mysteries* series (2002 to present, based on Elizabeth George's novels). These comparisons make it evident that literary adaptations, documentaries and quality drama alike present contemporary visual representations of the past with the tourist as focalizer. They visualize representations of the past that turn history into a sight, into a tourist attraction and into a spectacle, as history is turned into something to be viewed, something from which knowledge may be gained.

This observation leads back to the Pemberley scene in both book and adaptation. This scene verbalizes as well as visualizes the pleasures that may be derived from sightseeing, the more so if, as in the case of Pemberley and its owner, both are highly valued commodities which Elizabeth inspects and wishes to take possession of. Using "large and handsome" as modifying adjectives for both man and house leaves open precisely which of the two Elizabeth falls in love with. The film clearly decides for the man, Mr Darcy, who, in an obvious reversal of typically gendered perspectives, is frequently shown standing behind the window looking out. The audience is thus presented with a gazing man, who is at the same time intensely looked at and intensely framed. Colin Firth as Mr Darcy is fashioned as a compulsive spectator for the compulsive spectators. On fan web pages, one can find images called The Look.[11] Thus, still photography seems to be built into the adaptation, as shown by the multitude of screen shots you can also find on fan pages, proving the fans' affective investment.

Mr Darcy, re-created in Fielding's book and the film version of it, is the male fetish of heritage cinema, since the heritage on display is turned into a commodity; likewise, the man positioned within heritage becomes a commodity. Mr Darcy posters are still going strong on the Internet auction market. In fact, there is a regular Darcy-mania to be recognised. Fetishism in *Pride and Prejudice* (1995) thus clearly went two ways; it worked within an economic discourse and a sexual discourse with Mr Darcy as the object of desire at its centre. This object is fully displayed as a spectacle to excite

---

[11] Cf. http://www.coastal.net.au/~ddibd/jane/thelook.html.

pleasure in women and whoever else finds him exciting. The Austrian heritage-plus-crime series, *Kommissar Rex*, puts a similar character on display as the inspector who solves the crimes with the help of his German shepherd dog (mark the typically Austrian merging of nature and culture). The actor in this series also counts as one of Austria's sexiest men and is presently appearing in a number of quality literary adaptations and a biopic about an Alpine folk hero.

In the *New York Review of Books* the BBC mini-series *Pride and Prejudice* was called a *Pride and Prejudice* with "extra Darcy" (Menard 1996). This man featured in excess to enhance desirability is a useful element in discussing concepts of critical theory such as fetishism, as students are made aware of the fact that the notion of fetishism may be read within an economic discourse as well as within a discourse of sexuality and pleasure (cf. Bruzzi 1997). Students thus learn that the generic features that adaptations of classics share with documentaries and drama series displaying heritage bring about multiple signification. The stunning aerial tracking shots, the long shots, the close-ups, the non-diegetic moment of sheer looking all, via the workings of fetish, permit readings which accommodate both the more economically minded and the pleasure-seekers. And let us not forget that it is not just the man Elizabeth Bennett is interested in but also his £10,000 a year.

Higson's main thrust of argument was directed at the ideologically motivated beautification of the past, which denied the adaptations, and thus implicitly the novels, narrative space in favour of heritage space. What I discuss with my students is their side of the story. Can they as short-term or long-time inhabitants of Vienna enjoy heritage space? How do they react to the lingering shots of various parts of English heritage, of landscapes, of houses, of furniture, even of a man?

The pleasure side of heritage cinema is closely linked to the marketing of literary adaptations as romances, whereby producers specifically target an audience interested in romance. The description on the front cover of the presentation box of the DVD of *Pride and Prejudice* attempts to convince prospective buyers that what they get is "the celebrated BBC dramatisation of a classic romance". What is termed classic here is neither the BBC dramatisation nor the novel the dramatisation is based on, but the romance. *Pride and Prejudice* (1995) is consequently more firmly positioned within the genre of romantic comedies than within the genre of literary adaptations.

When key moments of British romantic comedies are explored, students are able to see the place of *Pride and Prejudice* within romantic comedies. They also gain deeper insight into the construction of the masculinities these comedies employ. Among the key scenes we can count Hugh Grant's declaration-of-love scene from *Four Weddings and a Funeral* (1994), Colin Firth's famous wet-shirt scene, and again Colin Firth as Mark Darcy declaring his love to Bridget Jones (Renée Zellweger). They all employ the same version of linguistically incontinent but emotionally constipated Englishmen. English or British in this case does not necessarily refer to British production, nor British actors (Renée Zellweger is from Texas), but to a version of post-modern, simulated Englishness which seems to sell well on the global market (cf. Seidl 2002). The Schönbrunn DVD on a smaller scale and the Austrian drama series *Kommissar Rex* sell equally well, and the latter's biggest fan club is based in the Netherlands.

Investigation of the BBC adaptation of *Pride and Prejudice* alongside similar romantic products, and the comparison with the tourist DVD and the Austrian series, which share a number of generic features, make explicit to students that literary adaptations sold worldwide work especially well as extensions of the tourist industry. These features commodify the past and at the same time play with the pleasurable aspect of a fetish, thus unleashing the emotional reactions of the audience.

Are we then back in a climate in which commodity fetish, misrepresentations of the past, and reactionary nostalgia thrive, back to heritage as a celebration of the middle and upper classes, thereby consciously disavowing the working classes? In a sense yes, but using the BBC production of *Pride and Prejudice* as an example, which has gone through various stages of appropriations, that is, various versions of *Bridget Jones's Diary*, can make students aware of the fact that each adaptation can also be seen as an act of acquisition, as an appropriation, as making something one's own.

In conclusion: Once there was *Pride and Prejudice*, a novel by Jane Austen, which went through a number of filmic adaptations, such as the one starring Laurence Olivier as Mr Darcy in the 1940s, or the one featuring Alan Badel in the same role in the 1950s/1960s. There was the version scripted by Fey Weldon in the 1980s, and then there was Andrew Davies' rewriting in the 1990s. Helen Fielding based her column and then her books on the BBC version. And finally there is *Bridget Jones's Diary* the film, and *Bridget Jones. The Edge of Reason*, the sequel which is currently in production. All together they continue to give meaning retroactively to something known under the name of *Pride and Prejudice*.

Maybe the essence of this something is not so important, in the sense of the structure of that which remains; maybe it is not so important to find out exactly what remains, in the sense of the core or the universally valid. Maybe it is more interesting to look at what remains, in the sense of particular cases, which follow particular rules, to look at what is still here in a particular example, like the tourist gaze that remains within *Pride and Prejudice*, and try to make sense of it from our specific vantage points.

Any adaptation of an earlier work retroactively adds meaning to what is adapted, and thus closes gaps the earlier text may have left open; at the same time an adaptation seems to open up other gaps. Adaptations are thus examples of what learners of a foreign language should be encouraged to do: intervene in texts, poach texts, and make texts their own. Similar activities are undertaken by fans, as can be seen on the Austen fan-pages, such as www.pemberley.com, where an avid fan community produces fan-fiction, prequels and sequels to novels, but also writes texts into what are perceived as gaps, or 'missing scenes' in the story. The fans deliberately do what reception theorists have described as the joys and thrills of literature. They fill gaps left through lack of descriptive detail, which are gaps continuously filled by filmic adaptations. They also fill gaps left through lack of dramaturgical motivation, which are gaps not necessarily filled by films. As I see it, students should be encouraged to regard adaptations above all as re-creations and appropriations, as translations in the widest sense, which all actualise in a different manner the meaning potentials, not of the original but of the chain of adaptations and appropriations that precede the one under examination. This insight may give students more confidence when it comes to their chief learning objective, which is making a foreign language and culture their own.

Bibliography

Anderson, Benedict (1983), *Imagined Communities. Reflections on the Origin and Spread of Nationalism*, London: Verso.

Bakhtin, Mikhail M. (1996), *The Dialogic Imagination. Four Essays* ([1]1981), transl. V. W. McGee, ed. Caryl Emerson & Michael Holquist. Austin: University of Texas Press.

Bhabha, Homi (1990), "The Third Space", in Jonathan Rutherford, ed., *Identity. Community, Culture, Difference*, London: Lawrence & Wishart, 207-221.

----- (1994), *The Location of Culture*. London: Routledge.

Bordwell, David (1997), *On the History of Film Style*, Cambridge, MA: Harvard University Press.

Bruzzi, Stella (1997), *Undressing Cinema. Clothing and Identity in the Movies*, London: Routledge.

Cardwell, Sarah (2002), *Adaptation Revisited. Television and the Classic Novel*, Manchester: Manchester University Press.

Dalle Vacche, Angela, ed. (2003), *The Visual Turn. Classical Film Theory and Art History*, New Brunswick: Rutgers University Press.

Hewison, Robert (1987), *The Heritage Industry: Britain in a Climate of Decline*, London: Methuen.

Higson, Andrew (1993), "Re-presenting the National Past. Nostalgia and Pastiche in the Heritage Film", in Lester Friedman, ed., *Fires Were Started. British Cinema and Thatcherism*. Minneapolis: University of Minnesota Press, 109-29.

----- (2003), *English Heritage, English Cinema. Costume Drama since 1980*, Oxford: Oxford University Press.

Jameson, Frederic (1998), *The Cultural Turn. Selected Writings on the Postmodern 1983-1998*, London: Verso.

Kieweg, Werner (2003), "Die Rolle der Emotionen beim Fremdsprachenlernen", *Der Fremdsprachliche Unterricht Englisch*, 37:63, 4-11.

Kramsch, Claire (1998), *Language and Culture*, Oxford: Oxford University Press.

----- (1993), *Context and Culture in Language Teaching*, Oxford: Oxford University Press.

McFarlane, Brian (1996), *Novel into Film. An Introduction to the Theory of Adaptation*, Oxford: Clarendon.

Menard, Louis (1996), "What Jane Austen Doesn't Tell Us", *The New York Review of Books*, 1 February, 13-15.

Metz, Christian (1981), *Film Language: A Semiotics of the Cinema*, Chicago: University of Chicago Press.

Pope, Rob (1994), *Textual Intervention. Critical and Creative Strategies for Literary Study*, London: Routledge.

----- (²2002), *The English Studies Book*, London: Routledge.

Reckwitz, Andreas (2000), *Die Transformationen der Kulturtheorien. Zur Entwicklung eines Theorieprogramms*, Weilerswist: Velbrück Wissenschaft.

Samuel, Raphael (1994), *Theatres of Memory*, London: Verso.

Seidl, Monika (2002), "Englishness in the Postmodern Condition. The Hugh Grant Case", in Gunther Kaltenböck, Dieter Kastovsky, Susanne Reichl, eds., *Anglistentag 2001 Wien. Proceedings*, Trier: Wissenschaftlicher Verlag Trier, 341-351.

White, Hayden (1988), "Historiography and Historiophoty", *American Historical Review* 93:5, 1193-1199, http://www.latrobe.edu.au/screeningthepast/classics/rr0499/hwrr6c.htm (1 November 2003).

Wolf, Werner (2002), "Das Problem der Narrativität in Literatur, bildender Kunst und Musik. Ein Beitrag zu einer intermedialen Erzähltheorie", in Vera & Ansgar Nünning, eds., *Erzähltheorie transgenerisch, intermedial, interdisziplinär*, Trier: Wissenschaftlicher Verlag Trier, 23-104.

Wright, Patrick (1985), *On Living in an Old Country: The National Past in Contemporary Britain*, London: Verso.

Appendix 1

Celebrity Vocabulary Task

Organise all the words in the boxes in a more memorable way. (Memory-network)

Write sentences describing a very famous man and a very famous woman (think in terms of internationally well-known celebrities, who might be, but not necessarily need be Austrian), giving information about their hair and face, their height and build and general appearance. Also write a couple of sentences hypothesizing about each one's character. For your descriptions, you may also use as many of the words provided as you want.

Bring pictures of your celebrities to class.

Write up your descriptions on separate sheets.

forbidding, taciturn, handsome, reserved, stiff, conceited, aloof, haughty, fastidious	skimpy, impulsive, effusive, pouting, excitable, gullible, poised, blissful, self-indulgent

Appendix 2

Expand Text

> Rebecca, feeling all the more than common awkwardness and anxiety of his situation, now forced herself to speak; and immediately, though not very fluently, gave him to understand that her sentiments had undergone so material a change, since the period to which he alluded, as to make her receive with gratitude and pleasure his present assurances. The happiness which this reply produced, was such as he had probably never felt before; and he expressed himself on the occasion as sensibly and as warmly as a man violently in love can be supposed to do. Had Rebecca been able to encounter his eye, she might have seen how well the expression of heartfelt delight, diffused over his face, became him; but, though she could not look, she could listen, and he told her of feelings, which, in proving of what importance she was to him, made his affection every moment more valuable.

> Ralph, feeling all the more than common awkwardness and anxiety of her situation, now forced himself to speak; and immediately, though not very fluently, gave her to understand that his sentiments had undergone so material a change, since the period to which she alluded, as to make him receive with gratitude and pleasure her present assurances. The happiness which this reply produced, was such as she had probably never felt before; and she expressed herself on the occasion as sensibly and as warmly as a woman violently in love can be supposed to do. Had Ralph been able to encounter her eye, he might have seen how well the expression of heartfelt delight, diffused over her face, became her; but, though he could not look, he could listen, and she told him of feelings, which, in proving of what importance he was to her, made her affection every moment more valuable.

Using the extract from a novel that seems more natural to you, decide how you could render the passage on film. Provide what you think should be the dialogue of the scene. What can you see in your mind's eye? What can you hear in your mind's ear? Decide on camera movement and position (framing of the image), shot length, editing, sound and lighting.

Appendix 3

Pemberley

Elizabeth, as they drove along, watched for the first appearance of Pemberley Woods with some perturbation; and when at length they turned in at the lodge, her spirits were in a high flutter.

The park was very large, and contained great variety of ground. They entered it in one of its lowest points, and drove for some time through a beautiful wood, stretching over a wide extent.

Elizabeth's mind was too full for conversation, but she saw and admired every remarkable spot and point of view. They gradually ascended for half a mile, and then found themselves at the top of a considerable eminence, where the wood ceased, and the eye was instantly caught by Pemberley House, situated on the opposite side of a valley, into which the road, with some abruptness, wound. It was a large, handsome, stone building, standing well on rising ground, and backed by a ridge of high woody hills; -- and in front, a stream of some natural importance was swelled into greater, but without any artificial appearance. Its banks were neither formal, nor falsely adorned. Elizabeth was delighted. She had never seen a place for which nature had done more, or where natural beauty had been so little counteracted by an awkward taste....

They descended the hill, crossed the bridge, and drove to the door;

Using this extract from a novel, decide how you could render the passage on film. What can you see in your mind's eye? What can you hear in your mind's ear? Decide on camera movement and position (framing of the image), shot length, editing, sound and lighting.

Index of Films

1900 House, The (Channel 4 1999) • 24
24 Hour Party People (UK 2002, D: Michael Winterbottom, Sc: Frank Cottrell Boyce) • 15
28 Days Later (USA / UK 2002, D: Danny Boyle, Sc: Alex Garland) • 15
Adventure of English, The (ITV 2002, D: Robert Bee, David Thomas, Sc: Melvyn Bragg) • 87, 96
American Beauty (USA 1999, D: Sam Mendes, Sc: Alan Ball) • 48
Another Country (UK 1984, D: Marek Kanievska, Sc: Julian Mitchell) • 138, 139
Ben Hur (USA 1959, D: William Wyler, Sc: Lew Wallace, Karl Tunberg) • 80
Big Brother (Channel 4 2000 to date) • 103, 108
Big Read, The (BBC 2003) • 12
Bill and Ted's Excellent Adventure (USA 1989, D: Stephen Herek, Sc: Chris Matheson) • 81
Billy Elliot (UK / F 2000, D: Stephen Daldry, Sc: Lee Hall) • 177
Blair Witch Project, The (USA 1999, D, Sc: Daniel Myrick, Eduardo Sánchez) • 13
Bleak House (in production, BBC 2004, Sc: Andrew Davies) • 17, 23
Bleak House (UK 1985, D, Sc: Ross Devenish) • 114
Boudicaa (ITV 2003) • 16
Bridget Jones's Diary (UK / F 2001, D: Sharon Maguire, Sc: Helen Fielding) • 15, 35, 41, 47, 164, 165, 175, 177, 188, 189, 193
Brideshead Revisited (UK 1981, D: Michael Lindsay-Hogg, Sc: John Mortimer) • 102, 110, 161, 162
Bright Young Things (UK 2003, D, Sc: Stephen Fry) • 39, 49
Byron (BBC 2003, D: Julian Farino, Sc: Nick Dear) • 16
Caravaggio (UK 1986, D, Sc: Derek Jarman) • 188
Carrington (UK / F 1995, D, Sc: Christopher Hampton) • 40, 102
Changing Stages (BBC2 2001, D: Jamie Muir, Roger Parsons, Sc: Richard Eyre) • 87, 88, 92
Chariots of Fire (UK 1981, D: Hugh Hudson, Sc: Colin Welland) • 39, 138, 169
Charles II (BBC 2003, D: Joe Wright, Sc: Adrian Hodges) • 16
Chocolat (USA / UK 2000, D: Lasse Halström, Sc: Robert Nelson Jacobs) • 164, 165
Clueless (USA 1995, D, Sc: Amy Heckerling) • 35, 36, 38, 41, 84, 164
Crying Game, The (UK / J 1992, D, Sc: Neil Jordan) •166
Culloden (BBC 1964, D, Sc: Peter Watkins) • 108, 110
Daniel Deronda (BBC 2002, D: Tom Hooper, Sc: Andrew Davies) • 13, 17
David Copperfield (BBC1 1999, D: Simon Curtis, Sc: Adrian Hodges) • 114
Dogville (USA / UK / F 2003, D, Sc: Lars von Trier) • 9-12
Dr Zhivago (ITV / Granada / WGBH 2003, D: Giacomo Campiotti, Sc: Andrew Davies) • 13, 16, 17
Draughtsman's Contract, The (UK 1982, D, Sc: Peter Greenaway) • 110, 188
East Enders (BBC1 1985 to present, P: Julia Smith *et al.*, Sc: Tony Holland *et al.*) • 95
Elizabeth (UK 1998, D: Shekhar Kapur, Sc: Michael Hirst) • 15, 25, 48, 62, 102, 177
Emma (UK / USA 1996, D: Douglas McGrath, Sc: Douglas McGrath) • 35, 36, 39, 41, 43-48, 65, 69, 71, 84, 151, 163, 164, 167, 188
Enchanted April (UK 1992, D: Mike Newell, Sc: Peter Barnes) • 45

English Patient, The (USA 1996, D, Sc: Anthony Minghella) • 151, 155
First Knight (USA 1995, D: Jerry Zucker, Sc: Lorne Comeron) • 151
Forsyte Saga, The (UK 2002, D: Christopher Menaul, Sc: Stephen Mallatratt) • 16
Four Weddings and a Funeral (UK 1994, D: Mike Newell, Sc: Richard Curtis) • 41, 164, 165, 192
French Kiss (USA / UK 1995, D: Lawrence Kasdan, Sc: Adam Brooks) • 164, 165
Full Monty, The (UK 1997, D: Peter Cattaneo, Sc: Simon Beaufoy) • 15, 177
Genius of Shakespeare, The (BBC2 2000) •87, 89, 92-94
Gladiator (USA / UK 2000, D: Ridley Scott, Sc: David Franmzoni, John Logan, William Nicholson) • 151
Goodbye Lenin (D 2003, D, Sc: Wolfgang Becker) • 23
Gosford Park (UK / USA / D / I 2001, D: Robert Altman, Sc: Robert Altman, Bob Balaban) • 39, 49
Great Britons (BBC2 2002, Prod: Mark Harrison) • 87, 89, 91-95
Great Expectations (UK 1946, D: David Lean, Sc: Anthony Havelock-Allan) • 114
Great Expectations (BBC 1999, D: Julian Jarrold, Sc: Tony Marchant) • 114
Hamlet (UK 2000, D, Sc: Mike Mundell) • 156
Hamlet (UK / USA 1996, D, Sc: Kenneth Branagh) • 20, 78, 79
Hamlet (USA / UK / F 1990, D: Franco Zeffirelli, Sc: Zeffirelli, Christopher DeVore) • 80
Hamlet (USA 2000, D, Sc: Michael Almereyda) • 20, 25, 81-83
Happy Birthday Shakespeare (BBC1, 2000, D: Nick Hurran, Sc: Mark Wallington) • 87, 90, 91
Hard Times (BBC 1994, D:, Sc: Peter Barnes) • 114
Heart of Me, The (UK / D 2002, D: Thaddeus O'Sullivan, Sc: Lucinda Coxon) • 49
Heat and Dust (UK 1983, D: James Ivory, Sc: Ruth Prawer Jhabvala) • 162
Heiress, The (USA 1949, D: William Wyler, Sc: Augustus & Ruth Goetz) • 58
He Knew He Was Right (UK 2004, D: Tom Vaughan, Sc: Andrew Davies) • 16
Henry V (UK 1944, D: Laurence Olivier, Sc: Dallas Bower, Alan Dent) • 13, 19, 20, 78, 80, 94
History of Britain, A (BBC 2000-2002, D: Claire Beavan, Sc: Simon Schama) • 125
Hours, The (USA 2002, D: Stephen Daldry, Sc: David Hare) • 40, 47
Howards End (UK 1992, D: James Ivory, Sc: Ruth Prawer Jhabvala) • 14, 110, 138, 144, 162, 167, 169, 170, 172, 174
I Capture the Castle (UK 2003, D: Tim Fywell, Sc: Heidi Thomas) • 16, 49
Ideal Husband, An (USA/UK 1999, D, Sc: Oliver Parker) • 127, 130, 131, 135-142, 145, 146
Importance of Being Earnest, The (USA / UK / FR 2002, D, Sc: Oliver Parker) • 130, 131, 135-138, 140-146
In Search of Shakespeare (BBC2 2003, D: David Wallace, Sc: Michael Wood) • 87
Inspector Morse (UK / USA 1987-2000, D: Roy Batersby, Sc: Julian Mitchell et al.) • 191
Inspector Lynley Mysteries (UK 2002 to present, D, Sc: various) • 191
Iris (UK / USA 2001, D, Sc: Richard Eyre) • 40
I´ve Heard the Mermaids Singing (Canada 1987, D, Sc: Patricia Rozema) • 57
Jewel in the Crown, The (BBC 1984, D: Christopher Morahan, Sc: Irene Shubik) • 161, 162
Jude (UK 1996, D: Michael Winterbottom, Sc: Hossein Amini) • 143, 177, 188
King John (UK 1899, D: Sir Herbert Beerbohm Tree, Sc: William Shakespeare) • 78
King, The Kaiser and the Tsar, The (BBC1 2003) • 105

Kommissar Rex (SAT1/ORF 1994 to date) 'Die Tote von Schönbrunn' (1994, D: Detlef Rönfeldt, Sc: Peter Hajek) • 191-193

Little Dorrit (UK 1987, D, Sc: Christine Edzard) • 114

Little Women (USA 1994, D: Gillian Armstrong, Sc: Robin Swicord) • 44, 46

Lock, Stock and Two Smoking Barrels (UK 1998, D: Guy Ritchie, Sc: Guy Ritchie) • 15

Lola rennt (D 1998, D, Sc: Tom Tykwer) • 23

Looking for Richard (USA 1996, D: Al Pacino, Sc: Pacino, Frederic Kimball) • 19, 79

Lord of the Rings, The (USA / NZ 2001-2003, D: Peter Jackson, Sc: Jackson, Frances Walsh, Philippa Boyens) • 12, 13

Lost Prince, The (BBC1 2003, D, Sc: Stephen Poliakoff) • 25, 102, 103, 105-107, 109

Love's Labour's Lost (UK / F /CAN 2000, D, Sc: Kenneth Branagh) • 79

Madness of King George, The (UK 1995, D: Nicholas Hytner, Sc: Alan Bennett) • 25

Mansfield Park (UK 1999, D, Sc: Patricia Rozema) • 35, 39, 41, 43, 46-48, 51, 53, 65, 163

Martin Cuzzlewit (BBC 1994, D: Pedr James, Sc: David Lodge) • 114

Maurice (UK 1987, D: James Ivory, Sc: Kit Hesketh-Harvey) • 168, 144, 169

Mayor of Casterbridge, The (2 parts, ITV 2001/03, D: David Thacker, Sc: Ted Whitehead) • 16

Middlemarch (UK 1994, D: Anthony Page, Sc: Andrew Davies) • 10, 11, 17, 119, 151

Midsummer Night's Dream, A (UK / I 1999 D: Michael Hoffman) • 20, 79, 81, 90

Mrs Brown (USA / UK 1997, D: John Madden, Sc: Jeremy Brock) • 25

Mrs Dalloway (USA / UK 1997, D: Marleen Gorris, Sc: Eileen Atkins) • 47

Much Ado About Nothing (UK / USA 1993, D, Sc: Kenneth Branagh) • 20, 80

Murder at Harvard (BBC2 2002, D, Sc: Eric Stange, Simon Schama) • 103, 104

Nicholas Nickleby (USA / UK / D / NL 2002, D, Sc: Douglas McGrath) • 16, 39

Notting Hill (USA / UK 1999, D: Roger Michell, Sc: Richard Curtis) • 15, 41, 47, 164

O (USA 2000, D: Tim Blake Nelson, Sc: Brad Kaaya) • 79, 81, 82

Oliver Twist (UK 1948, D: David Lean, Sc: Stanley Haynes) • 16, 114

Oliver Twist (BBC 1999, D: Renny Rye, Sc: Alan Bleasdale) • 114

Orlando (UK / F / I 1992, D, Sc: Sally Potter) • 102, 110, 177

Othello (USA UK 1995, D, Sc: Oliver Parker) • 80

Other Boleyn Girl, The (BBC2 2003, D, Sc: Philippa Lowthorpe) • 25, 102, 103, 105, 106, 108, 109, 156

Our Mutual Friend (BBC2 1998, D: Julian Farino, Sc: Sandy Welch) • 114, 116, 118, 119, 122, 123, 161

Passage to India, A (UK / USA 1984, D, Sc: David Lean) • 14, 167, 174

Persuasion (UK / F / USA 1995, D: Roger Michell, Sc: Nick Dear) • 35, 38, 41, 43, 44, 47, 65, 71

Piano, The (AUS / F 1993, D, Sc: Jane Campion) • 18, 27

Plain Jane (ITV 2001, D: John Woods, Sc: Lucy Gannon) • 16

Plunkett and Macleane (UK 1999, D: Jake Scott, Sc: Robert Wade) • 14, 48

Pride and Prejudice (BBC 1958, D: Barbara Burnham, Sc: Cedric Wallis) • 193

Pride and Prejudice (BBC 1985, D: Cyril Coke, Sc: Fay Weldon) • 125, 193

Pride and Prejudice (BBC 1995, D: Simon Langton, Sc: Andrew Davies) • 11, 12, 16, 37, 38, 42, 65-67, 69, 119, 121, 125, 129, 163, 165, 175, 177, 188, 189, 192, 193

Pride and Prejudice (USA 1940, D: Robert Z. Leonard, Sc: Aldous Huxley) • 37, 125, 193

Prospero's Books (UK / F / I 1991, D, Sc: Peter Greenaway) • 20, 80, 188

Ran (J / F 1985, D: Akira Kurosawa, Sc: Masato Ide, Akira Kurosawa) • 92

Remains of the Day, The (USA / UK 1993, D: James Ivory, Sc: Ruth Prawer Jhabvala) • 151, 167, 173, 174, 178

Revengers Tragedy (UK 2002, D: Alex Cox, Sc: Frank Cottrell Boyce) • 14, 15

Richard III (UK / USA 1995, D: Richard Loncraine, Sc: Ian McKellen) • 19, 20, 78, 79, 144

Romeo + Juliet (USA 1996, D: Baz Luhrmann, Sc: Craig Pearce) • 15, 19, 20, 78, 79, 144

Room with a View, A (UK 1985, D: James Ivory, Sc: Ruth Prawer Jhabvala) • 14, 39, 45, 80, 127, 128, 138, 144, 162

Russian Ark (RUS / D, D: Aleksandr Sokurov, Sc: Boris Khaimsky et al.) • 10, 21

Schönbrunn – Quelle der Schönheit (Arte / ORF 2002, D: Georg Riha) • 190

Schwarzwaldhaus 1902 (SWR 2002, D: Volker Heise, Sc: Rolf Schlenker) • 23

Schwarzwaldmädel (D 1950, D: Hans Deppe, Sc: Bobby E. Lüthge) • 23

Sense and Sensibility (USA/UK 1995, D: Ang Lee, Sc: Emma Thompson) • 10, 11, 35, 38, 39, 41-47, 57, 65, 66, 71, 73, 77, 78, 161, 163, 165, 167, 168

Shakespeare in Love (USA / UK 1998 D: John Madden, Sc: Marc Norman et al.) • 20, 40, 47, 48, 79, 80, 164, 177

Shakespeare, Man of the Millennium: South Bank Show (ITV 2000, D: Rex Bloomstein, David Hinton) • 87, 88, 90, 92, 94, 95

Shooting the Past (UK 1999, D, Sc: Stephen Poliakoff) • 103

Singing Detective, The (BBC1 1986, D: Jon Amiel, Sc: Dennis Potter) •161

Sissi (A 1955, D, Sc: Ernst Marischka) • 23

Sonnenallee (D 1999, D: Leander Haußmann, Sc: Detlev Buck) • 23

Sylvia (UK 2003, D: Christine Jeffs, Sc: John Brownlow) • 40

Tadellöser & Wolff (D 1975, D: Eberhard Fechner, Sc: Walter Kempowski) • 23

Tempest, The (UK 1979, D, Sc: Derek Jarman) • 20, 79

Ten Things I Hate About You (1999, D: Gil Junger, Sc: Kirsten Smith et al.) • 20, 79, 81, 82

Thin Blue Line, The (USA 1988, D, Sc: Errol Morris) • 166

Tipping the Velvet (UK 2002, D: Geoffrey Sax, Sc: Andrew Davies) • 16

Titanic (USA 1997, D, Sc: James Cameron) • 13

Titus (I / USA 1999, D, Sc: Julie Taymor) • 20, 79, 80, 94

Tom and Viv (USA / UK 1994, D: Brian Gilbert, Sc: Michael Hastings) • 40

Trainspotting (UK 1996, D: Danny Boyle, Sc: John Hodge) • 14, 48, 77, 78

Tromeo and Juliet (USA 1996, D, Sc: Lloyd Kaufman, James Gunn) • 20

True Romance (USA 1993, D: Tony Scott, Sc: Quentin Tarantino) • 16

Twelfth Night (UK 1996, D, Sc: Trevor Nunn) • 20

Vanity Fair (BBC 1998, D: Marc Munden, Sc: Andrew Davies, William Makepeace Thackeray) • 114, 119-123

Velvet Goldmine (UK / USA 1998, D: Todd Haynes, Sc: James Lyons) • 137

Video Diaries (BBC2 1991, Prod: Community Programme Unit) • 103

Washington Square (USA 1997, D: Agnieszka Holland, Sc: Carol Doyle) • 58

Way We Live Now, The (BBC 2001, D: David Yates, Sc: Andrew Dunn) • 16

Wilde (UK / D 1997, D: Brian Gilbert, Sc: Julian Mitchell) • 40, 137

Wings of the Dove, The (USA / UK 1997, D: Iain Softley, Sc: Hossein Amini) • 15, 47, 48, 177

Witchcraze (BBC2 2003, D: James Kent, Prod: Mark Hayhurst) • 108

Wonderful Britain: Shakespeare's Country (1926, Prod: Harry B. Parkinson) • 88

Wunder von Bern, Das (D 2003, D: Sönke Wortmann, Sc: Rochus Hahn) • 23

Wuthering Heights (ITV 1998, D: David Skynner, Sc: Neil McKay) • 152, 153, 156

Wuthering Heights (UK/USA 1992, D: Peter Kosminsky, Sc: Anne Devlin) • 152, 153, 156

Wuthering Heights (USA 1939, D: Wiliam Wyler, Sc: Charles MacArthur) • 152

General Subject Index

Aarseth, J. Espen • 150
Academy Award • 46, 151
action film• 13, 20
adaptation • 18, 25, 35-49 *passim*, 51, 52, 77, 113-123 *passim*, 125, 149-156 *passim*, 161, 162, 164, 184-194 *passim*
aestheticism • 136, 140
Agee, James • 78-79
Aldridge, Ira • 80
Alexandra (Queen) • 107
Almereyda, Michael • 20, 25, 79, 81-84
Altman, Rick • 23, 24, 123
Anderson, Benedict • 21
Andrew, Dudley • 18
Ankersmit, F.R. • 101
area studies • 174
art-house film • 20, 39, 44, 45, 47, 110, 162, 166
Arts and Entertainment • 38, 163
Arts Council • 163
Atkins Diet, The • 93
Austen, Jane • 11, 16, 25, 35-49 *passim*, 51-54, 59, 63, 65-73 *passim*, 78, 135, 151, 156, 164, 177, 190
Austenmania • 16, 38, 44, 47
auteur • 55, 105
authenticity/authentification • 9, 11, 12, 22, 26, 37, 43, 46, 77-79, 125, 126, 129, 135, 139, 142, 154, 156, 189
authorship • 10, 151
auto-referentiality • see self-reflexivity

Bacall, Lauren • 10
Badel, Alan • 193
BAFTA (British Academy of Film and Television Arts) • 17
Baier, Jo• 23
Baker, Henry • 143
Bakhtin, Mikhail • 183
Ballaster, Ros • 43
Barber, Lesley • 61
Barr, Charles • 14

Barthes, Roland • 188
Bate, Jonathan • 88, 89, 97
Baudrillard, Jean • 25, 133
BBC (British Broadcasting Corporation) • 10, 13, 14, 16, 17, 23, 24, 38, 44, 48, 87, 105, 114, 125, 149, 151, 161, 163, 177, 188, 193, film department 163
BBC Worldwide • 22
BBFC (British Board of Film Classification) • 15
Bean, Sean • 12
Beardsley, Aubrey • 139, 142
Beerbohm, Herbert • 78
Beja, Morris • 18
Belton House (Grantham) • 69
Berger, John • 108
Bergman, Ingmar • 45, 143
Binoche, Juliette • 152, 165
bio-pic • 20, 25, 40
Birtwistle, Sue • 69
Blake, William• 53
Blanchett, Cate • 12
Bleasdale, Alan • 114
blockbuster film • 20, 162
Blockbuster Video • 83
Bloom, Harold • 97
Bloomsbury group • 56
Bloomsbury Publishing • 40
Bogdanov, Michael • 80
Böhm, Karlheinz • 23
Boleyn, Anne • 103
Boleyn, Mary • 103, 109
Bond movies • 144, 145
Bordwell, David • 16, 184
Borgmeier, Raimund • 25, 171
Bourdieu, Pierre • 57
Bradshaw, Peter • 143
Brady, Orla • 154
Bragg, Melvyn • 88, 92, 95-97
Branagh, Kenneth • 15, 20, 79, 81, 97, 144
Brecht, Bertolt • 10
Breckman, Sam • 12, 69
Breloer, Heinrich • 23

Bristol, Michael • 77
British Screen •166
British Screen Classics • 88
British Tourist Authority • 42
Britishness • 22, 42, 164, 165
Brontë Myth, The (Miller) • 152
Brontë, Emily • 151, 152
Brontë, Emily • 26
Brook, Peter • 10, 97
Brownstein, Rachel M. • 66
Brusberg-Kiermeier • 11, 26
Bruzzi, Stella • 14
Buena Vista • 36, 48, 166
Bulandra Theatre Company • 92
Burt, Richard • 79
Butler, Judith • 14

Caan, James • 10
camp • 20
Campbell, Nancy • 173
canon • 10
captions • 128
Cardwell, Sarah • 18, 19, 149, 151, 191
Carey, Henry • 103
carnivalesque • 122
Cartmell, Deborah • 19, 25
Castle, Terry • 54, 60
Caughie, John • 113
Cavanah, Robert • 153
CBS/Fox • 163
Ceaușescu, Nicolae • 92
Channel 4 • 23, 44, 48, 162-166
chick lit • 36
Christianity • 51, 52
Christie, Agatha • 145
Christie, Julie • 41
Chumbawamba • 15
Church Gibson, Pamela • 14, 15, 25, 65, 78, 138, 143, 170, 171
classic TV serial • 13, 16, 17, 25, 37, 39, 44, 107, 113, 114, 119, 122, 164
collage • see history/historicity
Collingwood, Robin G. • 21
Collins, James • 39
colonialism • see post-colonialism
Columbia Pictures • 42, 44, 46, 164
comedy • 11, 15, 57, 137, 138, 140, 142, 146, 164, 165, see also romantic comedy
Conklin, Susie • 69

Cook, Pam • 14, 22, 129
Corner, John • 14
costume • 14, 54, 56, 77, 81
costume drama/film • 16, 19, 24, 25, 26, 36, 39, 40, 44, 45, 47, 61, 107
Cottrell Boyce, Frank • 15
Cox, Alex • 15
Craig, Cairns• 15
crossover film • 20, 39, 43, 44, 45, 47-49, 136, 141
culture areas (Anthony D. Smith)• 22, 23
Czar Nicholas II • 107, 108

Darcy-mania • 47, 191, 192, wet-shirt scene 67-69, 129-130, 151
Davies, Andrew • 12, 16, 17, 23, 119, 129, 193
Davis, Carl • 121
De Lauretis, Teresa • 55
Dead Certainties (Schama) • 103, 104
"Death of a Harvard Man" (Schama) • 103
Delft School • 56
Dench, Judi • 97, 145
Denton, Charles • 38
Department of National Heritage • 16
Dickens, Charles • 17, 24, 78, 114 -119 passim
discourse analysis • 169
docu-drama • 103, 104
documentary • 25, 103, 104
Dogme95 • 10-11, 102, 156
Dole, Carol M. • 71
Doran, Lindsay • 46
Driver, Minnie • 139, 141
Dunkley, Christopher • 121

Ealing Studios •141, 145
East Enders• 95
Easthope, Antony • 21, 22
Eccleston, Christopher • 15
Edward VIII • 103, 105
Edzard, Christine • 114
Eliot, George • 16, 17, 78
Elizabeth II • 15
Ellington, H. Elisabeth • 65-67
Elsaesser, Thomas • 162
Empire • 58
Eng.Lit. curriculum • 183, 184

England, England (Julian Barnes) • 18
English Shakespeare Company • 80
Englishness • 14, 18, 22, 42, 43, 125, 164, 168, 169, 176, 177
Eras of Elegance • 24
Ermarth, Elizabeth Deeds • 101
ethnicity • 13, 15, 22, 156, see also post-colonialism
Everett, Rupert • 138, 139, 141, 145
Everyman's Library /Knopf Publishing • 41
expressionism • 48, 116, 122
Eyre, Richard • 88, 92, 93, 97

Faulstich, Werner • 155
Featherstone, Mike • 22
Fechner, Eberhard • 23
Fellini, Frederico • 15
feminism • see gender
fetishism • 14, 151
fidelity/fidelity criticism • 18, 25, 36, 39, 72, 83, 135, 142, 149
Fielding, Helen • 165, 177, 193
Fiennes, Ralph • 152, 155
film analysis • 173
Film Council • 15
film music • see heritage film
FilmFour • 48
fin de siècle • 25, 77-84 passim, 139
Firth, Colin • 163, 165, 188, 192, 193
Flete Estate • 11
Fluck, Winfried • 172
Forde, John M. • 14
Forster, E.M. • 44, 135, 138, 174
Foucault, Michel • 54, 55, 93, 151
Fragile Films • 141
Francke, Lizzie • 152
Frears, Stephen • 165
Freeman, Hadley • 13
freeze-frame • 108
Freud, Sigmund • 185
frock-flick • see costume film

Gaines, Jane • 14
Gainsborough, Thomas • 128
garden • 25, 56, 65-73 passim
Garson, Greer • 38
gender • 9, 13, 14, 23, 41, 43, 48, 51-63 passim, 106, 107, 119, 129, 141, 169, 170, gendered narration, 153, see

also heritage film, sexuality, chick lit, scopophilia, lesbianism, homosexuality, costume, costume drama / film
Generation X • 82
George V • 102, 107, 108
George VI • 105
George, Elizabeth • 191
Gere, Richard • 151
Gielgud, John • 83
globalisation • 12, 22, 97, 140-141
Globe Theatres • 92, 94
glocalisation (Robertson) • 22, 43
Gold, Murray • 121
gothic • 48, 114, 122
Granada Television • 102, 161, 162
Grant, Hugh • 163-165, 192
Greenaway, Peter • 80, 109, 188
Greenblatt, Stephen • 80
Greer, Germaine • 97
Gregory, Philippa • 105, 109
Griem, Julika • 15, 113, 126, 150, 177
grotesque • 48, 119, 120, 122
Guardian, The • 13, 109, 143
Gunning, Tom • 151

HAL Films • 48
Hall, Peter • 93, 94, 97
Hamlet (theatre production, Welles 1936) • 92
Hands, Terry • 80
Hardy, Thomas • 16, 135
Harvey, Sylvia • 14
Hawke, Ethan • 82
Haynes, Todd • 137
Heckerling, Amy • 35
Heimatfilm • 23, 177
Held, Carolin • 25, 138
Henry VIII • 103, 108
Hensher, Philip • 121
heritage • anti-heritage position 113, in Austria 186, 187, 189, definition 9, 26, 187, in Germany 23, 175, heritage industry 16, 136, heritages 26, institutions 56, 176, and television 17, 21, 22, 25, 26, 35, 37-39, 42, 87-97, 161-166 passim, 17, 21, 22, 25-26, 101-110 passim, tourism 40-42, 88-98 passim, 121, 125,

126, 169, 175, 190, 193, World Heritage 186
heritage film • alternative heritage 13, 16, 19, 23, 138, 177, American involvement 43, anti-heritage 13, 56, 81, 120, 122, 152, and art history 125-133 *passim*, bourgeois heritage film 138, and class 42, and cultural memory 132, definition 9, 13, 26, 87-88, 102, 126, 135, 136, 175, and EFL teaching 167-179 *passim*, 183-194 *passim*, female heroines in 14, 119, female authorship 41, French 164, German 23, heritage space vs. narrative space 113, 170, 171, 186, 192, iconography 43, 45, 121, 122, 126, 127, as literary cinema 40, meta-heritage 13, 80, 81, 122, 152, music in 61, 121, 122, 128, not-heritage 13, 16, post-heritage 13, 16, 23, 25, 102, 138, and postmodern history 110, revisionist heritage 13, 16, 123, 177, Russian 21, and self-reflexivity 132, and Shakespeare 77-84 *passim*, 87-97 *passim*, and social critique 122, teaching of 151, origins in TV 161, 163, transnational 161-166 *passim*, 193, and video release 166,
Herzog, Charlotte • 14
Hewison, Robert • 14, 187
Higson, Andrew • 14, 16, 24-26, 57, 58, 65, 77, 88, 113, 114, 126, 127, 138, 141, 167, 169-172, 174, 176, 179, 187, 188, 191, 192
Hill, John • 14, 138
historical film • 16, 24, 26, 39, 108, 110, 125-127
History Channel, The • 22
history docusoap • 23
history/historicity • 21, 24-26, 36, 37, 39, 40, 77, 93, 95, 96, and art 125-130, as collage 109, historical re-enactment 79, 80, 83, historical television 101-110 *passim*, metahistory 21, New Historicism 80, and postmodernism 101-110 *passim*
Hodges, Adrian • 114
Hoffman, Michael • 20, 79, 81
Hogarth, William• 128

Holden, Anthony • 94
Hollywood • 10, 12, 20, 26, 37, 39, 43, 46, 49, 126, 152, 161, 163-166
Holm, Ian • 12
homosexuality • 135, 137-141, 145, see also lesbianism, sexuality, gender
Hopcraft, Arthur • 114
Hornaday, Ann • 143
How to Read a Film (Monaco) • 184
humanism • 25, 87, 91-93
Hutcheon, Linda • 101

imaginary community (Anderson) • 21, 23, 183
imperialism • see post-colonialism
interactivity • 150
intermediality • 10, 18, 26, 126, 128, 130, 133, 184
intermediality • 18
International Journal of Heritage Studies • 24
intertextuality • 24, 26, 130, 140, 145, 155, 169, 184
intertitles • 3
Iser, Wolfgang • 26, 66
Ishiguro, Kazuo • 173, 174, 178
ITV (Independent Television) • 13, 16, 38, 87, 152, 162
Ivory, James • 14, 23, 44, 127, 128, 138, 149, 162, 175, 176
Izzard, Eddie • 15

Jackson, Glenda • 92
Jackson, Peter • 12
Jacobi, Derek • 15
James, Henry • 23, 48, 135
Jameson, Fredric • 77, 188
Jarman, Derek • 121, 165, 188
JASNA (Jane Austen Society of North America) • 24
Jeffries, Stuart • 109
Jenkins, Henry • 101
John (Prince) • 102, 105, 106, 110
Johnson, Claudia • 51
Jonson, Ben • 97
Jordan, Neil • 166
Junger, Gil • 20, 79, 81

Kapur, Shekar • 62, 188
Keita, Salif • 59

Kellynch Hall • 71
Kemble, John Philip • 80
Kempowski, Walter • 23
Kidman, Nicole • 10
Kingsley-Smith, Jane • 77
Kirby Hall • 56
Knight Errant (Millais) • 143
Kosminsky, Peter •152
Krämer, Lucia • 23, 26
Kramsch, Claire • 185
Kreuzer Helmut • 18
Krewani, Angela • 26, 44
Kuhn, Annette • 14
Kureishi, Hanif • 165
Kurosawa, Akira • 92

LA Times • 47
Labour • 16
Lady Windermere's Fan (Wilde) • 140
Landeskunde • see area studies
Landy, Marcia • 109
Langton, Simon • 69
Lanier, Douglas • 95-96
Lean, David • 114
Lee, Ang • 11, 43, 46, 71, 163, 164, 188
Leigh, Mike • 121
lesbianism • 54, 55, 57, 60
Lionheart Television • 163
Littlefield, Ephraim • 103, 104
Loncraine, Richard • 19, 20, 79, 144
London Film Festival • 55
London Review of Books • 54
Lothe, Jakob • 17
Lowthorpe, Philippa • 102, 103, 105-
    107, 109
Luckington Court (Great Sherston) •
    69
Luhrmann, Baz • 19, 20, 79, 81, 82, 95,
    97
LWT (London Weekend Television) •
    152
Lyme Park (Disley) • 42, 69

MacLachlan, Kyle • 82
Madden, John • 20, 79
Maguire, Sharon • 189
Maier, Hermann • 189
Malham Rocks (Yorkshire) • 154
Man on a Meat Hook • 53
Mandela, Nelson • 92

Marchant, Tony • 114
Mary (Queen) • 102, 110
Masterpiece Theatre • 24
McDowell, Andie• 164
McFarlane, Brian • 17, 18, 149, 184
McGrath, Douglas • 43, 71, 151, 163
McKellen, Ian • 12, 97, 144
McLean, Gareth • 13
Medhurst, Andy • 16
media literacy • 167, 179
medievalism • 12
melodrama • 137, 138, 142
memory • 107, 130, 132
Merchant, Ismail • 14, 23, 44, 138, 149,
    162, 175, 176
Metro-Goldwyn-Mayer (MGM) • 37
Metz, Christian • 184
Michell, Roger • 43
Middle England • 63
Middleton, Thomas • 15
Millais, John Everett • 143
Miller, Jonathan • 83, 97
Miller, Lucasta • 152
miniseries • see classic TV serial
Mirage • 164
Miramax • 35, 46, 47, 48, 57, 62, 141,
    163, history of 165, 166
Monaco, James • 184
Monk, Claire • 9, 13, 15, 16, 53, 78,
    102, 113, 123, 135, 138, 169-171
Montacute House (Yeovil) • 73
Monty Python • 91
Moore, Julianne • 141
Morris, Errol • 165
Morris, William • 142
Morrison, Marion • 67
multiplex cinema • 21, 36, 39, 46, 47,
    57, 58, 63
Mulvey, Laura • 65, 66, 129
Mundell, Mike • 156
Munden, Mark • 121
Murdoch, Rupert • 15
Murray, Bill • 82
Muscular Christianity • 131

narration, unreliable • 173
narrative space • see heritage space
narratology, cognitive • 171
National Curriculum • 187
National Heritage • 56, 176

National Heritage Acts • 176
National Heritage Memorial Fund •
176
National Trust • 24, 42, 176
Nelson, Blake • 79
New British Cinema • 162
New Woman • 56
New York Review of Books • 192
newsreels • 87-88, 93
Newsweek • 38
Ninagawa Theatre Company • 92
nostalgia • 9, 11, 12, 14, 15, 22, 24, 38,
42, 77, 81, 126, 127, 146, 150, 156,
177, 193
nouvelle vague • 143
Nünning, Ansgar • 175, 176

O'Connor, Sinéad • 152
OED (Oxford English Dictionary) • 97
Olivier, Laurence • 14, 19, 38, 78, 83,
94, 193
Ontario New Wave • 55
Orion Pictures • 38
Oscar • see Academy Award
Otherness • 51
Our Town (Thornton Wilder) • 11

Pacino, Al • 19, 79
Paget, Derek • 77, 78, 81
Paltrow, Gwyneth • 46, 71, 163, 164
Parker, Alan • 14
Parker, Oliver • 26, 80, 130, 135-146
Parkinson, Harry B. • 88
Parkman, George • 103, 104
parody • 61
pastiche • 142
Paulin, Tom • 106
PBS (Public Broadcasting Service) •
162
Pearson, Roberta E. • 79
Pemberley • 67-70, 129, 190, 191
Penguin • 41
Percy, Henry • 108
period drama/film • 14, 16, 26, 39, 45,
142
Phoenix, Joaquin • 151
photography • 107, 108
pictorialism • 14, 25, 56, 102, 107, 113,
115, 126-130, 132, 142

Picture of Dorian Gray, The (Wilde) •
138
picturesque • 11, 43, 65, 66, 68-73, 81,
113, 190
Pidduck, Julianne • 43
Pilcher, Rosamunde • 23
Polanski, Roman • 16
Poliakoff, Stephen • 102, 103, 105-110
Polygram • 164
populism • 25, 87, 93-96
post-colonialism • 43, 48, 51-63 *passim*,
88, 185, 186, imperialism 97, slav-
ery 52, 53, 58, 59
postmodernism • 20, 22, 24, 25, 61,
179, 188 and history 101-110 *pas-
sim*, 146
Pope, Rob • 189
Potter, Cherry • 184
Potter, Dennis • 161
Powell, Sandy • 79
Powrie, Phil • 138
Pre-Raphaelites • 143
Pride and Prejudice (Jane Austen) • 12
Puccini, Giacomo • 128

queerness • 51, 53, 55
Quinn, James • 77

reality television • 102, 108
regenrification • 13, 24, 123
Reith, John • 114
resurrectionism • 24
retrovisions • 24
Richards, Jeffrey 114, 115•
Roberts, Julia • 164
Robertson, Robert • 22
romantic comedy • 20, 40, 41, 46, 47
rom-com • see romantic comedy
Rosenstone, Robert A. • 101, 102, 104-
106, 109, 110
Rozema, Patricia • 35, 43, 51-63 *passim*, 163
RSC (Royal Shakespeare Company) •
80, 88
Rylance, Mark • 89, 94

Said, Edward • 53, 59
Sakamoto, Ryuichi • 155
Saltram House (Plymouth) • 42, 72

Samuel, Raphael • 20, 24, 26, 88, 114, 187, 188
Sanditon (Austen) • 38
Sargeant, Pamela • 22, 126
Schaff, Barbara • 25, 143
Schama, Simon • 24, 25, 101, 103-106
Schneider, Irmela • 18
Schneider, Romy • 23
Schönbrunn • 190
Schwarzenegger, Arnold • 189
scopophilia • 55, 60, 65, 66, 129
Scott Thomas, Kristin • 155
Scott, Gerry • 11
Screen Language (Potter) • 184
Seibel, Ralph • 175
Seidl, Monika • 26
self-reflexivity/self-referentiality • 61, 104, 127, 130, 132, 133, 135, 142, 152, 188
Sentimental Journey, A (Sterne) • 62
sexuality • 53, 55, 59, 60, 120, 121, 145, 146, 156, see also gender
Shakespeare, William • 18, 19, 25, 61, 77-84 *passim*, *A Midsummer Night's Dream* 90, *Hamlet* 81-84, *Henry V* 78, 94, *Julius Caesar* 92, *King Lear* 95, and Elizabethans 94, Shakespeare Festivals 92, Shakespeare on TV (BBC/Timelife) 83, 87-97 *passim*, bardbiz 87-89, 96, Shakespeare Memorial Theatre 88, "Sonnet 116" 90, and Victorianism 93
Shaw, Fiona • 89, 91-95, 97
Sheen, Erica • 18, 149, 151
Signet Publishing • 41
Simpsons, The • 94
simulation • 9, 24, 133
Sinyard, Neil • 19
Skynner, David • 152
slavery • see post-colonialism
Smith, Anthony D. • 22
St Stephen's Cathedral (Vienna) • 190
Sternberg, Meir • 173
Sterne, Laurence • 62
Stewart, Maaja • 53
Stiles, Julia • 82
still life • 125, 127, 128, 130
Stone, Marcus • 115
Storz, Oliver • 23

Stratford-upon-Avon • 10, 79, 88-92, 96, 97
Street, Sarah • 9, 11, 21, 22, 25, 138
Studio Canal • 164
subculture • 20
Surkamp, Carola • 26

tableau vivant • 26, 54, 125-133 *passim*, 139
Tarantino, Quentin • 16, 38
Taymor, Julie • 20, 79, 80, 94, 97
teaching • see heritage film
teen film/teen-pic • 20, 25, 82
Teigh, Old Rectory (Oakham) • 70
television • see heritage and television, classic TV serial, reality television
Telewest • 22
temporality • 107
Thackeray, William Makepiece• 119
Thatcherism • 14, 125, 177
theatre • 10, 79, 80, 94, 95, 97, 139, 140
Theatres of Memory (Samuel) • 20
theatricality • 135, 139, 141, 142, 146
Thompson, Emma • 11, 42, 58, 71, 164
Times, The • 14
Tolkien, J.R.R. • 13
Touchstone • 166
tourism • see heritage
Town and Country • 42
Trafalgar House (Salisbury) • 72
transgression • 51, 53, 54, 60
travelogues • 87-88
Trollope, Anthony • 16, 24

UK History • 22
UKTV • 22
Urry, John • 121
Ustinov, Peter • 190

Variety • 46
Verona, Diane • 82
video release • 45, 48, 166
Vilsmaier, Joseph • 23
visual studies • 185
Vivendi Universal • 164, 165
voice-over narration • 11
Voigts-Virchow, Eckart • 15, 78, 79, 113, 126, 135, 150, 177
Von Trier, Lars • 9, 11

voyeurism • see scopophilia

Wallington, Mark • 87
Walt Disney • 46, 165
Washington Post • 143
Watkins, Peter • 108, 110
WBGH Boston • 10, 23, 152
Wearing, Catherine • 119
Webster, John • 103, 104
Weinstein, Harvey • 57, 166
Welch, Sandy • 114
Weldon, Fay • 161, 193
Welles, Orson • 92
Weta Workshop • 12
Wharton, Edith • 23
Whelehan, Imelda • 149, 155
White, Hayden • 21, 102
Whitley, John • 123
Wilde, Oscar • 25, 26, 130, 135, 139-
    146
Wiltshire, John • 36
Winterbottom, Michael • 143, 188
Winterson, Jeantette • 13, 17
Witherspoon, Reese • 141
Wolfe, George • 97
Wood, Michael • 87, 96
Woolf, Virginia • 47
Working Title • 164, 165
Wright, Patrick • 11, 14, 187
Wroe, Martin • 77
Wyler, William • 152

*Yellow Book, The. An Illustrated Quar-
    terly* (1894-1897) • 139

Zeffirelli, Franco • 19, 80
Zellweger, Renée • 192, 193

Contributors

Raimund Borgmeier holds a Chair of English Literature at Giessen University. He also taught as Visting Professor at the University of Wisconsin, Madison and Milwaukee. He has published widely, e.g. on Shakespeare, Romanticism, and SF. He is also series editor of *Die englische Literatur in Text und Darstellung*, 10 vols. (Reclam, 1982-1986). Most recently, he edited a book on *Interpretationen: Englische Short Stories* (Reclam, 1999).

Stefani Brusberg-Kiermeier wrote her PhD thesis *Körper-Inszenierungen in Shakespeares Historien* (1999) at the Free University Berlin, and is currently completing her post-doctoral dissertation, *Victorian Laughter*. She is co-editor of *Shakespeare in the Media* (2004) and has published on Shakespeare, Aemilia Lanyer, and contemporary British drama and film. She has taught English Literature and Gender Studies at Free University Berlin, Humboldt University Berlin, Siegen University and since April 2004 at Potsdam University.

Deborah Cartmell is Subject Leader and Principal Lecturer at De Montfort University, Leicester. She is author of *Interpreting Shakespeare on Screen* (2000) and co-editor of *Adaptations: From Text to Screen Screen to Text* (1999), *Talking Shakespeare* (2001) and six volumes in the Film/Fiction series, published by Pluto Press. She is currently working on adaptations of children's literature.

Pamela Church Gibson is Reader in Cultural Studies at the London College of Fashion. She has published widely on film, fashion, fandom, history and heritage and has edited three collections of essays – the most recent, *More Dirty Looks: Gender, Power, Pornography* was published by the British Film Institute in 2004. She is currently writing on women, cinema and consumption in the post-war period.

Carolin Held was Assistant Lecturer at the Department of English Literature, University of Tuebingen fom 2001 to 2003. She is currently finishing her PhD thesis entitled *'The Disturbance of Anticipation': Ausformungen von Progressiveness im britischen Television Drama*.

Andrew Higson is Professor of Film Studies, and Head of the School of Film and Television Studies, at the University of East Anglia. He has published widely on British cinema, and his most recent book is *English Heritage, English Cinema: Costume Drama since 1980* (OUP, 2003).

Lucia Krämer is Lecturer in English Literature at the University of Regensburg, where she studied English and French. She took her PhD in 2002 for a thesis on fictional biographies of *Oscar Wilde in Roman, Drama und Film* (Lang, 2003) and has published various articles on this subject.

Angela Krewani is Professor of History and Theory of the Digital Media at the University of Marburg. She has published on British cinema and television drama, Hollywood and media art and theory. She is currently working on digital film.

Roberta E. Pearson is Professor of Film Studies and Director of the Institute of Film Studies in the School of American and Canadian Studies at the University of Nottingham. She is the author, co-author and co-editor of numerous volumes and articles and is planning a monograph on Shakespeare and British national identity.

Barbara Schaff took her PhD on contemporary English bio-plays at Passau University in 1990. From 1992 to 1996, she held a post-doc position for Gender Studies at Munich University, where she has been a Lecturer since 1997. The title of her post-doctoral dissertation is _War, Gender and Memory. The First World War in British Cultural Memory_ (2002). She has co-edited books on authorship, English fantasies of Venice and bi-textuality, and published on travel literature, war literature, fakes and forgeries, and female authorship.

Monika Seidl is a teacher with a PhD in English Literature and a post-doctoral qualification in Cultural Studies. She has recently completed a book-length study on a theory of adaptations of classics. She was a full-time exchange lecturer at the German Department of St Andrews University, Scotland, has taught a Film Studies course for the Cultural Studies Module at Klagenfurt University and is currently in charge of the Cultural Studies Introductory Module at the English Department of Vienna University.

Sarah Street is Professor of Film at the University of Bristol, Department of Drama: Theatre, Film, Television. Her books include _British National Cinema_ (1997) and _Transatlantic Crossings_ (2002). She is currently completing _Black Narcissus_ for I.B. Tauris. Her current research interests are set design and European cinema in the 1930s.

Carola Surkamp received her PhD at Giessen University in 2002 for a thesis on the concept of the perspective structure of English novels from Victorianism to Modernism. She currently works as a Lecturer at Giessen in the Department of Teaching English as a Foreign Language. Her main research interests include narratology, drama and film theories, and their implications for the teaching of fictional texts in the foreign language classroom.

Eckart Voigts-Virchow is Associate Professor at the University of Giessen. He also taught English Literature and Cultural Studies at the Universities of Madison and Milwaukee, Wisconsin, and Frankfurt/Main. He has published widely on contemporary drama, film and media studies, and Dennis Potter. Both his post-doctoral dissertation (on metaphors of technology in Victorian industrial novels and proto-SF) and his _Introduction to Media Studies_ (Klett) are forthcoming.